South Asian Union

Problems, Possibilities and Prospects

South Asian Union

Problems, Possibilities and Prospects

Ranjit Kumar

Manas Publications
New Delhi - 110 002 (India)

MANAS PUBLICATIONS
(Publishers, Distributors, Importers & Exporters)
4858, Prahlad Street,
24, Ansari Road, Darya Ganj,
New Delhi - 110 002 (INDIA)
Ph.: 23260783, 23265523 (O); 27131660(R)
Fax: 011- 23272766
E-mail: manaspublications@vsnl.com
www.manaspublications.com

ISBN 81-7049-219-X
Rs. 695

Typeset at
Manas Publications

Printed in India at
Nice Printing Press
and Published by Mrs. Suman Lata for
Manas Publications, 4858, Prahlad Street
24, Ansari Road, Daryaganj
New Delhi 110002 (INDIA)

To the memory of my father

Foreword

Ask most United Kingdom citizens — even well educated ones—how the European Union is structured, and they will be unable to provide an informed answer.The relationship between the Council and the Commission and the Parliament is a closed book to them. For many of them, in this notably eurosceptic country, the EU means domination by "Brussels".

I am of course exaggerating, but not much. The fact is that after many years of EU membership the concept of Europe has not caught on well in Britain. There are many reasons. They include the historical, the political (notably a lack of enthusiastic political leadership) and the legal (the legal systems in the UK and the other member countries are different). It is not easy to guess whether the UK will join the Euro. Nor is it easy to predict what Britain's final decision will be on the proposed new European constitution.

What is quite clear, however, is that co-operation in the EU has had a huge (and largely beneficial) effect on all the member states, including the UK. It has affected people's lives. It has turned Europe from a group of states whose strength and influence had been greatly diminished by the second world war into an economic force to be reckoned with. There is, of course, no "United States of Europe" but there is an entity which is greater and stronger than the sum of its parts.

Could something similar work in South Asia? The straightforward and simple answer is probably yes, but of course in practice the issue is neither straightforward nor simple.

One of the lessons from the European experience is that difficult decisions are always political rather than economic. (That was something that was never taken fully into account in the early days of the European Economic Community—as the EU then was. As it became clear that the logical development was from an economic to a political community, fears and apprehensions grew.)

It would, surely, be the political dimension of inter-state relations that would be the major factor dictating whether SAARC could be transformed into something more akin to the EU. From an outsider's perspective, there would be at least two aspects of that political dimension which would make such a transformation difficult.

One is the history of wary relations (to put it euphemistically) between India and Pakistan. The second is the huge disparity in size between India and the other SAARC countries. What is relevant here is not just the dramatic difference between India (with its population of 1048 million) and the Maldives, with 0.28 million, but the fact that India is so much bigger than even its large neighbours. I remember at a seminar which I organised in Chennai in 1993 how readily participants from Bangladesh and Sri Lanka described India as "big brother" (using the term with more suspicion than family friendliness). Admittedly the discussion was good-humoured—particularly when one of the Indian participants lightened the tone with the comment: "I blame the British"—but the size factor will remain a real hurdle.

It is much less significant in Europe, because there is no one European "big brother". The populations of the largest members are: Germany 83 million; France 60 million; the UK 60 million; Italy 58 million; Spain 40 million. Notwithstanding this demographic balance, there have been from time to time suspicions between the big members themselves about undue dominance by others.

Ranjit Kumar most certainly does not share the widespread British ignorance about the EU. He demonstrates detailed knowledge and understanding. For example, he describes the different roles of the European Parliament, the Council and the

Commission and neatly and aptly characterises them as the "institutional triangle" which forms the European Union.

In this book Ranjit Kumar has pursued, with remarkable results, what can best be described as his "big idea". He has analysed the development of the European Union, setting his analysis well in context, and applied it to South Asia.

His approach is positive and optimistic. He is convinced of the benefits that would flow from closer collaboration by the member states of SAARC. His strength is that he has not allowed his optimism and his enthusiasm to cloud his judgement. He has no illusions about the difficulties (for example the difficulty implicit in the huge size and strength of India by comparison with the other member countries). His study of the development of the EU, however, enables him to point to difficulties overcome in the European context.

He rightly points out that this process has been slow and steady. The difficulties have not vanished overnight. Suspicions have always stood in the way of the political development of the EU, and they still do (as witness the debate over the proposed new constitution).

He recognises the significance of the major changes in post-second world war Europe. Born of the need to rebuild Europe and to provide a counterpoise to the Soviet Union, the EU could have been characterised initially as a union against something. The collapse of the Soviet Empire in 1989 removed that need—and, it can plausibly be argued, made it possible to concentrate on the case for the European concept. Positive thinking is often much more difficult than negative, but that is not an argument against it. And Ranjit Kumar is a strong proponent of positive thinking among the members of SAARC.

To return to my question: Could something similar to the EU work in South Asia? If the positive thinking is nurtured, and if a slow process of growth is recognised as inevitable, and not dispiriting, the author's "big idea" is certainly not a wholly fanciful vision.

Sometimes Ranjit Kumar's enthusiasm makes him less critical of the EU than I would be. For example, he describes, accurately, the extraordinary system which gives the European Parliament different locations, and requires movement between them at great cost, but does not use that as an example of the kind of preposterous inefficiency which invites eurosceptic scorn.

He is probably wise to avoid that kind of controversy, because it would detract from the value of his approach. He provides a great deal of information about both the EU and SAARC. This includes information about the structures and the constitutional background to them, but it includes also well-researched information about the political realities of the organisations. For example, he emphasises the significance of sector interests, especially agriculture, in the EU. He is skilful at pointing to parallels between the European and the South Asian situations.

Ranjit Kumar carried out the research for his book, and wrote the first draft, during his ten-week period as a Press Fellow at Wolfson College, Cambridge, from April to July 2004. That represents a prodigious labour. The result is informative, challenging and stimulating.

It is a privilege to have been invited to write this foreword.

Bill Kirkman

Bill Kirkman, an Emeritus Fellow of Wolfson College, Cambridge University, UK.

Preface

To think of a confederation of states of South Asia called South Asian Union patterned on the European Union may be an utopian dream but after living in Cambridge (UK) and traveling to various parts of Europe one cannot help but dream only of a similar cooperative living of nation states in South Asia also. This is an area, where one fifth of humanity lives and which is under the dire need of peace, progress, development, stability and economic upliftment. In Europe, when one comes across an Italian, an Irish or a Polish citizen one is convinced that the integration of Europe was perhaps the greatest peace project undertaken during the latter half of last century and which is likely to flower to full bloom soon though there may be lots of pricks in the European plant called European Union. Though there are dissenting voices also largely in Britain, and a few other countries, where there is a new political party called UK Independence Party thriving on the people's sentiments claiming all the time that it is fighting for the independence of Britain as if the greatest colonizer of previous centuries is itself going to be colonized by none other but its own European colleagues.

However, considering the ground realities in South Asia which is vastly different from Europe. one can always say that the region is not ready for such kind of cooperative living. True, South Asia is mostly known for poverty, illiteracy, hunger, malnutrition, poor governance, a few democratic regimes, insurgency, ethnic conflicts, hub of terrorism, fundamentalism, military tensions and what not? Whereas Europe is known for its richness, widespread problem of obesity due to abundance of food, total democracy, rule of law, good governance, extreme stage of development, etc. At the same time South Asia can boast of being one of the most talented and qualified human resources on this earth besides huge wealth of natural resources whereas Europe also has many areas of conflicts, communal tensions and underdevelopment requiring state intervention. Most of the South Asian States fear each other's dominance and pinpricks if they come on a single platform whereas the European States have opened their borders for each other's citizens and for free trade and commerce. If a South Asian Union takes shape in due course of time as desired by the South Asian leaders from the platform of SAARC Summits, the biggest immediate peace dividend would be in the form of a hugely reduced defence expenditure of India and Pakistan.

However, the obvious questions are: Can and should an European model be implanted on South Asia? When the European Union itself is becoming too unwieldy after the enlargement to 25 member states and lot of contradictions emerging in the foreign and defence policy front, should the South Asians look towards European Union as a role model? When all the regions of Europe are not happy with the common agricultural policy of EU, should the South Asians not emulate the concept of having common policies in many areas for common governance? Would the European Union model be feasible in South Asia? Are the South Asians ready to adopt this model? Or is the European Union not an ideal model that should be adopted considering the controversies in some of the European countries regarding the utility of EU and it acting like a hard taskmaster, regulator, or inspector or superstate in most spheres of life that may deter the South Asians to think of a similar "undesirable and hence unworkable" model?

Questions like why should Europe have a constitution when all the member countries have a constitution are often asked and why should individual European countries be deprived of the sovereign right of having its own foreign and defence policies? Would the Pakistanis, Bangladeshis and the Indians be able to mix freely with each other and have a common foreign and defence policy and live under the same constitutional umbrella as the European Union is trying to achieve? Would the constitutions of the member countries become redundant after an European constitution is adopted and would the South Asian countries be prepared for such an eventuality? No doubt this is thinking to the extreme position when the Europeans themselves have not reached that level of political unity at the moment and have lots of problems and controversies. But, definitely most of the Europeans especially in the smaller European countries aspire to live in not only economically integrated but politically united Europe. The Europeans have come to this stage after they started dreaming of such an Europe in the late forties of the last century. Some of the visionary South Asian leaders now a days talk of the successes of the European Union in giving its people a more relaxed and better life and where there are no possibility of military conflicts between the member states. So they talk of the possibility of emulating this example so that the impoverished people of South Asia can also achieve that level of life for majority of its population in a few decades if not in years and eliminate the widespread poverty and hunger and war like situation from the area.

The conditions right now do not exist in South Asia for a fully-fledged South Asian Union because of lack of cooperative mentality among South Asian countries. One of the basic prerequisites of becoming a member of European Union for any European country is to have a democratic regime and respect for human rights. Some of the South Asian states would not qualify to be a member of such kind of an union patterned on European Union as they cannot fulfill these basic criteria of the membership. The former authoritarian, communist regimes of East Europe could qualify for the membership of EU only after throwing off the yoke of dictatorship of the proletariat and embracing the concept of democracy and free market.

Yes, the criteria required for becoming a member of EU cannot be met by South Asian countries if South Asia also wants to have similar model. Does it mean that the common masses of South Asia cannot aspire for a similar cooperative living of nation states in South Asia so that they get a better life? Can't they dream of a similar economic and political set up in South Asia? A political union may be aiming too high but the immediate dream of South Asians should be to achieve the economic union the kind of which EU has been very successful to achieve. Should not a poor man dream of becoming a wealthier person to lead a better life? Should these South Asians be left at the mercy of the self serving, incompetent and autocratic rulers and bureaucrats who want to perpetuate their rule through demagoguery and corruption with an iron hand? Should the people of South Asia be deprived of the opportunities the ordinary Europeans are getting after the evolution of EU in it's present form? Is the EU too idealistic an organisation to be copied by the South Asians and would it be unworkable and impractical in South Asia? The EU of today is not politically united and no political union is expected in near future but the way the Europeans have integrated their economies is quite impressive and has brought lots of good to the masses especially to the poorer regions of Europe.

There would definitely be problems of management, vested interests, pulls and pressures and different perceptions on various issues among member states in a huge organisation like European Commission responsible for executing the policies of European Union but the gains of common governance far outweigh the disadvantages and problems to a few groups of Europeans. This is why there are eurosceptics in many European countries mostly in United Kingdom, always doubting the relevance and necessity of having a common system of governance through European Union, there would be lot of asiasceptics in South Asia also doubting the requirement of a federation of south Asian states similar to the European Union. People in authority in South Asia would fear losing their positions of power and authority so there would be lot of resistance for a common system of governance like the European Union has achieved over the years.

Since South Asia is inhabited by one fifth of the world population, any social and economic instability in this part of the world would definitely have an impact on the peace and stability of the rest of the world. The region requires suitable conditions and opportunities for faster economic growth so that people come out of poverty and hunger, which breeds fundamentalism, terrorism and other kinds of social and religious extremism and problems. The South Asian region cannot be deprived of a better model of cooperative governance as the EU has developed simply because conditions do not exist right now. But should not one dream of a similar living standard in South Asia also? The EU of today was dreamt of more than five decades ago. If the South Asians also start dreaming of a similar cooperative regime then it will definitely take shape may be two, three or four decades later. Better late than never. There may be shortcomings in EU and sometimes it may be overplaying its desired role to give a better and secure life to the ordinary Europeans but the sincerity and intention to achieve this aim cannot be doubted. Similarly to give a better life to the ordinary South Asians one has to think of a development model working largely successfully elsewhere. Perhaps the EU best fits in this criteria as there are lot of similarities that exist between South Asia and Europe, that makes the case stronger for a similar model in South Asia.

As a South Asian it was exciting for me to get a first hand experience of the way the European Union is working and delivering wonderful results to its people. Seeing Europe from own eyes for a few months when there was intense debate going on about the political future of Europe and talking to various policy planners of the new emerging Europe was an eyeopener. It's difficult not to start dreaming of a similar model in South Asia also. A borderless, visaless travel between South Asian countries, every South Asian aspires for. As the pains pf partition of the subcontinent have not yet subsided and there is urgent desire among South Asians to cross the border and see their near and dear ones without any restrictions and police verifications, such a borderless regime like the EU has developed would be widely welcomed in South Asia. As the East Europeans of last decade could not have imagined in their dreams of crossing the border of any European country and be able to work there without any questions of immigration being asked is really an astonishing experience in their life. Similarly the South Asians of today cannot think of crossing the border without having a passport and visa in their pocket and be able to get a job and buy property there, as the Europeans are able to do today.

People in some parts of Europe may be resenting the growth and evolution of European Union into a nation State but there seems to be overwhelming desire among Europeans to have a common governance through common state structures and institutions. How these institutions work and what are the basic foundations and principles on which they work and how they have been structured and evolved over last five decades is an interesting study in exercise. How these institutions are proving to be very beneficial for the common Europeans is interesting to know. And how the functioning of these European institutions should be studied by the South Asians so as to give similar model to the people of South Asia to improve their economic lot.

The purpose of this book is to present to all those interested in the South Asian affairs and to the common readers the problems, roadblocks and possibilities in giving a similar model of European Union to the South Asia and also to tell how these common European institutions are working. As the South Asian countries have formed an organisation called South Asian Association for Regional Cooperation (SAARC) almost two decades ago in 1985, but have only moved an inch forward in the shape of a free trade area agreement to be implemented at snail's pace from 2006 over ten-year period. However, from the very beginning, during each summit meeting the SAARC leaders have expressed great ambitions to make South Asia free from hunger and poverty. But no concrete steps have been taken to convert these ambitions into reality. The Free Trade Area agreement signed during Islamabad Summit was perhaps the first major step, which was agreed after great deal of deliberations. The SAARC leaders have also expressed their desire to have a South Asian economic union on the pattern of European economic union during the 11th SAARC summit and reiterated during the 12th SAARC summit but no time frame has been specified to achieve this. The very first step of economic integration i.e. free trade area would take more than a decade to be implemented so one can imagine how long a fully-fledged economic union could take to materialise. Perhaps two decades. But that would be too slow a process considering the speed with which other regions of the world are pooling their resources together for the welfare of their people.

The EU also integrated its economies very slowly in the initial years but last decade saw the fastest integration process giving to Europe a common single currency EURO and a common monetary policy. This is the kind of integration the SAARC members require and should consider EU as a model to improve the economic life of the South Asians and for which they would have to study the European integration process. This book gives an historical account of the development of EU, its structure and functioning and also of the SAARC so that readers can make a comparative understanding and draw conclusion on the feasibility of a South Asian Union on the pattern of European Union. Also, I have included in the book in the annexure part the declarations of the SAARC summits 1985 onwards, which has become quite heavy, though, as a study material. for all those interested in South Asia.

This book was made possible during my tenure as a visiting Wolfson Press Fellow in the Wolfson College, University of Cambridge in the Easter term, 2004. I am obliged to Dr M.S.S. Pandian, Visiting Fellow, South Asia Deptt, University of Cambridge, for revising the manuscript and giving valuable suggestions. I am grateful to the EU Commission delegation in New Delhi for organising meetings with senior officials in EU Commission Headquarters in Brussels (Belgium) to get comprehensive idea of the way the European Union is functioning. I am also indebted to Prof John Naughton, Director, Richard Synge, Asstt Director, for providing necessary guidance and to Ms Hilary Pennington, Administrator, for extending necessary support and assistance.

Ranjit Kumar

Special Correspondent

Navbharat Times, New Delhi

Contents

Annexures

1

A South Asian Union

During the 10th SAARC summit at Colombo in 1998, the SAARC leaders recognised that South Asia, while reflecting a rich, complex and varied plurality of cultural and religious traditions, was heir to a profound common civilizational continuum of great antiquity. This constitutes a historical basis for sustaning harmonious relations among the people of the region. They acknowledged that the SAARC process could draw more deeply from the vitality and strength of South Asia's shared cultural heritage as a source influencing and enhancing creative energies in all fields.

These strong cultural linkages can be exploited to create an atmosphere of goodwill and harmony among all the nationalities of South Asia. Inspite of cultural and linguistic diversities, if the European countries can come together to form an Union why not the South Asians? This is why the unique example of cooperative living, sharing of skills, assets, resources and pooling of sovereignty by European countries, who had a long spell of cold war, for the welfare of its people has also inspired the South Asian leaders. When the SAARC Heads of States constituted an Eminent Persons Group to recommend a roadmap of the future of SAARC, the wise men of South Asia recommended the setting up of a South Asian Economic Union, and the SAARC Heads of States followed it up with a declaration during 11th SAARC summit at Kathmandu by stating the intention of achieving the goal of an Economic Union of South Asia.

During the 1998 SAARC summit the Eminent Persons Group (EPG) of SAARC presented its vision document which laid out a road-map with distinct milestones to achieve: a Free Trade Area by 2008, a Customs Union by 2015 and an economic union by 2020. During the 11th SAARC summit at Kathmandu the leaders agreed to the vision of a phased and planned process eventually leading to a South Asian Economic Union but no timeframe was set to achieve this target. It simply remains a vision for the SAARC leaders. There seems to be a strong desire among South Asian leaders to achieve this ambitious target but lack of sincerity and will power is preventing the members to rise above political differences to give a strong push to this idea.

In these circumstances, perhaps as a bigger partner of SAARC and one of the top ten economies of the world, India has a responsibility to take sincere initiatives even if it means losing some advantages but for the time being India has to forget about the principle of reciprocity and take unilateral measures to win the confidence of the smaller neighbours. Perhaps, in a way, India has been practicing this with Pakistan by not asking for a reciprocal WTO commitment of extending Most Favoured Nation status to India.

But India has to go beyond that and offer easy visa regime for common citizens and access to Indian markets to the Pakistani exporters. The Gujral doctrine enunciated by ex. PM I.K. Gujral in 1997 should perhaps be the guiding principle in India's neighbourhood policy which may promote the concept of cooperative living in South Asia faster. During his tenure as PM one of the first orders issued by Mr Gujral was: No acrimonious war. No war of words. This was the essence of the Gujral doctrine of nonreciprocity so far as neighbouring countries were concerned. Gujral doctrine aims at building a tension free South Asia and simultaneously building bridges of development cooperation with its neighbours. Talking of inter state relations especially India's immediate neighbourhood, Mr. Gujral himself says, "Gujral doctrine, if I may call it so, states that, first, with its neighbours like Bangladesh, Bhutan, Maldives, Nepal and Sri Lanka, India does not ask for reciprocity, but gives and accomodates, it can, in good faith and trust. Second, we believe that no South Asian country should allow its territory to be used against the interests of another county of the region. Third, that none should interfere in the internal affairs of another. Fourth, all South Asian countries must respect each other's territorial integrity and sovereignty. And they should settle all their disputes through bilateral negotiations."[1]

Also the concept of Panchsheel is very much relevant in South Asian context. If it is sincerely adhered to by the SAARC members the political environment in South Asia will improve to a great extent. The Panchsheel, or the Five Principles of Peaceful Co-existence, were first formally enunciated in the Agreement on Trade and Intercourse between the Tibet region of China and India signed on April 29, 1954, which stated, in its preamble, that the two Governments "have resolved to enter into the present Agreement based on the following principles:-

i. Mutual respect for each other's territorial integrity and sovereignty,

ii. Mutual non-aggression,

iii. Mutual non-interference,

iv. Equality and mutual benefit, and

v. Peaceful co-existence."

During the visit of Premier Zhou Enlai to India, he and Prime Minister Jawaharlal Nehru issued a Joint Statement on June 28, 1954, that elaborated their vision of Panchsheel as the framework, not only for relations between the two countries, but also for their relations with all other countries, so that a solid foundation could be laid for peace and security in the world. Panchsheel, as envisioned by its creators, gave substance to the voice of newly established countries who were seeking the space to consolidate their hard won independence, as it provided an alternative ideology dedicated to peace and development of all as the basis for international interaction, whether bilateral or multilateral.

Panchsheel was incorporated into the Ten Principles of International Peace and Cooperation enunciated in the Declaration issued by the April 1955 Bandung Conference of 29 Afro-Asian countries. The universal relevance of Panchsheel

1. Speech by Mr. I.K. Gujral at the Bandarnaike Center for International Studies in Colombo, January 20, 1997.

was emphasised when its tenets were incorporated in a resolution on peaceful co-existence presented by India, Yugoslavia and Sweden, and unanimously adopted on December 11, 1957, by the United Nations General Assembly. In 1961, the Conference of Non-Aligned Nations in Belgrade accepted Panchsheel as the principled core of the Non-Aligned Movement.

In today's world, it is not enough that Panchsheel be promoted as an alternative ideology that empowers the less-developed. It should be made clear that Panchsheel is an ideology for the entire world, and is as relevant to the developed countries of the globe as it is to the less-developed. What should be stressed today is that the principles of Panchsheel are not just empowering principles,. they are also guiding principles that enshrine a certain code of behaviour. Their essence is the non-use of power, the approach of tolerance, "of living one's life, learning from others but neither interfering nor being interfered with", and the obligation to do unto others as you would have them do unto you.

Perhaps all these points find mention in various SAARC declarations also but the South Asian countries have not been following these principles scrupulously. This is why the concept of cooperative living in harmonious manner remains a dream. However, to realise the dream of making South Asian Association For Regional Cooperation a really homogenised economic entity we have to study the experiences of other international economic groupings like ASEAN, NAFTA etc., and evolution of European Union to its present day form and take similar steps suitable to our socio-economic and political conditions. In just half a century, the European Union has achieved remarkable things. It has delivered peace between its member states and prosperity for its citizens. It has created a single European currency, and a frontier free 'single market' where goods, people, services and capital move freely. The EU has grown from six to 25 countries and it is preparing to embrace a few more. It has become a major trading power and a world leader in economic field only because economic strengths have been combined to make it a single bloc. Is it not an example worth emulating ?

Yes, if we go by the strong views expressed by various South Asian leaders. To quote a Sri Lankan leader,[2] "I see a new star rise in the skies of South Asia. I see new star rise, the star of Economic Emancipation and Economic Opportunity for South Asians. The South Asian region has a common and shared history. We speak the same languages. Our colour is the same. We have a multi-religious society. Each in our country believes in the freedom of religion. We all have similar per capita income. All are in similar stages of economic development, all share a common legal system based on common law, all have free market based economies, all share English as a common language for government and business transactions, and all share a common history and culture. The logical choice for the nations of South Asia is to come together under a 'South Asian Free Economic Zone,' which would include all SAARC countries. We could embark on a development journey, where in the first phase, to conclude by the year 2010, the member nations could reach a critical phase in their economic development and per capita income, with liberal trade agreements and co-operation in all sectors. This could be done on the pattern of the European Commission with a common trading currency, a common central bank, a revolving Presidency, a common travel document".

Five Steps

If we go by standards achieved by the European Union then five steps would be required to develop SAARC into a South Asian Union. First step will be to create a Free Trade Area. The second step will be to establish a customs union, third will be to create a common market, then an economic union and finally the fifth step would be the political union. The European Union has not yet been able to achieve fifth level of unity and it seems to be a far cry now, in the background of mutual acrimony over the proposed European Constitution among the major member states, but the way the EU has gradually integrated its various facets of common governance the day is not far off, may be a few years down the line, when

2. Anura Bandarnaike, M.P. Sri Lanka, address on 20th Martyrdom anniversay of Zulfikar Ali Bhutto; 8 March, 1999.

the member countries especially the smaller and insignificant on the world stage would start emphasizing the need of a collective political voice of a united Europe and to assert a common foreign and security policy agenda to show their importance on the world scene.

Though international issues are hotly debated in European Parliament and resolutions are passed expressing European views, they are not taken seriously by the world community as they do not carry the weight of individual governments. However if EU has its foreign and security policy decided in Brussels backed by its own combined military and economic might and all member states agreeing to it then world community would listen to the EU opinion on various issues with great respect. If it happens the EU will become a true political union and then international community will start lobbying among the member countries to vote in their favour in the European Parliament and also in the decision making European Council and then a true European political union will emerge. Then each member state will be respected much more on the world scene. However major powers of European Union have sharp differences on various world issues and they do not present themselves with a collective voice whereas in the economic arena EU for all practical purposes is one entity, a single collective voice of 25 States, as it is always represented by its trade commissioner in all the trade bodies like WTO and fight Europe's case single handedly.

Europe took more than five decades to reach to the level of Economic Union so it would be unrealistic to think of a South Asian Union in a timeframe of few years though the process can be hastened if member states give priority to their economic well being and utilise the opportunity of economic cooperation under the aegis of SAARC as a win-win situation for all while trying to resolve their political differences simultaneously. In Europe also, from the very beginning, the European countries talked of economic cooperation only and this unification process was speeded up when in the early nineties Soviet Union was dissolved and East European countries got themselves freed from Soviet influence.

Views from Pakistan

A noted Pakistani academic and management expert Dr Khawaja Amjad Saeed presenting[3] his thoughts on the theme of a dream about SAARC economic union by 2010 says," The sincerity and commitment by the Governments and the people of SAARC are the crying need of today. Status quo is never a permanent feature. Change is an on-going process. South Asian Economic Union by year 2010 can be the result of a positive thinking approach. An excellent debate has been initiated in this respect. It is hoped that this subject of vital importance will be discussed and debated at various levels namely Government, Private, Public, NGOs institutional and even individual levels. Ideas need to be pooled. Experiences need to be shared. Dimensions of cooperation need to be identified and a framework needs to be evolved to serve as a basis for the proposed South Asian Economic Union by 2010. Clear cut principles for SAARC were spelled out at the time of its establishment and these require firm commitment by all the SAARC countries. The cooperation among SAARC countries cannot be a substitute for bilateral and multi-lateral cooperation but shall complement them. Further, such cooperation shall not be inconsistent with bilateral and multi-lateral obligation.

"Principles on which cooperation shall be based include respect to the following:

1. Sovereign Equality
2. Territorial Integrity
3. Political independence
4. Non-interference in internal affairs of other states and mutual benefit.

"The foregoing principles represent strong conceptual logistics on the basis of which South Asian Economic Union can be strongly visualized by 2010. All the SAARC countries must strictly adhere to the above principles as a mark of respect to each other and help realize the goals for which SAARC has been established."

---

3. *Defence Journal*, Pakistan, May 2002.

The Kathmandu SAARC Summit visualising the establishment of South Asian Economic Union elaborated certain pre-requisites to this dream which were identified as:

1. Promote mutual trust and understanding, peace, stability and amity and accelerated socio-economic cooperation.
2. Foster good neighbourly relations, relieving tensions and building confidence.
3. Finalize a regionally agreed investment framework to meet investment needs of the member states.
4. Promote South Asia as a common tourist destination by upgrading infrastructure, air linkages, simplification and harmonization of administrative procedures and joint marketing.
5. Combat the problem of poverty with a new sense of urgency.
6. Focus on rural micro-credit programmes for women and disadvantaged, widen opportunities for gainful employment and reconstitute the independent South Asian Commission on poverty alleviation.
7. Finalize the SAARC Social Charter including:
   a) Poverty eradication.
   b) Population stabilization.
   c) Empowerment of women.
   d) Youth mobilization.
   e) Human resource development.
   f) Promotion of health and nutrition and projection of children.

Making a strong case for emulating the example of European Union, former Prime Minister of Pakistan Benazir Bhutto said,[4] "First and of precedent-setting importance is the example that you, the European Union, are providing to the rest of humanity. Let us not mince words: The European Union is a revolutionary breakthrough in international relations, the ramifications of which are not yet fully understood.

4. Address before the London Breakfast Club—Free Trade and South Asia, 16 April, 1999.

"Many around the world have been watching with both astonishment and some envy as the European nations have been able to create one of the world's largest single markets in human history, and this without bloodshed or military conquest. Let us not underestimate the accomplishment of creating the European Common market by states whose entire history together has been one of war, animosity and mistrust.

"The desire for the creation of 'super-economic zones' like the European Community was driven by smaller states seeking to effectively compete economically with the economic superpowers of the day, namely the United States and Japan. The GNP of America is (US$ 8 trillion) and of Japan (US$ 5 trillion). Only after combining the 10 'First World' European economies can the combined EC GNP compete (at US$ 7 trillion).

"All this has been accomplished without a single bullet being fired. Huge territories, nations and populations peacefully agreed to redefine their economic borders, and to co-exist with each other in the better interests of their future well being. The EC's formation is truly a model case of the new paradigm, where economically we enter an increasingly 'Borderless World' while maintaining our national sovereignty. In essence, the EC member states are 'pooling' their economic sovereignty in creating a free trade zone and a common currency, thus submerging their narrow national interests for the greater good of the whole European Community."

The economic route to peace

It is hoped that sanity will prevail among all South Asian leaders to plan a faster integration of their economy by listening to the saner voices of their own accomplished countrymen to drop their insistence on "politics first and economy later" as it would lead to nowhere. The noted Malaysian leader Daim Zainuddin[5] has a word of advice for the South Asians, "Asia and India have the strategic advantage of being able to draw lessons from the European model of integrating and expanding markets.

5. Former Finance Minister of Malaysia. Address at the 3rd Asia Pacific Forum, February 22-24, 2004, New Delhi.

Europe has taught us that low level irritants between neighbours who had fought many wars in the history can fester but prosperous neighbours will be too busy making money to quibble over trivial issues. The BBC says that England and France are the best enemies; when formerly feuding neighbours get together to promote prosperity, as we hope India and Pakistan will, they create wealth and opportunities." However, when one state is determined not to progress in economic cooperation unless bilateral disputes are resolved then not much cooperation can be expected from that state to open the doors of its markets, for promoting regional trade, which always expresses the apprehension of being swamped away by a giant Indian economy. It took two decades for SAARC to agree to a South Asia Free Trade Area agreement (SAFTA), and before this preferential trade regime called SAPTA was very hesitantly implemented, though it was considered first major move towards economic cooperation. During last two decades the political rivalries between member nations, specially between India and Pakistan, have increased to such an extent that both acquired nuclear and ballistic missiles capability and very often threatened to annihilate the other side. In this atmosphere it was difficult to imagine an atmosphere of economic cooperation in South Asia.

So, one can guess how the SAARC could not even reach the stage of the very first step of creating a free trade area even after two decades of its existence. Though the Islamabad summit on 4-6 January, 2004, signed an agreement, to set up a free trade area in the region, called South Asia Free Trade Area (SAFTA) by 2006, experts still fear attitudinal roadblocks in its implementation. Though this declaration was described as historic as any small step forward in South Asian cooperation is considered a big step. However this was the third and not the first time that the member states of SAARC have laid down a target date for setting up a free trade area. The agreement signed in Islamabad visualises a graded reduction in import tariffs over the next decade. The first milestone will be in 2006 when the more advanced members of SAARC will have to bring average tariffs down to 20 percent and the Less Developed Countries will have the flexibility of retaining customs duties at

30%. These targets are still not ideal one that characterise a free trade area having minimum or no tariff, but it is more realistic target considering that the SAARC member states now have some of the highest import duties in the world. The more difficult task would be to cut tariffs after 2006 to between zero to five percent over five to eight years. In fact the way the existing preferential trade arrangement (SAPTA) has been implemented shows that no SAARC country is willing as yet to make major tariff concessions. Perhaps the economic insecurity among smaller countries of South Asia added by India-Pakistan tensions is stopping the march ahead of South Asian economic cooperation in a more integrated fashion. Even if the SAARC countries start implementing the SAFTA it will require creation of basic infrastructure to handle increased volume of trade between the members. India and Pakistan will have to open more trading routes in Rajasthan and Punjab, reopen the sea traffic between Mumbai and Karachi that existed before 1965, and goods train services between Lahore and Delhi in addition to increased air services not only between the two capitals but Mumbai and Karachi also. Similarly India and Bangladesh also have to agree for more trading routes and transit facilities to India to link its north eastern states with shorter and economical road routes.

Trade will increase

Even if this extended term SAFTA is implemented seriously the trade volume between the countries would increase very much requiring huge investments of billions of dollars in road and transport sector to link the land border, rail and air routes as only one land crossing point exists between India and Pakistan at Wagah in Amritsar and Lahore. To drastically increase the infrastructural facilities for road, rail and air transport between various South Asian cities, as we see the excellent network of fast lane highways, high speed rail and air network between various European cities, heavy investments would be needed for which the South Asian countries need to pool their efforts, skills and resources together. India being the largest country can take the lead in setting up a infrastructure development fund but augmenting its coffers would be difficult for India, as it is not a cash rich country, so adequate policies would be needed to attract private sector involvement for build, operate, transfer kind of arrangement. The gradual integration of South Asian economy would also dramatically boost the demand of air services from Dhaka to Karachi, Islamabad to Chennai, Thimpu to Lahore, Colombo to Kathmandu and so many other trade and tourist destinations for which heavy investments in airports and hotels would also be required in which foreign investors would willingly participate. The infrastructure development projects will fuel the South Asian economy in a big way by increasing the demand for steel and cement and boost trade and tourism simultaneously which will provide employment to millions of people. This will give a big fillip to the minuscul five percent trade that is presently being conducted among SAARC members. In fact the SAFTA agreement if implemented faster can make South Asia a magnet for foreign investment and lead to restructuring of the economies. In its present form it is not strong enough. According to Mr. Muchkund Dubey[6], this agreement does not measure up to the Eminent Persons Group recommendations. Some of the important measures recommended by the EPG and missing from the Agreement are: finalisation of the pending draft investment agreement, the creation of the SAARC investment area, a South Asian Development Fund, a South Asian Development Bank and an Asian Energy grid; vertical industrial integration, harmonisation of the fiscal and monetary policies. A crippling drawback of the SAFTA is that it does not provide for the creation of any mechanism for pursuing 'the additional measures' under article 8. This casts doubts on the seriousness of the contracting parties to pursue these measures. A major limitation of this treaty is that it leaves out trade in services. However given the political will this Agreement has the potential to acquire a momentum of its own, which can lead to the transformation of economic relations in the region."

After a free trade area agreement is implemented in totality the next step would be to create a customs union. The experience of European Union in this area should be studied deeply to give a similar model for SAARC. For a customs union—the first step

---

6. Ex-Foreign Secretary, India (*The Hindu*: SAFTA a perspective; 10.01.2004)

towards common market—means two quite simple things: that goods of all kinds move freely from one member country to another, unhindered by customs or quotas or other restrictions of any kind; and that goods from the rest of the world are subject to an identical level of duty wherever they enter the area. In fact the customs policy of the EU is a foundation of the Union and essential element in the functioning of the single common market. The single market can only function properly where there are common rules applied in a common way at its external borders—customs administrators of the 25 member countries acting as one. These common rules go beyond the customs union as such—with its common tariff—and extend to all aspects of trade policy, such as preferential trade, health and environment controls, the common agricultural and fisheries policy, the protection of the economic interests of the EU by non tariff instruments and external relations policy measures. Now the European Union is running into new phase of customs cooperation which started on 1st January, 2003, and will continue till 31 December, 2007. Under this phase legal and financial basis will be provided for electronic information exchange systems between national administrations, training seminars for customs officials and experts, the exchange of officials between national administrations and the basis for an electronic system which will allow business to move towards paperless customs environment. According to the objectives laid down by the EU customs have an important role to play to combat fraud and criminal activities. The EU is becoming a strong economic and trading player in the world economy. Customs Union is playing an important role in ensuring the competitiveness of the European trade environment. Can South Asian countries have similar arrangements in future to improve the competitiveness of their economy by creating common customs procedures and laws and regulations on the boundaries of SAARC?

Single Market

After the Customs Union provisions are introduced the establishment of a single or common market will become easier. Launched in 1985, the 1992 Internal Market programme (IMP) in EU was an ambitious attempt to fulfill the original aims of the

Treaty of Rome by sweeping away obstacles to the four freedoms: free movement of goods, services, capital and labour. Liberalisation, deregulation and freedom of movement are, therefore the principal watchwords of the IMP. The underlying aims of the IMP were both political and economic. From the former perspective it was seen as a means of restoring the dynamic of European integration and thus of taking forward the aim of binding the countries of Europe together. In other words the IMP sought to reduce costs by eliminating barriers to free movement.[7] The ultimate aim of the common market is to merge the economics of the member states into one, by breaking down the barriers between them and working out common policies. The European Common Market, officially called the European Economic Community, has affected the economic, political and military policies of all countries and especially the United States. It has been emulated in Latin America, Africa and even within Europe itself. It has induced other neighbouring countries to become part of it as either full or associate members. It does indeed represent peaceful revolution of our times.[8] Thus one can imagine the positive impact that can have on the South Asian economic integration after the introduction of the Common Market. For common market to become successful the member countries should have undisputed boundary but a disputed boundary can also become peaceful after the introduction of the customs union and the common market as the economic benefits to the ordinary masses will be so great that people will ignore the disputes since they will enjoy the free movements across the border and get a feeling that the border no longer divides them. It will encourage cross border investments, movement of labour and business. The economic benefits will be so enormous that the countries would be encouraged to address peace and security issues jointly and sincerely.

Currency

Since in the common market people still would have to change the currencies each time they cross the borders they

7. Commentary: The Single Market: Ian Begg.
8. Lawrence Krause; *The Common Market.*

would prefer to have a single currency to avoid losing money each time they change their currency notes. So there will be popular pressure from the people to introduce a single currency over the entire region. For which an economic union has to be established. The last stage of the economic integration of a regional grouping will be the economic and monetary union. Since the mid-1980s the process of European integration has assumed more significance than ever before in the economic and political life of the Continent. In 1985, the European Community launched its single market programme, with the objective of liberalizing its internal trade including capital movements. Seven years later, at Maastricht in the Netherlands, the EC went much further and agreed the Treaty on European Union. The new Union (EU) was to have a 'Common Foreign and Security Policy' and co-operation in matters of Justice and Home Affairs. But the most radical and historic shift contained in the Treaty was the establishment of an Economic and Monetary Union. With these new elements the integration process was set to challenge the traditions of Europe's nation-states like never before in the post war period.

"EMU was the single most important strand of what was seen as the 'relaunch' of European integration in the 1980s and 1990s. At Maastricht the EC member states agreed, subject to two 'opt-outs', a timetable for replacing existing national currencies like the D-mark, French franc, and Italian lira with a single European currency. There was to be a single monetary policy, managed by a European Central Bank (ECB) that was independent from national governments. It would, in consequence, possess considerable power over the economic fate of the Continent. In order to qualify for entry EC states had to show that they could abide by a set of tough fiscal disciplines represented by the 'no bailout' provision and the convergence criteria."[9] Today 12 nations of EU use one single currency EURO which has revolutionised peoples, thinking in these countries towards one Europe and it gives them a feeling of becoming citizens of Europe. This kind of an economic and monetary union would be an ideal setting for South Asia but

---

9. *The Road to Maastricht*: Kenneth Dyson

given the current state of relations between the member countries it does not seem feasible in the near future. However it should be the job of the academic community and the think tanks and also the Chambers of Commerce and Industry to push for this ideal stage of economic integration which would lead to interdependence among South Asian people and nations and which in turn will lead to permanent peace and stability in the subcontinent.

Common Parliament

After the economic and monetary union in South Asia is achieved, the South Asian countries can think in terms of a common foreign policy and security agenda, though it may seem improbable at the moment. A borderless visa free regime as it has evolved in European Union can be thought of in SAARC region also. The Association of South East Asian nations (ASEAN) has successfully introduced this visa free travel among their member states long back which has helped faster integration of their markets. After all three major countries of South Asia India, Pakistan and Bangladesh were one political entity though under British rule and partition of the region in 1947 is still considered artificial as the people of the region speak similar languages and have the same culture and lifestyle. Only six decades ago they belonged to same British colony called India though much water has flown in the Ganges and Jhelum since then. The world political and economic scene has changed a lot. East and West Germany have merged once again. Cold War scenario is no more. South Asian politics was also very much influenced by the super power politics. Pakistan was considered to be in American camp and India in the Soviet camp. Now Soviet Camp is no more. Though rivalry between India and Pakistan continues it may evaporate with the passage of time as people will soon realise the futility of having a permanent state of enmity between the two nations. The resumed cricket series between India and Pakistan hosted by Pakistan in the first half of 2004 displayed vividly the common peoples urge to interact with each other. Similarly, the organisation of a Made in Pakistan exhibition in New Delhi Talkatora gardens in March 2004, also drew huge response and warmth from Indian public. The way the Pakistani businessmen and women played Holi (Hindu festival of colours) with their Indian counterparts during the exhibition period also reminded the observers of the South Asian affairs that Hindus and Muslims can live amicably in the subcontinent inspite of the rising trends of Hindu fundamentalism in India and the Jehadi culture in many parts of the subcontinent. After the resolution of political differences the countries of the region can come on one platform with independent sovereign national identities and to discuss their common issues and problems. For this, the proposed South Asian Union can also think of a common Parliament after total economic integration has been achieved, as it would require framing of common rules and procedures for trade and business, customs and issues of taxation etc. The Parliament can discuss common problems and arrive on a consensus decision to deal with those issues effectively. The European Parliament is an excellent model where the pan-European parties are emerging and fighting elections on an European agenda. (See Chapter-12)

2

A dream for South Asia

This writer had a brush with history as a only South Asian witness to the epoch making enlargement ceremony of European Union at Dublin (Ireland) on May 1, 2004. As the flags of 10 new member States along with 15 existing States of European Union were hosted in the huge lawns of the Presidential Palace amidst thunderous applause of the Heads of states and governments of all the 25 members, at the famous Phoenix Park, people all over Europe especially in eastern region declared no more war in Europe. In Germany, Dr Helmut Kohl, the former Chancellor, told a crowd outside the eastern city of Zittau at the meeting point of the German, Polish and Czech borders that "a peaceful future in Europe was the simplest and the most important reason for European integration. We want to honour the dead and tend the graves but we don't want any more soldiers graves in Europe." On this evening, he said, he could see his entire life before him: the second world war, the dictatorships and division, but most of all Germany's zero hour from which we could never have imagined coming to this point. Dr. Kohl called for an end to talk of old and new Europe, saying that, from today (May 1) there was only one Europe, "Europe pure". In the Czech capital Prague people gathered at the Wencesias Square from where 15 years ago they had assembled to demand the resignation of the Communist politburo. In Warsaw, Lech Walesa, whose Solidarity Movement toppled the country's communist regime in 1989 said, "Poland's entrance into the European Union fulfills my dreams and lifetime work." The

EU's commissioner for enlargement, Gunter Verheughen said, "May 1, will be milestone in the history of Europe. It is the Europe's response to the end of cold war and an opportunity to heal the wounds of the past, wounds of war and dictatorships. Of the ten new countries eight are communists. Latvia, Lithuania, and Estonia were part of the old USSR and a further five—Poland, Czech Republic, Slovakia, Slovenia and Hungary—were Soviet satellites. Malta and the Greek controlled half of Cyprus were also admitted to the European Union.

Accession of ten new members in European Union making it to 25 is being hailed as world's greatest peace project, healing not just the divisions of second world war but of the cold war wounds too. On May 1, 2004, the European leaders put a final seal on the reunification of a continent divided by cold war, as the EU expanded to 25 nations, becoming world's biggest free trade area. Leaders of states once under Moscow's iron grip for the first time took their place as full members of EU, alongside western European counterparts, in a summit at Farmleigh House in the salubrious Phoenix Park in Dublin. The new enlarged Union will be one of 450 million people and 20 official languages, stretching from the Atlantic to the border of Russia across three time zones and deep into the territory of the old Soviet Union. The accession of ten new including eight communists into EU has turned the wheel of history. They created the third biggest moment in the post 1945 reconstruction of a peaceful Europe, following the Franco-German rapproachment of the 1950's and the end of dictatorships in southern Europe in the 1970's. In fact what began with the fall of Berlin Wall in the night of 8/9 November 1989, was finally completed in May 2004.

Milestone

This enlargement will be remembererd as one of the milestones of the early 21st century. With the so-called eastward enlargement of EU what has been achieved is just not the demolition of the remnants of the Berlin Wall, which artificially divided Europe into West and East, it is an unprecedented step towards a Europe—whole and free. Never before in

European history have so many countries of central and eastern Europe been together with their western neighbours as democracies in the same political, economic and security community, with equal rights and obligations. For decades they have been second class citizens, poor relatives, objects of other's designs. For decades they have had a complex of backwardness and exclusion, while west Europeans have caricatured them as exotic, eccentric and obscure. The eight former communist states who joined the EU are often regarded in the existing member states as being on the continent's easternmost fringe and as poor cousins who should be grateful to be admitted to an exclusive club. But the new EU members such as Poland, Hungary or the Czech Republic regard EU membership as a return—after an enforced estrangement—to the heart of Europe where politically, culturally and economically they have always belonged. Before Communism, the same customs, culture and ideas that swept through London, Paris and Berlin were seen in Budapest, Prague and Warsaw It was only the cruel division of postwar Europe that cast the East adrift. Now there is a sense of homecoming in these countries.

Now with the accession of ten new states It would create immense potential for the economic future of the region as their purchasing capacities rise due to increased prosperity in the coming years. In fact a vast trade empire of 450 million consumers is being created. After the accession of ten new members the population of EU will increase by around a fifth but its economic might will increase by somewhere between four to six percent. Ten new members will account for 25 percent of Europe's population but only five percent of its GDP. Estimates of how long it will take their living standards to catch up with the present EU average range from 15 years or 50 or more. The combined gross product of the old 15 EU members is some Euro 9,000 bn whereas the accession states muster just Euro 500 bn. This enlargement will also cause lot of social unrest in both the developed and the developing region of EU as the poorer citizens would try to grab a share from the rich.

Thus there is a concern that although the accession countries will not add hugely to the EU's economic muscle, they could complicate life for the bloc's trade policy makers especially in the common agricultural policy. For example, Poland will be the country asking for a big slice of the agricultural subsidies extended by EU which swallows up half the EU's entire budget. Poland has the potential to play a dominant role in European farming and from May 2004, the Polish farmers will be entitled to share in the distribution of those 50 billion Euro Common Agricultural Policy funds. The impact of accession on central Europe's agriculture is likely to be felt right across the union's rural communities. A third of Poland's population lives on land. It has large as well as small farms and food already forms a substantial percentage of its exports, but its agriculture uses minimal agrochemicals, because the Polish farmers have never been able to afford them. There are also millions of small holders and it is feared that a large number of them will go out of business. Finding jobs for them will be a problem as they would not be able to survive the competition of the new big investors in the farms sector. The American agribusiness like the Cargill has been eyeing up the opportunities and is ready to use Poland as a bridgehead into lucrative EU markets. So change is likely to be dramatic and fast.

Benefits

At the moment for the large number of the population of the new accession states the only tangible benefits of full membership would be the free movement of labour as the agricultural subsidies and the cohesion transfers have not been fully made available to them. The new members will face huge domestic pressures to squeeze more economic rewards out of EU membership than are currently on offer and to resist further losses of national sovereignty. Still the arrival of 75 million new consumers in EU is not being sniffed at by economists, even if their incomes are below the EU average. In overall terms Germany is expected to be the big winner. It is estimated by an Austrian Bank that Germany's trade with the new entrants will be around Euro 100 billion which will be five percent of German

GDP whereas the Austrian trade is tipped to reach the equivalent of 10 % of GDP over a decade. Austria has always been a gateway to the east. Although Britain does not have the same geographic proximity or the historical ties, a study by the British Deptt of treasury suggests that some 100,000 jobs are linked to exports to the new ten members.

As the old EU members fear immigration, chaos and competition from cheap skilled labour or more favourable tax regimes, for the moment the East Europeans will have the right to work only in Britain, Ireland and probably Sweden and the Netherlands. All other EU member countries will deny them employment rights for up to seven years. Agricultural subsidies to the Eastern European farmers will remain a fraction of those paid to existing members and the net flows of money from cohesion funds will be derisory after the budget contributions which new members start paying from Ist of May are taken into account. It is also feared that the ten new members could prove a disruptive presence in EU councils, demanding a say out of all proportion to their economic power and unyielding in their defence of national interests, as their sometimes unruly electorates perceive them. This enlargement will make the EU an even more argumentative body. And with further expansion approaching, the high-watermark of Europe's institutional integration has surely been reached. The more EU grows, the clearer it will surely become that it must remain an association of 30 or so independent countries, linked by history, geography, a common cultural heritage and mutual economic interests but far too diverse and idiosyncratic ever to merge into a single federal state.

Membership

The EU is open to membership to any European country that meets certain political and economic criteria. The possible number of members of the EU is therefore, theoretically well over 40. In the short term, three other countries are lined up to be members in the near future. Bulgaria and Romania will so long as there are no major problems, whereas the third aspirant Turkey is more problematic. Proposed Turkish membership of the EU has been and continues to be one of the most divisive elements in EU affairs. Turkey first applied to join in 1959 and since then progressive forces within the country have been implementing reforms—particularly in relation to the Kurdish minority—and have advanced their arguments for these by referring to the ultimate goal of the EU membership. Many of the criticisms of Turkey's membership focus on its perceived status as a 'Muslim' country. However Turkey is an avowedly secular republic not a Islamic state. While many Turks are practising Muslims, Islam is no more a state religion. However, Turkey with only Istanbul on the European geographic mainland has always been a problem. If a country is somewhat in Europe and mostly in Asia then there are dissenting voices on its admission to EU. There is a widespread feeling that Turkey just would not fit in the EU. Many Europeans argue now that it is time for a pause and take a breath before further enlargement. Negotiations with Turkey, can begin if it meets the socalled political criteria regarding human rights, democracy, rule of law as well as respect for and protection of minorities. But there are deeply European countries wanting to join EU and the big question is how to refuse them. Countries like Croatia, Serbia, Macedonia or even Georgia would be eager to join EU. So, questions are being asked 25 today, how many tomorrow?

Attracted by the advantages of living together in a joint European family, new European countries are eager to join EU. At the first level, the objective is to ensure that Bulgaria and Romania, the current candidate countries who were not yet ready for accession in 2004, can enter the European Union as early as 2007. Then the application of Turkey will also be taken up. A review of whether Turkey has met the political criteria will be done and if it is positive negotiations will begin. Turkey has a standard of living which is about 25% of the EU average—roughly the same as Bulgaria and Romania. It's population of about 70 million people would make it the biggest EU country after Germany. Beyond these candidates there are potential future members. These are the countries of the western Balkan regions, consisting of Albania and the former Yugoslav countries of Croatia, Macedonia, Bosnia-Herzegovina and Serbia-

Montenegro. The EU needs to help these countries to step up their preparations for potential EU membership. In February 2003, Croatia submitted an application for EU membership, which is being examined by the European Commission.

The rest of the western Balkan countries will be encouraged to follow their respective roadmaps towards eventual EU membership. Less clear, however will be the impact of enlargement on the early remaining possible candidate for membership—the countries of the European Free Trade Area Association(EFTA) namely Iceland, Liechtenstein, Norway and Switzerland. Norway twice completed membership negotiations but these were twice rejected in a national referendum. Switzerland appplied for membership in 1992 but has chosen not to pursue its application. It is not clear whether Switzerland will review its application in near future or not. People very often ask—how many more members will join EU in a decade or so.

With the enlargement the big question now being raised among Eurosceptics is whether the individual national identities be devoured by a European superstate, a Europa or United States of Europe run by bureaucrats in Brussels? There are fears that the Council of Europe will be too large a body to agree unanimously to a decision so it will become a debating house and if a decision taken after a long debate is enforced by a majority vote it will result in divisions and mutual suspicions and pressure lobbies working against each other. But if the Europeans are able to manage their affairs in a more cohesive manner EU will be an extraordinary community, unique in the world, of going on 35 democracies and 455 million going on 600 million citizens, living together in mutually reinforcing freedom, peace and prosperity. It seems to be a tall order right now but who could have predicted this kind of Europe when the present state of EU was never thought of during cold war days. It is natural for the size of an organization like EU to have severe management problems and controversies which attract media attention and sensationalism and thus an impression is formed among the gullible public that EU is not a workable solution for their problems. However, experts describe EU as a "work in progress " and it will take several years to mature to its full potential.

It is not surprising that the journey from the overthrow of communism in 1989 to Union membership took 15 years. The adjustment process to meet the entry conditions can be tough and long. It took the United Kingdom two attempts before it joined in 1973, along with Denmark and Ireland. Greece became a member in 1981, within six years of applying, whereas Spain and Portugal joined in 1986 after 10 years of effort. The entry of Austria, Finland and Sweden in 1995 was a relatively rapid affair. The new member states from central and eastern Europe had a long way to travel. They lacked the established political, economic and legal structures that would allow them rapidly to join the Union. It was therefore clear that the accession process would take time, although EU leaders began sending positive political signals encouraging their membership shortly after the Berlin Wall fell in 1989. But helping the candidates move to a market economy and a stable pluralist democracy were the first priorities. The actual entry negotiations began later, in March 1998.

Support for reforms

Support for economic and democratic reforms in the candidate countries in preparation for EU entry began in 1989 when the Union created the so called Phare programme initially for the benefit of Poland and Hungary, the first countries to free themselves from Communism. Along with Phare two other programmes called ISPA and Sapard were started. ISPA supported the development of infrastructure whereas Sapard helped the newcomers modernise their agriculture. Together these programmes provide Euro 3 billion a year to help adapt to European Union membership. Under a separate deal for preaccession assistance, Cyprus and Malta were jointly allocated Euro 95 million for the 2000-04 period. With this expansion all the members would benefit significantly. However new large additions in a family is always an issue for management concerns and the EU is no exception. The experience of previous EU enlargements has shown that old and new integrate smoothly and that (if they arise) short term strains are soon offset by long term gains. Because of its sheer size, the latest enlargement raised extra questions for people on both sides about the impact on their lives and jobs. Some people in the west worried that their jobs would be threatened, if new EU citizens willing to work for relatively low wages, moved towards the developed countries in the EU in large numbers. There were also concerns of environmental standards or the possibility of more illegal immigrants entering the EU via the new member states. People in the new members of EU often asked whether their economies could withstand competition from western firms or whether their farmers could survive against the counterparts bolstered by years of support from EU's agricultural policy. Others worried that the richer EU citizens would push up the price of property.

On a political level, some asked whether such a big enlargement might slow European integration or dilute current achievements. Others in the new member countries wondered whether they might be surrendering sovereignty to Brussels so soon after shaking off the Soviet yoke. These questions were all addressed and answered during the accession negotiations and in practical action taken during that period. Moreover, enlargement in itself will create further economic growth and prosperity and will thus sustain the positive trends. And for the short term, transitional measures have been agreed to deal with any unexpected negative effects on the economy of any member state. Countries that were already members before 2004 can, for a period of up to seven years, freely decide when workers from the new member states can enter job markets. Experience with previous enlargements has shown that in any event, relatively few workers emigrate.

Similar would be the concerns in various South Asian countries also as Pakistanis fear competition from Indian industries and Indians apprehend flood of illegal immigrants entering India from Bangladesh in search of livelihood. With the gradual movement towards the final stage of integrated economy, the South Asian leadership need to allay these fears in advance by taking remedial measures and creating awareness among all the

South Asians, especially among opinion makers. The experiences of European Union should be studied by South Asians to remove all the apprehensions among the common masses and political leaders also to counter practical difficulties in opening the borders without any customs barriers.

Efforts are in hand to reinforce border controls by new entrants along the Union's new eastern frontier. It is in their own interests to apply them strictly as they themselves become end destinations for illegal immigration, or criminals, from outside—not just transit points to other EU countries. Internal frontiers between the newcomers and other Union members will only be removed once external frontier protection is deemed to be adequate, based on a unanimous decision of the member states. Although farmers of new member states will receive full scale EU-support only after a ten-year transitional period, they will stand to receive Union funding worth about Euro 10 billion in the period 2004-06 and will therefore be the first direct beneficiaries of accession. The new member countries who feared a massive sell off of their agricultural land and property will for several years be free to decide whether or not to allow sales to citizens from other EU countries. Generally the period agreed is seven years, while for Poland it was extended to 12 years. The experience of small countries within the EU suggests that the concern of newcomers about losing sovereignty and independence to Brussels is misplaced. Each of them, starting with tiny Luxembourg, has a greater influence in European and world affairs than it would on its own, thanks to the institutional framework of the EU, which is especially designed to give each country, and its citizens, their say. The EU treaties also allow a certain number of member states to move ahead as a group in a particular policy area, leaving the other countries to catch up later.

Commitments

The membership terms agreed by the new entrant states include a commitment to adopt the Euro and accept the disciplines of economic and monetary union(EMU). But the process of joining the Euro area is not automatic and no timetable has been set. As was the case with the older member states, each will join according to its own timetable. None has an opt-out from the Euro as obtained by the United Kingdom and Denmark. However, before being able to adopt single currency, new members will have to meet normal EMU requirements on budget deficits, debt, inflation, long term interest rates and exchange rate stability. This means that, in practice, the first of them cannot adopt the Euro before 2006 at the earliest. A number of newcomers have signalled their intention to adopt the Euro as rapidly as possible. On the one hand early membership will ensure monetary stability, encourage inward investment and probably lead to lower interest rates for businesses and consumers. On the other hand, keeping a currency out for a while will provide enough flexibility to manage exchange rates, deficits and inflation in a way which may deliver faster growth rates than might be possible under the disciplines of EMU(in particular the Stability and Growth pact).

The new member states have a number of things in common. They are all poorer than the average of the other 15 EU countries. Except Malta and Cyprus they have recently emerged from 40 years of communist dictatorships. They have limited resources yet major needs for infrastructure projects and social programmes. While they will therefore, wish to obtain as much of the EU's structural funds as possible, their absorption capacity may be limited. The fact that all the newcomers with the exception of Poland are small countries was partly responsible for launching the process to draw up a new constitutional treaty for the enlarged Union. One of the prime concerns of the drafters of the treaty was to facilitate the decision taking process in a Union of 25 or even more members. In terms of sheer numbers, decision taking is anyway more cumbersome with 25 ministerial delegations attending each meeting of the Council of the European Union. The linguistic complexity increases as nine more official languases are added to the previous eleven. A Slovenian member of the European Parliament or minister sitting in the council are just as entitled to speak in the language of the people he or she represents as one from Germany, France or the United Kingdom. The extra costs of interpretation are marginal to the equivalent of one cup of coffee per Union citizen per year that preserves EU multilingualism, says the European Commission.

The dream Hugo saw

Victor Hugo's dream can very well he seen by any South Asian visionary leader or thinker with remarkable similarity in South Asian context. The fast changing face of Europe with disappearing boundaries and customs barriers and a unified currency and a possible fully-fledged joint army with common security and foreign policy can only be a dream for the people of ever feuding South Asian countries as they are presently struggling towards an effective regime of deeper economic interaction and trade exchanges. However, in the words of President A P J Abdul Kalam, to realise one's goal one has to dream and dream a lot so as to make that dream become true. The Europeans had begun dreaming right since the middle of 19th century when the French writer Victor Hugo started propagating the idea of a United States of Europe. This dream was shattered by two world wars of the 20th century. Inspite of the division of Europe in the communist and anti-communist camp the idea of United States of Europe started getting concrete shape only after the end of second world war when in May 1948, the Congress of Europe was held at The Hague and attended by more than 800 politicians from all over Europe. It's President of honour was Winston Churchill. This Congress was organised by the International Committee of the Movements for European Unity and led directly to the foundation in October 1948, of the European movement.

The Congress adopted a message to Europeans which called for a United Europe, throughout whose area the free movement of persons, ideas and goods is restored. This would be accompanied by a charter of Human rights, a court of justice to guarantee those rights and a European Assembly where peoples representatives of all the nations would sit as a legislative member to chalk out plans for their common welfare. These ideas were worked out in more detail in a political report considered by the Congress which prompted a number of specific resolutions adopted unanimously.

The Congress represented the high watermark of enthusiasm for European integration in the immediate post-war world. It sought on an all party basis to bring pressure on governments to elicit popular support for integrationist idea. Although it had substantial impact at the time, the Congress may be seen in retrospect to have been not wholly successful. The main ideas put forward were embodied the following year in the statute of the Council of Europe. In fact to celebrate the birth of the idea of a united Europe the European Movement organised in May 1998, a Congress of Europe at The Hague to mark 50th anniversary of the first congress. The idea of a united Europe moved forward when French foreign affairs minister Robert Schuman took up the idea originally conceived by Jean Monnett and proposed on 9 May 1950, the treaty of Paris establishing the European Coal and Steel community (ECSC) and then the Treaty of Rome was signed in 1957, to establish the European Economic Community (EEC). At the same time an European Atomic Energy Committee was also set up. In 1992, the Treaty on European Union was signed in Maastricht. In 1997, the treaty of Amsterdam was signed which came into force in May 1999. Since the entry into force of the Maastricht Treaty in November 1993, the European Community became a component part of European Union. European Union or the Union is used to be known as European Community or earlier still as the Common Market. From 1981 till 1998, the ECU (European Currency Unit) was used in all areas of the Union's finances including the grants to member states under the structural funds from European Investment Bank. On first January, 1999, the Euro replaced the ECU on 1:1 basis and fixed exchange rates applied between Euro and the currencies of participating states until such time as these currencies are phased out. Rates between the Euro and all other currencies were determined on daily basis. And finally the Euro became a currency of daily use from 2002.

The dream of Victor Hugo

A day will come when you will no longer wage war, when you will no longer raise men of arms against each other. You would still have differences to settle, interests to discuss, certainly disputes to solve, but do you know what you will have in place of men on foot and horseback, in place of guns, falconets, spears, pikes and swords? You will have a small box made of wood, which you will call a ballot box. And do you know what this box will bringforth? An Assembly in which you will all feel you live, an assembly which will be like your own soul, a supreme and a popular council which will decide, judge and solve everything in law, which will cause the sword to fall from every hand and justice to rise in every heart. And this event will say to you, there ends your right, here begins your duty, lay down your arms! Live in peace.

On that day you will be conscious of a common thought, common interests and a common destiny. You will clasp each other's hands and you will acknowledge that you are sons of the same blood and the same race. On that day you will no longer be hostile tribes but a nation........on that day your name will no longer be war, but civilization.

A day will come when there will be no battlefields, but markets opening to commerce and minds opening to ideas. A day will come when the bullets and bombs are replaced by votes, by universal suffrage, by the venerable arbitration of a great Supreme Senate which will be to Europe what Parliament is to England, the Diet to Germany and the legislative Assembly to France. A day will come when a cannon will be a museum piece as instruments of torture are today. And we will be amazed to think that those things once existed!

A day will come we shall see those two immense groups—the United States of America and the United States of Europe, stretching out their hands across the sea, exchanging their products, their arts, their works of genius, clearing up the globe making the deserts fruitful, ameliorating creation under the eyes of the creator and joining together to reap the well being of all.

Speech at the International Peace Congress held in Paris in 1851

Common Institutions

After expanding in all directions and having created a huge infrastructure to run its institutions the 15 members of European Union strongly felt the need to have a common constitution to run their affairs in a more systematic manner with set principles and laws for which an European Parliament has already been created. Attracted by the benefits of living together the smaller European states are queuing up to join the Union.

This is why when 10 new European states joined EU on first of May 2004, a watershed was crossed which will lead towards a nation state based Union which is much closer to the kind of Europe which the founding fathers of Congress of Europe envisaged in 1948. Though the British illustrious leader Winston Churchill referred to the idea of a United States of Europe way back in 1948 but faltered on this grand vision later on, the present British leaders still have to clear the minds of people that the European Union will not be renamed United States of Europe. Prime Minister Blair declared in British Parliament that the Queen will not be replaced as Head of State by an EU President. He also tried to dispel the impression that Britain will be forced to join the Euro without a referendum and regardless of the economic tests being passed. Nor Britain will loose its seat in the UN Security Council. But the Europeans are not bothered. The only thing that bothers them is that the British attitude will delay the adoption of a new European constitution for which Britain has already been warned by the EU Commissioner Chris Patten that it will have to live in the margins of EU forever. That in effect will create an EU without Britain. In a democratic society there are peoples of various shades and opinions and it is natural for the leaders to fight over issues keeping in mind the domestic constituency but it does not mean that the system will collapse. These kind of debates in fact strengthens the democratic and political fabric of a state.

New Europe

The South Asian countries will have to deal with this newly emerged powerful democratic Europe and get ready to increase its own internal strength so as to be able to deal and interact with the Europeans in a more effective manner. This is why the leaders of South Asia have started referring to European Union as a model for the South Asian countries to make themselves prosperous, peaceful and stable society. No doubt the European countries also took more than fifty years to realise this dream of a unified Europe at least economically the South Asian countries may also take a few decades to achieve the level of integration the way the Europeans have achieved. The 25 countries of European Union have surrendered their economic management to the authority in Brussels which is controlled by European Council comprising Heads of State and Prime Ministers of the member countries, though they are still struggling to implement a common constitution for all.

To ask South Asian countries to think of a common constitution would be asking too much in the present circumstances and in the foreseeable future it does not seem feasible. But to move towards that goal with step by step approach as the Europeans have done would be desirable. The South Asian leaders may react violently to this idea as none of them would like to subjugate themselves to a new common South Asian administrative regime which they would naturally fear be dominated by India. Similar are the fears right now in Europe where Britain is hesitating to surrender its political authority to the regime in Brussels. Britain and a few other countries may ultimately succeed in preventing the European countries from adopting a common constitution for the European Union and thus save themselves from surrendering their foreign and defence policies to the Brussels administration but the heights achieved by the European countries even without a common constitution would be a dream achievement for the South Asian countries as they are the most poor region of the world. Their coming together would mean a lot of economic interaction among themselves which would definitely uplift the impoverished people of South Asia.

As the Europeans have made life easier for the citizens of the member countries by integrating their economies the South Asians would also be benefited by similar approach. With this aim in view the then Indian Prime Minister Atal Bihari Vajpayee drew a roadmap at a peace seminar in December 2003, for a harmoniously integrated South Asia. He said that open borders and even a single currency for the region were not unrealistic and utopian if "we can put aside mistrust and dispel unwarranted suspicion and develop mutual sensitivity to each others' concerns." The dream that Victor Hugo saw one and a half century ago is now being realised in Europe. Can we dream of a reunited South Asia, of course, with each state maintaining their sovereignty, but where there will be open borders with peaceful coexistence and free movement of people, ideas and commerce as we now see in Europe?

Source: Facts and figures sourced from European Commission documents

3

South Asia: Possibilities

Amidst sea of poverty, malnutrition, illiteracy and hunger lie the small and big islands of prosperity, high technology and excellence. This is the broad scene of South Asia today. With a combined population of more than 1.3 billion, it's huge market, rising middle class, cheap but qualified labour and abundant natural resources, South Asia is waiting to be tapped not only by foreign investors but by the domestic entrepreneurs and businessmen also. For this a climate conducive to growth and cooperation with spirit of cooperative relations and partnerships needs to be created among all the seven member states of South Asian Association of Regional Cooperation (SAARC) i.e. Bangladesh, Bhutan, India, Maldives, Nepal, Pakistan and Sri Lanka. Peace, prosperity and stability is not only vital for the economic and social upliftment of the impoverished people of South Asia but for peace, security and stability of the entire Asia and the world also as this region comprises one fifth of humanity. There is no dearth of desire among the political and business leaders of the region to create an environment of peace and friendship to improve intra-SAARC trade, as is evident from their various statements.[1]

Any economic and social imbalance affecting 20% of world population (having 44% of the world's poor or approximately

---

1. (i) The foreign minister of Bangladesh Morshed Khan in an address to Confederation of Indian Industries (CII) said, "We should shed mental barriers and increase intra-SAARC trade from the present 5% to 20%. There is a need to establish a new (Contd.)

522 million people living on less than a dollar a day) in a single region will definitely impact on the peace and prosperity of the rest of the world. It is therefore imperative that the countries of South Asia develop understanding of the magnitude of the issue of peace and prosperity and start cooperating extensively in the economic arena. Politics, religion, language, ethnicity have kept the South Asians apart from each other inspite of and perhaps due to their geographical proximity. The Indian subcontinent which was a conglomerate of loosely organised kingdoms and which was brought together under one empire by the Britishers is now known as South Asia comprising mainly of India, Pakistan and Bangladesh came into being as independent political entities only in 1947 (Bangladesh separated from Pakistan in 1972) and since then there has been little economic interaction among them though trade between India and Bangladesh has picked up during

---

identity for South Asia by creating a pan-Asian organization. A time-bound task force is needed to be formed to increase intra-regional trade, come what may. The formation of common platform of standardization is needed which would help intra-SAARC trade immensely. The need of the hour was to create a synergy between industry and politics so that the poor of the region, who comprise 1/5th of the global population, benefit. After the Islamabad SAARC Summit there is a new found confidence and friendship among the member countries, and governments should resolve all outstanding issues. Bigger steps are needed to be taken towards confidence building measures between India and Bangladesh as both cannot divorce each other. India and Bangladesh together could become an economic force to reckon with (2nd June, 2004).

(ii) A Pakistani businessman Jalil Baig (Chairman, Pakistan Hardware Merchants Association) talking to the members of CII said," India and Pakistan share a common history, culture, language, sentiments and business ethics, hence trade and economic relationship between the two countries are inevitable. The businesses of the two countries need to forge closer relations. There was a need to expand, widen, enlarge and deepen the relations. Despite the proximity between the two countries, the businessmen have to procure each others' products through a third country which makes it upon 30% costlier. (3rd June, 2004)

the last few years due to better interaction and understanding of the importance of the neighbourhood trade between the two countries. But the same is not true between India and Pakistan. It's a win-win situation for the two neighbouring countries if both import and export to the maximum from each other. Considering the low transportation cost and time it would always be cheaper and logical to do so and thus benefit the consumers of each other's countries. But politics has denied the cost advantages of living in the neighborhood to the consumers. Of course there are political grievances of one South Asian state against the other and since there has been no willpower among the two warring states to solve the territorial and boundary issue through peaceful means or the issue of the demarcation of the boundaries the tension between three major South Asian countries has been growing and often comes to the point of acute border tensions between them. Due to the political tensions the countries of the region have been spending more and more on guarding their thousands of kilometres long borders and strengthening their military muscle on the one hand and snapping all the economic links on the other.

Fighting economic battle individually

Three of the biggest economies of SAARC—India, Pakistan and Sri Lanka—account for 89 percent of the GDP and 87 percent of the population of the region. They are developing economies having large concentration of people below poverty line, while the rest four are considered less developed countries. Average per capita income for over 1.3 billion people is around $460, against the world average of $ 7,000, and it varies between $250 in Nepal to $2040 in Maldives. The economies of the region are not globalised by world standard especially when compared to neighbouring South East Asia or China. Therefore, in this age of cooperation and competition it is an irony that South Asian economies are fighting their battles individually and independent of each other because of political tensions. If political tensions are there to stay due to the intractable national positions of the neighbouring countries on the issues dividing them the question is for how long the leadership of three major countries can deny the benefits of neighbourhood trade to their citizens?

Due to political tensions the countries of the region have not been investing on road and other transport linkages and in fact those existing are not used properly. If political issues remain unresolved, a mechanism should be developed to have economic interactions among businessmen of the region, so as ordinary people are not deprived of the benefits of a cooperative and interdependent economy. The road, rail and shipping linkages that existed between the three countries have in fact deteriorated over the time and have become unserviceable so a fresh investment would be required to restore them. Consequently, the people of South Asia are paying the price of low growth. There are examples galore of how other regional groups of countries are cooperating specially in the economic field to develop their joint bargaining power not only in the economic but political arena also. But South Asians are still struggling to put their two decade old SAARC on rails so as to speed up the growth train. As the three major members of SAARC are the major negotiating partners for having Free Trade in the SAARC region there is a talk of restoring road and transport linkages between them. The three most populous countries India, Pakistan and Bangladesh would be the prime movers of the SAARC and hence a better economic understanding between them is very essential for the smooth conduct of trade relations in the SAARC area.

Driving Force

With increased prospects of a robust economic growth of 7.2 % in South Asia in the year 2004,[2] India would be the driving force of South Asian economy in the years to come, which should attract world attention on the region. If South Asian countries cooperate with and take advantage of India's developed market and technological supremacy in the field of Information Technology, biotechnology, pharmaceuticals and in the auto sector etc., they will help themselves. The Global Economic Development Finance 2004 report says that sustaining such high level of growth in future is possible. Continued reforms in India including tax cuts early in 2004 and capital account liberalisation will contribute to future growth. Considering the

2. A World Bank forecast.

high GDP growth of India in 2004, the report forecasts that economic growth is expected to be 7.2% in South Asia boosted by IT exports from India and the growing practice of outsourcing from OECD economies. The South Asia GDP rise in 2003 was 6.5%, a sharp pickup from the 4.3% registered in 2002 and is expected to be 7.2% in 2004. According to the World Bank, peace talks between India and Pakistan coupled with the regional trade initiatives of the SAARC may further boost international confidence in the region.

Much depends on South Asia whether the Millennium Development Goals can be reached by 2015.[3] South Asia has 40% of the problem, which means it has 40% of the solution. It is the place where 40% of the population lives on less than a dollar a day, and where 35% of the children do not get primary education. So this region is most going to drive whether we reach the targets or not. Expressing confidence on the ability of South Asians to deliver, "India has been graduating from receiving assistance and is on track to itself becoming a donor nation. Aid flows in South Asia are relatively insignificant. It is the quality of decision making by government officials and the private sector that will make the critical difference. If the West can play a role, it will be through facilitating improved trade access to world markets, rather than through development assistance. I am a great admirer of the Indian model. They are standing on their own feet, not holding out their hands for dollars or euros."[4]

Challenge

However, South Asia continues to remain an underdeveloped region—a hub of poverty and economic backwardness. Low quality of life in the region as a whole is both a cause and an effect of underdevelopment. For each of the South Asian economies, the challenge is to achieve higher growth amidst volatilities of world economic environment. Achieving higher GDP growth is a critical necessity for tackling the problems of unemployment and poverty. However there are number of hurdles

3. Human Development Report, 2003, UNDP.
4. Mark Brown, Administrator, UNDP.

to overcome. Much of the responsibility of pulling the region out of poverty and underdevelopment and putting it on higher growth path is on the big three i.e. India, Pakistan and Sri Lanka. Development of these three economies may drive the Less Developed countries of the region through demonstration as well as integration effect.[5] This will reduce the trade dependence on countries geographically situated far away from the region. The South Asian countries exchange goods principally with countries outside the region. Their largest trading partners, accounting for more than 50 percent of their total trade, are the major industrial countries in the European Union, along with the United States and Japan. A substantial portion (40 percent) of the region's trade is with countries in the Asia-Pacific region, including China, the Southeast Asian countries, Australia, New Zealand, and the high-income East Asian countries (Hong Kong, Japan, Korea, Singapore, and Taiwan). It is then no surprise that the total external trade of the region amounts to 0.8% of world exports and 1.3% of world imports. Intra-regional exchanges represent only 5.3% (exports) and 4.8% (imports) of the total.

However, there is encouraging trend also. In 2002-03, India's trade with SAARC countries in rupee terms has grown by 21% (19% in dollar terms) as compared to the previous year, according to an analysis by the PHD Chamber of Commerce and Industry (of India) released in January, 2004. The President of the Chamber, Mr. Ravi Wig, says that "it is good turning point for India to consolidate the trade with SAARC countries and to take it to a higher orbit of growth. Care has also to be taken to encourage the other SAARC countries to increase their exports to India since some of the countries are very keen to enhance their market access to the expanding Indian market."

PHD analysis points out that in rupee terms India's trade with Bhutan has registered maximum growth during 2002-03 at 109%, although from a low base. In absolute terms India's exports to Bhutan has gone up from Rs 362 million in 2001-02 to Rs 1,890 million in 2002-03. However India's imports from Bhutan have gone up from Rs 1141 million in 2001-02 to Rs. 1254 million

5. CII study: South Asia: Regional Economic and Trade Cooperation.

in 2002-03. Says Mr. Wig, "Unless we take some concrete measures to enhance the imports from countries in SAARC, the response from other member countries for taking SAARC concept to its logical conclusion will be less than enthusiastic."

Comparison of trade statistics of neighbouring SAARC countries reveals that inspite of the size of the Pakistani economy being much larger than other SAARC members, the total trade of Pakistan with India is much less. With a proper trade climate, the trade with Pakistan can increase between US $ 6-8 billion. This includes the legalisation of US $2 billion of unofficial trade.[6] With Bangladesh India's total trade was almost $ one billion, with Sri Lanka it was close to one billion and with Nepal it was around US $ 600 million in 2002. But with Pakistan it was around US $ 200-250 million (official trade). The volatile political relationship has overwhelmed attempts to encourage trade between the two countries and has also impacted on economic integration in the South Asian region as a whole. There are both political and economic obstacles to expanding trade between the two countries. Greater economic cooperation could, however, provide mutual economic benefits, such as lower prices for consumers, much needed revenue for the governments, and cost effective gas import to India via Pakistan. Perhaps most importantly it could generate new linkages between the two business communities, thereby nurturing constituencies for peace in the region.

Trade with Pakistan

According to FICCI in 2002-03, India exported only US $ 216.52 million worth of goods to Pakistan, out of the US$ 48 billion of total exports. Pakistan's exports totalled US $ 8.8 billion, but only US $ 46.83 million went to India. This export to India in fact declined in 2002-03. In 1998-99, it was US $ 213.28 million. According to the PHD Chamber India's trade with Pakistan has grown by 22% in 2002-03 as compared to previous year. India's exports to Pakistan have gone up by 45%, whereas imports from that country declined by 30% in 2002-03 as compared to previous year. According to Federation of Pakistan Chambers of

---

6. A FICCI study report.

Commerce and Industry, before partition and immediately after independence, India was Pakistan's most important trading partner. In 1948-49, 56% of Pakistan's total exports were directed to Indian market, and 32% of its imports came from India. Lahore and Amritsar were important economic hubs, as trade flourished with a free flow of goods and services. However, by the early 1950's trade between the two countries was reduced to a trickle, which has not revived since. There are infrastructural bottlenecks in the way of improved trade also which can be removed only with improved political and security environment. Both the countries are working on the proposal of the then PM A.B. Vajpayee to open road routes between Rajasthan and Sindh and also the shipping link between Mumbai and Karachi. Presently the road route is nonfunctional. The opening of road route through Wagah border (Amritsar-Lahore) and the start of container services would greatly facilitate the movement of high bulk, low value cargo. Also the railway connectivity between India and Pakistan for movement is not sufficient and suffers from shortage of wagons and lack of coordination between the Pakistani and Indian Railways authorities. Efforts should be made to restart the old Sindh-Rajasthan rail route. The shipping link is very expensive and uneconomical especially for high bulk and low value products. The bilateral shipping arrangements do not permit loading of ships by one country's cargo meant for third countries at the sea port of the other country. This is another constraint for bilateral sea borne trade on the Karachi-Mumbai route.

Energy Cooperation

The greatest economic benefit of trade relations between India, Bangladesh and Pakistan would occur in the sphere of energy cooperation. India is one of the most rapidly growing energy markets in the world and will be able to absorb new sources of supply as they materialize in the region. Pakistan's potential role in fulfilling this need is not as a supplier but as a potential transit route for energy from Iran and Central Asia. The economics of gas supply looks very promising. A project proposal submitted by Iran to both countries estimated that Pakistan would gain between US $ 600 to 800 million per year in transit fees. It would also be able to use the pipelines to fulfill its own energy needs. India would benefit from diversified sources of pipeline gas and lower dependence on more expensive liquid natural gas (LNG). Even with LNG prices dropping, industry sources believe that there would be a significant cost advantage, especially to a pipeline from Iran. Similarly Bangladesh has also huge resource of natural gas which if sold to India would not only change the face of Bangladesh economy but will also benefit hugely India's energy sector. The energy cooperation would not only energise the economies of India, Pakistan and Bangladesh but South Asia as a whole which will also increase interdependence on each other. This will act as a major confidence building measure which would enable the SAARC to emerge not only as a global player in trade and investment but will also present to the world trading community a huge attractive market for their products and investment. It will also enable the deeper integration of SAARC area with the rest of the world. Actually, South Asia has abundant natural resources but not enough domestic finance, skill and entrepreneurship to exploit these resources gainfully. Lack of infrastructure besides institutional framework in smaller countries is another major problem coupled with absence of cooperation with bigger partner India. This is why South Asia is called resource rich poor economic region.

Removing the Fears

Allaying the fears that India's bigger economy will dominate over the rest of SAARC, Indian officials refer to the trade with Sri Lanka. Officials say that India's bilateral trade with other SAARC countries has not been to the disadvantage to them nor has it been to the sole advantage to India. For example, there has been a remarkable increase in the level of trade with Sri Lanka following the free trade agreement signed in 2001. In 2002 alone exports of Sri Lanka to India grew by around 137%. Consequently, India has now created a joint study group which is studying how to take Sri Lanka into the next generation of economic partnership with a focus on trade in services and investments in each other's countries. Similarly India also hopes to commence negotiations on a Free Trade Agreement with Bangladesh. The then Indian foreign minister Yashwant Sinha assured the SAARC members especially Pakistan'—We in India have no intention to overwhelm Pakistan's economy through trade. Our aim is only to have a normal trade relationship and promote trade in a manner that people of both countries benefit.

Role of Chambers

The industry and commerce chambers of the major countries of SAARC have an important role to play in promoting faster integration of the South Asian economy. The chambers can act as a driving force in the creation of a South Asian Economic Union. The role played by them in emphasizing upon the leaders of South Asia to speed up the process of integration would be crucial. The chambers are indeed acting as pressure groups on the respective governments to take more and more measures to facilitate improved trade interaction between the countries of the region. The chambers of South Asian countries have combined together to form SAARC Chamber of Commerce and its major members are Federation of Indian Chambers of Commerce and Industry (FICCI), Bangladesh Chambers of Commerce and Industry and the Federation of Pakistan Chambers of Commerce and Industry. The chambers of the region have formed joint business councils to promote trade and economic interaction between the countries which is linking businessmen and investors of the region.

The chambers are acting as important nongovernmental bodies to recommend action plans and release study papers which will go a long way in bringing the South Asian Economies together. SAARC Chambers of Commerce and Industry (SCCI) was established in 1994. The signing of SAPTA created an excellent opportunity for the SCCI to translate the political decision to much enhanced trade exchanges between the countries of the region. SCCI has since then organised several South Asian Economic Cooperation conferences which provided opportunities for business networking between businessmen of SAARC countries including India and Pakistan—the two major economies of the region.

The first major step in promoting bilateral trade was taken in January 1995, when FICCI in collaboration with the India Trade Promotion Organisation (ITPO) organised a first ever SAARC trade fair. It was a big success and exhibitors from all the SAARC countries participated in large numbers in which Pakistan had the largest pavilion. The second SAARC Trade Fair took place from 8th to 15th September, 1998, at Colombo, Sri Lanka, whereas the third SAARC Trade fair took place at Kathmandu from Oct. 25-29, 2002. Indian businessmen participated in these fairs in a big way. The SAARC trade fair should have been organised annually but perhaps political tensions among the countries forced the postponement of these fairs. Nevertheless, these fairs boosted the confidence of businessmen of SAARC countries on each other, where they got an opportunity to showcase their best products. Similarly the Confederation of Indian Industries (CII), India's other leading chamber, has developed mutual relations with the Bangladesh Chambers of Commerce and decided to organise fairs in each other's country. CII has also formed a CEO's forum with Pakistani business leaders to coordinate their efforts to improve trade interactions in the region.

SAARCNET

To facilitate business promotion in the SAARC region a special information service centre called SAARCNET was set up by the SAARC Chamber of commerce. This facility is sourced from FICCI business information services network (BISNET). The member federations of SCCI serve as national focal points of SAARCNET. This facility is on internet and extensively used by businessmen of the SAARC region for matchmaking and joint venturing. It has vital information on trade and industry of all SAARC countries including India and Pakistan. Getting visa was a major problem for south Asian businessmen to visit the neighbouring countries especially between India and Pakistan for trade and business talks. This issue was very often raised by FICCI with the concerned authorities which resulted in the Indian Government announcing unilateral visa relaxations including multiple-entry visas for Pakistani businessmen and since then a large number of Pakistani businessmen visited India. FICCI also liaisoned with FPCCI to put pressure on Pakistani Government to allow Indian businessmen to visit Pakistan by granting visas exempting police reporting. Pressure from businessmen led to SCCI visa exemption for the traders of all SAARC countries and this facility is being successfully availed by the businessmen of both India and Pakistan to travel to each other's country. Through second track diplomacy FICCI has been trying to undertake several confidence building measures between the business communities of India and Pakistan.

Trade Delegations

After a gap of 10 years, FICCI sent a trade delegation in 1995 which held very fruitful bilateral meetings with Federation of Pakistan Chambers of Commerce and Industry and also had occasion to meet the commerce minister. Next year three large business delegations were received by FICCI from Pakistan and useful parleys were held with the Indian counterparts. Again in 1997 a 24-member FICCI delegation toured Pakistan from April 27 to May, 1997. The delegation called upon several government dignitaries at Karachi, Islamabad and Lahore. Again a 100-member strong SAARC Chamber of Commerce and Industry visited Pakistan in March 1998. Where several business deals were struck but in the following months the nuclear explosions by India and Pakistan once again spoiled the business atmosphere between the two countries which affected the growth of SAARC trade as a whole. However the organisation of trade fairs resumed with the "Made in Pakistan" exhibition held in New Delhi in March 2004. This was highly successful trade fair attended by large numbers of visitors. A similar "Made in India" exhibition would be organised later in the year in Pakistan. To facilitate trade between the SAARC nations, FICCI under the umbrella of SAARC Chamber of Commerce and Industry undertook a study on Motor Vehicular Agreement in the SAARC region with special emphasis on movement of people and goods between all the five countries of SAARC i.e. Pakistan, India, Bhutan, Nepal and Bangladesh which enjoy land contiguity.

In an interesting development the businesswomen of India and Pakistan have also come forward to jointly work together for the economic and social development of women entrepreneurs in both the countries. The Pakistani businesswomen in their first ever visit to India as representative of Women's Chamber of Commerce and Industry of Pakistan (WCCI) signed an MOU with FICCI Ladies Organisation (FLO) with a view to increased interaction between businesswomen of the two countries. Ms Namita Ghosh, President of FLO, and Ms Salma Ahmad, President of WCCI, signed this MOU on 11 June, 2004. As part of the understanding the two parties have agreed to initiate measures to foster friendship and understanding between the businesswomen and promote cooperation in trade, investment, services and women empowerment. The two businesswomen groups are also likely to submit recommendations to the respective governments for promoting more effective economic relations between women entrepreneurs of India and Pakistan.

The Pakistani businesswomen also signed a MOU with Confederation of Indian Industries, to work together for the economic and social development of women entrepreneurs in India and Pakistan. CII and WCCI would exchange professional experience relating to services rendered to their respective regions. Reflecting on the need for women's empowerment within the SAARC region, Begum Ahmad mooted the creation of SAARC Women's Entrepreneurs Council, which would also boost trade within the SAARC region.

Joint Ventures

A study commissioned by SAARC Chamber of Commerce and Industry and formulated by Tata Economic Consultancy Services outlines the industrial investment opportunities and scope for joint ventures in SAARC countries. How the two biggest economies of the region India and Pakistan can establish cooperative and fruitful trade and business links comes out revealingly in this report.

Areas of cooperation and potential joint ventures

Industry Group	Project Focus
Information Technology	Software Exports Training Centre/ Centre for software training and management (CSTM), Software Development Centre. Pakistan has the potential to become an important software exporting and training centre. India can become a role model and both the countries should cooperate and collaborate to tap the large global market for software.
Fish processing	Processed frozen/canned fish products. Future thrust should be on value added canned products exports to the developed countries.
Drug and Pharmaceuticals	Bulk Drugs Expansion of formulation sector (Tablets, capsules, ointments, injections, etc) Expansion of healthcare products (IV fluids, disposable syringes, diagnostic kits, etc) Indian pharma industry can provide the necessary support and assistance to Pakistan for the expansion of its industry.
Agro Chemicals	A pesticides manufacturing unit in Pakistan. With the expansion of agri business, demand for agro chemicals will grow in future. Indian major players can play an important role through transfer of technology.

(Contd.)

Industry Group	Project Focus
Chemicals	Dyes and pigments manufacturing units in Pakistan. Pakistan has a strong maufacturing base for textiles and leather. Indian players and multinationals can assist Pakistan in developing this sector.
Auto mobile Ancillary	Integrated auto component complex. Next to India, Pakistan is the only country in the SAARC region to manufacture and assemble passenger cars. Pakistan may also consider assembling of HCV and LCV in collaboration with Indian companies.
Light Engineering	LPG cylinder manufacturing units in Pakistan for which technology can be sourced from India. This has scope for production of cylinders for industrial gases.
Leather processing	Manufacturing complex for a variety of value added products, leather footwear, leather garments and leather bags for exports.

The report concludes by saying that Pakistan and India should cooperate to tap the global market and expand marketshare. Similar potential exists between India and Bangladesh, Pakistan and Bangladesh and likewise between two chambers of the countries. Only in last May 2004, the President of Federation of Pakistan Chambers of Commerce and Industry (FPCCI) and President of Bangladesh Chambers of Commerce and Industry agreed to activate Pakistan Bangladesh Joint Business Council. In this very first meeting held in Dacca, the business leaders decided to take measures to enhance bilateral trade between them. They decided to meet regularly at least on annual basis. This is a welcome sign that through chambers the business communities of the SAARC region will be able to develop mutually beneficial relations that will ultimately benefit the organisation in furthering its economic integration.

India-Pakistan Bilateral Trade (In US $ million)

Year	Exports to Pakistan	Imports from Pakistan	Balance of Trade	Total Trade
1997-98	124.97	32.86	92.11	157.83
1998-99	105.22	213.28	(-)107.76	318.80
1999-2000	92.97	68.05	24.92	161.02
2000-01	183.04	62.90	120.14	245.94
2001-02	140.70	63.40	77.30	204.10
2002-03	216.52	46.83	169.69	262.35

Source: *DGCI&S,* Kolkata

India's trade with neighbouring countries

Trends in India-Bangladesh Trade (in US million $)

Year	India's exports Bangladesh	Imports from Bangladesh	Total Trade
2002-2003	1151.56	57.12	1208.68
2001-2002	922.80	57.89	980.69
2000-2001	857.67	72.57	930.24

Trends in India-Pakistan Trade (in US $ million)

Year	India's exports to Pakistan	Imports from Pakistan	Total Trade
2002-2003	216.52	46.83	263.35
2001-2002	140.07	63.04	204.01
2000-2001	183.04	62.09	245.94

Trends in India-Sri Lanka Trade (in US $ million)

Year	India's exports to Sri Lanka	Imports from Sri Lanka	Total Trade
2002-2003	968.83	95.96	1064.79
2001-2002	616.21	66.01	682.22
2000-2001	618.04	43.09	662.03

Trends in India-Nepal Trade (in US $ million)

Year	India's exports to Nepal	Imports from Nepal	Total Trade
2002-2003	216.52	46.83	263.35
2001-2002	140.07	63.04	204.01
2000-2001	183.04	62.09	245.94

Source: *DGCI&S,* Kolkata

Table 1: Economy of South Asia

Country	Population Million	GNP $ Billion	Per Capita ($)	GDP Growth (%)					
				1997	1998	1999	2000	2001	2002
Bangladesh	136	48.5	356.62	5.4	5.2	4.9	5.9	5.3	4.4
Bhutan	0.851	0.5	587.55	7.2	6.4	7.6	5.3	6.6	7.7
India	1048	501.5	478.05	4.8	6.5	6.1	4.4	5.6	4.4
Maldives	0.28	0.59	2107.14	10.4	9.8	7.2	4.8	3.5	4.3
Nepal	24	5.6	233.03	5.1	3.2	4.5	6.0	4.6	-0.6
Pakistan	145	59.2	408.28	1.7	3.5	4.2	3.9	2.5	3.6
Sri Lanka	19	15.9	836.08	6.3	4.7	4.3	6.0	-1.4	3.0
Total	1373.131	631.79	460.15						

Source: *World Development Report,* 2004

Table 2: Quality of life in South Asia

Country	Daily per capita calorie supply, 2000	Child malnutrition (% of Children under age	Population with access to safe water (%), 2000	Population with access to sanitation (%), 2000	Life expectancy at birth (per 1000 live births) 2001	Infant mortality rate (per 1000 live births),2001	Maternal mortality Ratio (per 100,000 live births) latest available
Bangladesh	2158	48 (1999-2000)	99(U) 97(R)	71(U) 41(R)	62(F) 62(M)	51	300 (1998)
India	2489	47 (1998-1999)	95(U) 79(R)	61(U) 15(R)	62(F) 60(M)	67	407 (1998)
Bhutan	NA	19 (1999)	86(U) 60(R)	65(U) 70(R)	63(F) 61(M)	74	NA
Maldives	2552	30 (1997-1998)	100(U) 100(R)	100(U) 41(R)	64(F) 64(M)	58	NA
Nepal	2446	48 (2001)	94(U) 87(R)	73(U) 22(R)	58(F) 59(M)	66	539 (1996)
Pakistan	2456	38 (1999-2000)	95(U) 87(R)	95(U) 43(R)	65(F) 62(M)	84	340 (2000)
Sri Lanka	2345	33 (2000) (2000)	98(U) 70(R)	97(U) 93(R)	74(F) 67(M)	17	23 (1996)

Source: *Asian Development Bank*

U: Urban, R : Rural F: Female. M: Male

4

The Evolution of SAARC

Inspite of lofty declarations of deeper economic cooperation from summit to summit from 1985 onwards for the economic and social upliftment of the poor and downtrodden people of the South Asia, SAARC has not been able to achieve its desired objectives. Marred by political tensions among member states SAARC had a chequered history having only 12 summit level meetings in the last 19 years. Though the SAARC heads of states are supposed to meet annually, political tensions due to territorial and boundary disputes, forced the postponement and the cancellation of the summit meetings. The pious declarations adopted by the SAARC leaders could not be executed on ground as the governments did not follow the directives of their heads of states as most of the time they were not on talking terms. As people of South Asia continue to suffer due to lack of joint programmes and people friendly policies for their economic upliftment, the region has been boiling with extremist movements. The Maoists in Nepal, the Tamil Tigers in Sri Lanka, the Naxalites in India, the Jehadis in Pakistan and Bangladesh all are flourishing because of continued deprivation of the masses. Lack of employment and economic opportunities are forcing the people to take recourse to extremism of various kinds. Often one extremist group is aiding and abetting another extremist group of the neighbouring countries. A new form of cooperation among these groups at the ground level started brewing to force the corrupt bureaucracy of these governments to take people friendly economic measures.

In fact, in every summit of SAARC the same question is raised: can this grouping of one fifth of the world's population ever get its act together to achieve any of its goals? In the nearly two decades of its existence, SAARC has been little more than acronym for unrealised potential. While other regional associations—most notably the Association of South East Asian Nations (ASEAN) and the European Union—are growing economically stronger by leaps and bounds but SAARC has made little progress on the high ideals promised in its charter. The charter of SAARC formally adopted in 1985 by the SAARC leaders assigned the goal to the seven nations to cooperate together to promote the welfare of the peoples of South Asia and to improve their quality of life. Towards this end the charter called for efforts to accelerate economic growth, social programmes and cultural development in the region, and also to promote and strengthen collective self reliance, contribute towards mutual trust and understanding, appreciations of one another's problems, promote active collaboration and mutual assistance in the economic, social, cultural, technical and scientific fields. SAARC has been in existence for nearly two decades but it's presence is not felt on the international scene. Just think of ASEAN which has now become a force to reckon with as world's major powers make it a point to send top level representations to attend its annual summit meetings. Its high profile deliberations on economic cooperation and security issues attract leaders like the US, Chinese and foreign ministers of other leading powers. India being the only member of SAARC as a Full Dialogue partner of ASEAN and member of its security platform—ASEAN Regional Forum—is able to draw benefit from this both politically and economically. But same is not true with SAARC as it has not been able to present itself as a cohesive economic grouping with which the world could interact seriously as the international community is doing with ASEAN and other economic groupings. The SAARC meeting always gets projected as India-Pakistan affair and the world always looks forward for a positive dialogue between India and Pakistan at this forum. Actually, whenever a summit meeting of SAARC is held the media of SAARC countries concentrate only on India-Pakistan talks whereas the world attention focuses on the issue whether India and Pakistan are talking to each other on this regional forum or not.

Initiative of Zia ur Rahman

When the idea of SAARC evolved in the early eighties the world was passing through a period of intense cold war. The international power politics divided the countries of the region. Added to these were domestic politics of the South Asian countries. One country accusing the other for the social and political instability on their lands. Inspite of this when the then President of Bangladesh Zia ur Rahman proposed in 1980 that the seven countries should explore the possibility of establishing some institutional arrangements for regional cooperation it received enthusiastic response from the leaders of these countries, though initially India was wary of such proposal as this came during the height of the cold war and the neighbouring countries had allegiance with India's rival powers. However India picked up on the idea, and to give concrete shape to this proposal initial meetings were held at foreign secretary level followed by the meetings at foreign minister level. After consultations, the foreign secretaries of the seven countries met for the first time in Colombo in April 1981. This was followed a few months later, by the meeting of the Committee of the Whole, which identified five broad area for regional cooperation. The foreign ministers at their first meeting in New Delhi in August 1983, formally launched the Integrated Programme of Action (IPA) through the adoption of the Declaration on South Asian Regional Cooperation (SARC).These countries eventually took a grand decision to establish South Asian Association for Regional Cooperation (SAARC) on 7-8 December 1985, at Dacca attended by their heads of states. The seven countries affirmed their commitment to achieve economic integration for prosperity. Another important goal enunciated during this summit was to gain bargaining strength vis a vis non members.

Though the goal of economic integration is not explicitly mentioned in the charter of SAARC, the objectives under clause no. 7 and 8 (as stated in the charter) would indicate a goal to increase the bargaining strength. The charter simply recognised the possibility that increased cooperation, contact and exchanges would contribute to the promotion of friendship and understanding among the member states and promote the welfare of the people of South Asia. However inspite of the charter clearly enunciating the principles of sovereign equality, territorial integrity, national independence, non use of force, non interference in the internal affairs of other states and peaceful settlement of all disputes, the member countries have obviously not been respecting these sovereign commitments to fellow member states resulting in continued political and military tensions in the region and consequently less and less economic and trade exchanges thus defeating the purpose of forming a regional organisation for mutual economic cooperation for the welfare of their masses.

Dhaka Summit

The Dhaka Summit of SAARC declared eight broad basic objectives : (1) To promote the welfare of the peoples of South Asia and improve their quality of life, (2) to accelerate economic growth, social progress and cultural development in the region, and to provide all individuals opportunity to live in dignity and to realize their full potentials, (3) To promote and strengthen collective self reliance among the countries of south Asia, (4) to contribute to mutual trust, understanding and appreciation of one another's problems, (5) to promote active collaboration and mutual assistance in the economic, social, cultural, technical and scientific fields, (6) to strengthen cooperation with other developing countries, (7) to strengthen cooperation among themselves in international forums on matters of common interests, and (8) to cooperate with international and regional organisations with similar aims and purposes.

Broad objectives are fine but ways and means to achieve these objectives have not been clearly delineated. However to achieve these objectives several steps were taken to give institutional shape to SAARC. A permanent secretariat was established in Kathmandu on 16 January, 1987, which facilitated the management of joint programmes for the member countries and holding of ministerial meetings and promoted people to people contacts through nongovernmental initiatives. An institutional structure was given to SAARC with a decision to organise annual summits. The highest authority of the Association rests with the Heads of State or Government. The next decision making authority is the Council of Ministers, which comprises the Foreign Ministers of member states and who are responsible for the formulation of the policies, reviewing the progress, deciding on new areas of cooperation, establishing additional mechanisms as deemed necessary, and deciding on other matters of general interest to the Association. The council meets twice a year and may also meet in extraordinary session by agreement of member states. After the Council of Ministers, a Standing Committee has been formed which comprises the foreign secretaries of the member states. This committee is entrusted with the overall monitoring and coordination of programmes and the modalities of financing, determining intersectoral priorities, mobilising regional and external resources, and identifying new areas of cooperation based on appropriate studies. It may meet as often as deemed necessary but in practice it meets twice a year and submits its reports to the Council of Ministers. Then there is a programming committee which comprises senior officials which meet prior to the standing committee sessions to scrutinize secretariat budget, finalise the calendar of activities and take up any other matter assigned to it by the standing committee. Technical Committees have also been constituted which comprises representatives of member states, formulate programmes and prepare projects in their respective fields. They are responsible for monitoring the implementation of such activities and report to the standing committee. The chairmanship of each Technical Committee normally rotates among member countries. At present there are 12 technical committees. It is clear that a very comprehensive institutional structure has been given to SAARC to meet its objectives.

In the second summit at Bangalore, in 1986, the grouping took note of the issue of terrorism and all heads of states affirmed that cooperation among SAARC states was vital if terrorism was to be prevented and eliminated from the region. They unequivocally condemned all acts, methods and practices of terrorism as criminal and deplored their impact on life and property, social economic development, political stability, regional and international peace and cooperation. They recognised the importance of the principles laid down in the UN resolution 2625 which among others required that each state should refrain from organising, instigating, assisting or participating in acts of civil strife or terrorist acts in another state or acquiesing in organised activities within its territory directed towards the commission of such acts. However an atmosphere of violence and terrorism has continued in the South Asian region affecting the creation of a climate conducive to growth and development and bilateral economic and trade exchanges. The Kathmandu declaration in November 1987, reemphasised the need for promoting peace, stability, amity and progress in the region. The SAARC leaders during this summit also signed a SAARC regional convention on suppression of terrorism and considered it a historic step towards the prevention and elimination of terrorism from the region. But these were hollow commitments meant for public consumption as is evident from increasing tensions due to the terrorist acts in the region.

Symbolic Measures

However the SAARC nations continued to take symbolic measures of cooperation. Development initiatives like SAARC integrated programme of action were undertaken. A SAARC audio visual exchange programme was launched. To promote understanding between the academic communities a SAARC chair was instituted. Fellowships and scholarship programmes were launched. A decision was also taken to commence organised tourism among SAARC member countries. A SAARC documentation centre was also setup and a SAARC Youth Volunteer programme was launched. Earlier the countries of South Asia had closed not only their borders but exchange of academics and even newspapers were not allowed to cross the borders. These measures were initiated with a view to create better understanding among each other. Definitely a lot of goodwill exists between the peoples of South Asian region but this was not helpful in creating a climate of trust among the member countries. No doubt an important decision was taken during the third summit to establish a South Asian food security reserve to provide a much needed cushion against food shortages and scarcity situations in the region. Perhaps this reserve has never been utilised.

The 1988 Islamabad declaration reaffirmed the objectives of SAARC and reemphasized the need for promoting peace, stability, amity, and progress in the region. Due to tensions between India and Pakistan the scheduled annual summit could not be held in 1989 and the fifth annual summit held at Male reviewed the progress and issued Male declaration on 23 November, 1990, which continued the momentum of various SAARC activities but not of great relevance as far as encouraging bilateral trade and investment among the members is concerned. During 1985-88, SAARC attempted to create vitality and efficacy of regional cooperation. Four regional centres were set up to supplement the work of the technical committees to share information and coordinate activities in priority areas identified by the member states. These centres are SAARC Agricultural Information Centre, SAARC Regional Meteorological Centre, SAARC Documentation Centre and SAARC Tuberculosis Centre. During the sixth SAARC summit in Colombo the heads of government decided to establish an independent South Asian commission on poverty alleviation consisting of eminent persons from each SAARC member state to conduct an indepth study of diverse experiences of seven member countries and report their recommendations on poverty alleviation in the region. They also established a committee for economic cooperation as an important outcome of the regional study on trade manufactures and services. Though neither the SAARC charter nor the declarations during the five summits took note of the need of liberalising trade the Colombo summit in 1991 declared the commitment to trade liberalization with a view to increasing intra-regional trade and investment in such a manner as will ensure that the countries in the region can share the benefits of trade expansion equitably.

Once again the summit could not be held in 1992 but the 1993 Dacca summit took a major step forward in promoting economic cooperation with the signing of South Asian Preferential Trading Arrangement (SAPTA). The preferential trade agreement aimed at promoting and sustaining mutual trade and economic cooperation among the member countries on the basis of reciprocity. Under SAPTA provision was made for member countries to negotiate tariff concessions productwise. Member countries agreed that both tariff and non tariff barriers will be removed phasewise selecting specific group of commodities. It was anticipated that the trade expansion through SAPTA will increase economic activities leading to enhanced intra-regional trade, which will in turn help the region alleviate its poverty by generating new employment opportunities for the people at different levels of production and export services and help securing higher standards of living for their populations. This was considered to be the first step towards higher levels of trade and economic cooperation in the region.

Preferential Trade

Under SAPTA tariff concessions were offered for a total of 226 products. Four member countries identified as least developed (Bangladesh, Bhutan, Maldives and Nepal) were offered 100 products for which they could get special treatment from the relatively more developed members namely India, Pakistan and Sri Lanka without any reciprocity requirement. In the second round of negotiations, some 2013 products were offered for tariff concessions of which 764 were especially earmarked for least developed countries of the region. It is an irony that the SAARC members were till now trading with non SAARC members. When SAPTA was initialled the SAARC members were conducting three percent of trade among themselves but after SAPTA they could improve this figure to five percent, though still a minuscule proportion considering the large volume of trade being conducted by members of ASEAN and European Union among themselves. The figure is 22% for ASEAN and 52% for European Union. Actually the South Asian countries never cared to provide reciprocal and adequate market access for themselves. However the increasing pressure of globalisation and with the advent of World Trade Organisation rule based regime and a provision for Most Favoured Nation Status on mutual basis to all the WTO members the SAARC members were also forced to think in terms of removing trade barriers among themselves. With the increasing trend worldwide to sign bilateral free trade agreements, the SAARC members also got encouraged. Sri Lanka was the first SAARC member to sign bilateral free trade agreement with India. Similarly almost free trade regime exists between India and Nepal and India and Bhutan. After great deal of debate the SAARC summit in Islamabad in January 2004, gave a great boost to the integration of south Asian economy when they agreed to implement a free trade agreement from 2006.

Besides the SAFTA agreement another very important achievement was the signing of the additional protocol on terrorism to deal effectively with financing of terrorism. The Islamabad declaration reaffirmed the commitment of SAARC to the regional convention on suppression of terrorism, which among others, recognised the seriousness of the problem as it affected the security, stability and development of the region. The signing of the additional protocol was described as a further manifestation of our determination to eliminate all forms and manifestations of terrorism from South Asia. It is interesting to note that concerns on national security have been extended to the SAFTA agreement, which allows member states to take action and adopt measures in the interest of national security. The SAARC declaration said that terrorism violates the fundamental values of the United Nations and the SAARC charter and constituted one of the most serious threats to international peace and security. It was agreed to fully implement the relevant international conventions to which the member countries were parties. The declaration added that they were convinced that terrorism, in all its forms and manifestations was a challenge to all states and to all of humanity, and could not be justified on any ground, whatsoever.

Major Milestone

Describing SAFTA as a major milestone, the Islamabad declaration says "that it is important to maintain the momentum and move towards further broadening of economic cooperation and to ensure equitable distribution of benefits of trade....."

The SAFTA agreement has suggested a number of measures that members may adopt, including the removal of barriers to intra-SAARC investment, harmonisation of customs facilities, transit facilities for efficient intra-SAARC trade and simplification of procedures for business visas. Any dispute that may arise among the contracting states regarding the interpretation and application of the provisions of SAFTA agreement or any instrument adopted within its framework concerning the rights and obligations of the member states will be amicably settled through a process initiated by a request for bilateral consultations. The agreement allows any contracting state to pull out of the treaty at any time after it comes into force on January 1, 2006. Such withdrawal shall be effective on the expiry of six months from the date on which a written notice thereof is received by the Secretary General of SAARC.

Also the other remarkable achievement of the historic Islamabad summit was the agreement on the South Asian Social Charter which has been described as a grassroots strategy for economic cooperation. The social charter will provide a road map for collective struggle against poverty. India has called for a professionally managed Poverty Alleviation Fund, which can finance specific poverty alleviation programmes and projects in SAARC. India also offered an initial contribution of US$100 million which would be utilized for poverty alleviation projects in the region but outside India. India's gesture can be described as emulating the footsteps of European Union which has similar programmes for economic upliftment of the poorer regions of Europe in which the developed members of EU contribute a lot. A similar fund needs to be created for the infrastructure development to improve the connectivities at various levels, road, sea and air, to allow easy movement of goods and passenger traffic. India is the only big country which can be expected to fund this initiative but due to fund crunch it cannot contribute substantially. Therefore, the private sector should be allowed to develop and manage these facilities which will go a long way in improving trade and economic cooperation in the region.

A major concession was given to the Pakistani viewpoint in the Islamabad declaration that suitable political and economic environment would help the birth of the proposed South Asian Economic Union. The declaration also talks on enhancing political cooperation among SAARC members, which said," We envision South Asia to be a peaceful and stable region where each nation is at peace with itself and its neighbours and where conflicts, differences and disputes are addressed through peaceful means and dialogue." The South Asians can only hope that these pious declarations would not remain empty slogans and would be executed on ground to create a conducive atmosphere for deeper economic cooperation between SAARC members. However these declarations put the 12th SAARC summit in Islamabad way ahead of the results of the previous summits and has paved the way for more action oriented future summits.

Source: Declarations of SAARC Summits since 1985.

5

SAFTA : First Major Initiative

The 12th SAARC summit in Islamabad was a landmark summit in the sense that during last 19 years of its existence it took first real, meaningful step towards economic integration by signing the South Asia Free Trade Area Agreement. From preferential trade (SAPTA) to free trade (SAFTA) was a major step, but the timelag between SAPTA and SAFTA was too long and timeframe of implementation of SAFTA is also very lengthy which actually nullifies the possibility of an early dramatic change in trade exchanges. SAPTA was decided in 1993 and partial implemention started in 1995 and a consensus among SAARC leaders was reached in 1995 to finalise an agreement on SAFTA but it took nine years to sign it and since it's execution will start only in 2006 at a very slow pace over a period of ten years, it's impact will not be visible early. SAFTA was meant to be operationalised since 2001 but a further five-year delay would rob much of its cream. Considering the fact that other regional economic groupings are integrating their economies very fast, South Asia will miss the bus of the advantages of an integrated economy and other economies will continue to exploit the lack of requisite cooperation between SAARC members and thus deny this area of a faster growth rate.

Though there was a plenty of desire expressed by the SAARC leaders to make South Asia attractive place for the world to invest in and the declaration of the 12th SAARC summit in Islamabad also reiterated its commitment made at the 11th SAARC summit at Kathmandu in January 2002, for the creation of South Asia

Economic Union the much belated SAFTA agreement raises hopes of a better trade environment. However, if we go by the slow pace of staggered implementation of SAFTA the realisation of the dream of a SAARC Economic Union would take no less than two decades. An economic Union would require the creation of a Customs Union and a single market of goods and services, which seems to be a far cry now. In an increasingly open environment of free trade worldwide South Asian countries cannot keep its borders closed or restrictive for trade and commerce. However the statements of South Asian leaders were very encouraging, perhaps with only note of caution from the President of Pakistan, General Pervez Musharraf, that "we must expand SAARC charter to discuss bilateral issues at regional level. We must put behind us the tarnished legacy of mistrust, bitterness and tension. We feel there is a need to continue a mechanism to even discuss bilateral issue at regional level. There can be no development in the absence of peace. There can be no peace, so long as political issues and disputes continue to fester." However, the SAARC charter makes specific commitment not to allow to raise bilateral disputes and issues as members would not be able to rise above these issues and this would retard the process of cooperation. On the other hand the Nepalese Prime Minister Surya Bahadur Thapa had very encouraging words to say, "we should transform South Asia into a region in which peoples, goods, services and technology move freely across the borders, the motor and railways systems are integrated, and pipelines, transmission lines and telephone lines are connected in a grid. We should respond to the world's problems such as the challenges and the opportunities of globalization as a united bloc."

Valuable Option

President Chandrika Kumartunga of Sri Lanka added, "we conclude the SAFTA arrangement at a moment when the world has realised disadvantages of the present multilateral trade processes, such as the WTO. This situation has given a new relevance to regional cooperation. We believe that the SAARC can provide valuable options for South Asia." Prime Minister Khaleda Zia of Bangladesh, whose late husband and the then

President of Bangladesh Zia ur Rahman had originaly initiated the proposal of SAARC said," trade promotion critically calls for reducing tariffs, dismantling non-tariff barriers and impediments of an institutional and attitudinal nature affecting exports from smaller to larger SAARC countries."

Giving priority to economic cooperation the then Indian Prime Minister Atal Bihari Vajpayee said, "The development of greater economic stakes in each other would naturally result in greater sensitivity to the concerns of each other. This would pave the way for the more ambitious—but entirely achievable—goals such as a Free Trade Area, an Economic Union, open borders and a common currency for our region. Much more remains to be done. In its 18 years of existence, SAARC has created high expectations amongst the people of the region. We should be candid in accepting that these expectations have not been fulfilled in the measure of the potential. The benefits of SAARC have not yet touched the lives of ordinary people. The UN Millennium Development Goals aim to achieve these targets by 2015. With our rich natural resources, our technical manpower base, and our recent economic resurgence, South Asia can—and should—achieve these targets faster. Let us now resolve that we will try to achieve all the Millennium Development Goals by 2010."

SAFTA as a foundation

With the first step of relevance being taken, it is hoped that the SAARC leaders will move faster towards the goal of a South Asia Economic Union as envisaged in the 11th and 12th SAARC summit declarations. However it seems to be a distant dream considering the attitudinal roadblocks. But one has to dream first. The roadblocks would be cleared in course of time. With SAFTA the foundation of a highway of progress interconnecting South Asia has been laid on which the vehicles of trade and economy would run. To allow movements of goods and services a network of road, rail and air transport infrastructure is to be developed. Necessity being the mother of invention and business being the creator it is hoped that constructions of highways and rail networks would also start in due course of time. To make

SAFTA an effective vehicle for a fast regional economic cooperation, the Federation of Indian Chambers of Commerce and Industry (FICCI) has suggested following steps:

1. Free movement of people—easy visa regulations and ability of businessmen to visit freely within the region is an important pre-requisite for enhancing both trade and investment. Visa for business purposes should be multiple entry, for a minimum duration of five years without the provision of citywise visa. However, for tourism and other purposes one time visa may be given without any delay. Goods and services—SAFTA should include not only free trade in goods but also in services.
2. Physical infrastructure i.e. linkages through road, railways, shipping and appropriate air links is most crucial for increasing intra-regionl trade to substantial levels. In fact, the current level of trade can be doubled provided regional agreements on roads, rail, shipping and air are put in place which enable seamless movements like that happens in the European Union and other trading blocs.
3. Harmonization in Customs, Banking, Insurance, quality standards and arbitration procedures would be required for easy conduct of trade in the region.
4. SAARC region agreement for investment promotion and protection should be signed alongside SAFTA. Such an agreement is imperative for promoting joint ventures and intra-regional investment amongst member states given the volatile political situation in the countries of the region.
5. The SAARC countries can take advantages collectively of several projects in energy, infrastructure and tourism. For example, the national highway and express development programme of India can be extended to include destinations in Pakistan, Bangladesh, Nepal and Bhutan. Similarly, the national energy grid can be enlarged to make it into a regional energy grid which shall balance the energy demand and supply of the region.
6. However, SAFTA which shall be implemented from 2006 has a rather long timeframe of 10-12 years. FICCI strongly

recommends an early harvest wherein the countries of the region especially the non-LDCs can identify a list of products that can become freely tradable and duty free from the very start. This shall give a jump start to the process of regional economic cooperation and integration and place South Asia in a competitive position vis-a-vis other trading blocs.

7. SAFTA is not our ultimate aim. The region has to eventually move to an economic union and we suggest the following roadmap to this process:
   a) SAFTA
   b) Capital account convertibility
   c) Integration of central Banks of SAARC countries
   d) Common political institutions for South Asian governance
   e) Common Governance
   f) SAARC Economic Union.

New Hope

Perhaps the South Asian countries wasted much of their last decade labouring on a time consuming process of commodity by commodity preferential tariff negotiations under SAPTA and inspite of having completed four rounds could hardly make a significant impact on intra-regional trade transactions, between member states, still languishing to below 5% of global trade of South Asia. The total number of items exchanged between member countries has now risen to 5500. Out of these Pakistan's 773 and India's 2927 items are eligible for preferential treatment. The reasons for SAPTA being ineffective are several. The very first problem was with the commodity by commodity approach adopted by the number of governments, which is very tedious and slow by its nature. A sectoral or across the board preferential tariff would have been far more useful in increasing substantially the intra-regional trade. According to FICCI, the tariff concessions granted by member governments were sometimes on commodities and products, which were either non-tradable, or with a low trade potential. Also, the tariff concessions granted by the member states fell within a range of 15-50% and were not always steep enough to trigger trade creation or diversion in the region. Hence, SAFTA is a welcome departure from SAPTA and a new hope for the region's economic integration.

SAFTA will be implemented in two phases from 1st January, 2006, under which tariff will be reduced to 0-5% and it will be fully executed and enforced by December 2015. The countries have been divided in two groups non-LDCs (India, Pakistan and Sri Lanka) and LDCs (Bangladesh, Bhutan, Nepal and Maldives). The adoption of SAFTA for both groups of countries, seven years for developing countries and for least developing countries in a span of ten years would vastly help in bringing down the custom duties drastically which will promote the cross-border investment and more crucially in formalizing the trade which is right now happening through third countries and unauthorized routes. The non least developing countries i.e. India, Pakistan and Sri Lanka, will scale down tariff from the existing levels to 20 percent, while the least developing countries like Bangladesh, Nepal, Maldives and Bhutan will curtail their tariff rates to 30% within two years of the coming into force of the agreement. The second timeframe stipulates 5-8 years, respectively. The number of products in the sensitive lists which remained undefined shall be subject to a maximum ceiling, to be mutually agreed among the states. The products, whose preferential imports could cause serious injury to domestic industry may fall in this list. The South Asian region presents a diverse scene which is the largest economic bloc in terms of consumers. Unlike other regional blocs, the size and pattern of the economic development of SAARC countries is not uniform and identical.

Win-win for all

A FICCI study says that that SAFTA will be a win-win situation for all the SAARC members. Smaller countries like Nepal, Bhutan, Maldives and Bangladesh often express fears that they will gain less through the process of SAFTA as compared to bigger economies like India, Sri Lanka and Pakistan. However, the experience of other trading blocs and Free Trade Areas reveal the opposite. For example there has been a remarkable increase in the level of India's trade with Sri Lanka following the FTA signed in 2001. In 2002 alone, exports of Sri Lanka to India grew by around 137%. Encouraged by the economic gains, Sri Lanka is now negotiating with India the next generation of economic partnership with a focus on trade in services and investments in each other's countries.

Similarly Indian industry was apprehensive of trade with China and the perception was that the Indian market may get flooded with Chinese goods to the disadvantage of domestic industry. However, the reality is that from 2000 onwards, trade volumes increased dramatically, both in terms of total volume and rate of growth, indicating the potential of huge untapped markets in both the countries. Trade volume increased from a low base of US $338.5 million in 1992 to US $7 billion in 2003. During this year India's exports to China rose sharply at 86.9% to US $4.2 billion, while the imports from China increased by a modest 25.1% to US $3.3 billion only. Another example is that of NAFTA where the intra-regional exports of all the member countries increased substantially (1993 to 2002). Canada's exports to its NAFTA partners increased by 87% in volume. Exports to the US grew from US$113.6 billion to US $213.9 billion. The US exports to Canada and Mexico grew from US$147.7 billion to US $260.2 billion. Mexican exports to the US grew by an outstanding 234% reaching US$ 136.1 billion. Exports to Canada also grew substantially from US$2.9 billion to US$ 8.8 billion, an increase of almost 203%. It is evident that the region as a whole benefited from NAFTA and it was a win-win situation for all. However, it needs to be understood that to take maximum advantage of SAFTA, all countries of the region have to carry out the necessary fiscal, monetary and trade reforms and work towards regional integration of their economies.

Great Scope

Countering another argument that the gains of free trade in the region are minimized by the facts that most countries are exporting competing products and hence do not have a high trade potential, FICCI says that there is great scope of cooperation amongst the countries at various stages of production of the commodities like textiles, tea, jute, sugar, leather etc., in which the member countries are competing in world markets. Giving an example, FICCI says that the superior quality of cotton of Pakistan can be used to produce yarn in India which in turn can be made into a finished fabric in Bangladesh and Sri Lanka. Not only does this open up an opportunity for intra-regional imports and exports but also certain joint ventures which can collectively take advantage of the entire South Asian and other world markets. Also there are sectors like Information Technology and tourism which shall again gain form a regional approach rather than narrow nationalistic one. The need of the hour is to create and market a South Asian identity and brand especially in select sectors where South Asia enjoys a competitive advantage to begin with.

Also the flow of FDI in South Asia was only 0.7% (US$ 4.58 billion) of total FDI in world which was US $374.38 billion in 2002. This is negligible inspite of the fact that the population of the area is more than 1.3 billion, representing one fifth of world consumers and abundant man and material resources. Once free trade area is operational and South Asia becomes a single integrated market, it shall certainly have a positive impact on the FDI inflow in the region as a whole. India being the largest market in the region, other neighbouring countries shall benefit even more once South Asia is perceived as a single destination by the foreign investors who could then establish base in any country of South Asia and freely export in the entire region.

A comparison of intra-regional exports across trading blocs reveal that while as a percentage of its total world exports, intra-EU exports are 55.2%, and intra-NAFTA exports 51.7% intra-ASEAN exports 20.4%, and the intra-SAARC exports are languishing at 5.3% even after having a preferential trade arrangement among the members. It has revealed the ineffectiveness of SAPTA even after a decade of its existence. SAFTA aims to bring down the trade barriers which will provide a framework for a faster and intensive process of economic integration. It is expected that with free flow of trade in the region, the current level of US $6 billion shall move up to US $14 billion annually within two years of SAFTA's existence.

According to FICCI, if SAFTA is implemented in right earnest, the intra-regional trade can move up to 8% of the total trade of the region in five years. In fact, SAFTA's significant contribution shall be the opening up of trade between India and Pakistan since the dispute over non-extension of MFN treatment by Pakistan to India will finally get resolved. The extension of MFN principle is explicit in the concept of free trade. This give and take between the two countries under SAFTA shall play an effective role in opening as well as freeing trade between the two countries. SAFTA would immensely benefit Pakistan, as it would enable it to import tea, auto parts, consumer durables, drugs and films from India at cheaper prices. At present Pakistan, which has one of the highest per capita consumption of tea, imports 150 million of tea mainly from Kenya, which could be exported from India at a competitive price with a lower transportation costs. Presently India accounts only for less than four million kg of Pakistan's tea imports. Apart from cheap imports from India, Pakistan could benefit by exporting cotton and textiles to India. An increase in India-Pakistan trade would boost infrastructural developments to facilitate faster trade between the two countries which will further energise the economies of the two countries. The spinoff effects would be visible in other SAARC members also, thus increasing the economic activity in the area.

AGREEMENT ON SOUTH ASIAN FREE TRADE AREA (SAFTA)

The Governments of the SAARC hereinafter referred to as "Contracting States", motivated by the commitment to strengthen intra-SAARC economic cooperation to maximise the realization of the region's potential for trade and development for the benefit of their people, in a spirit of mutual accommodation, with full respect for the principles of sovereign equality, independence and territorial integrity of all States;

Noting that the Agreement on SAARC Preferential Trading Arrangement (SAPTA) signed in Dhaka on the 11th of April 1993 provides for the adoption of various instruments of trade liberalization on a preferential basis;

Convinced that preferential trading arrangements among SAARC Member States will act as a stimulus to the strengthening of national and SAARC economic resilience, and the development of the national economies of the Contracting States by expanding investment and production opportunities, trade, and foreign exchange earnings as well as the development of economic and technological cooperation;

Aware that a number of regions are entering into such arrangements to enhance trade through the free movement of goods;

Recognizing that Least Developed Countries in the region need to be accorded special and differential treatment commensurate with their development needs; and

Recognizing that it is necessary to progress beyond a Preferential Trading Arrangement to move towards higher levels of trade and economic cooperation in the region by removing barriers to cross-border flow of goods; Have agreed as follows:

Article 1 Definitions

1. Concessions mean tariff, para-tariff and non-tariff concessions agreed under the Trade Liberalisation Programme;
2. Direct Trade Measures mean measures conducive to promoting mutual trade of Contracting States such as long and medium-term contracts containing import and supply commitments in respect of specific products, buy-back arrangements, state trading operations, and government and public procurement;
3. Least Developed Contracting State refers to a Contracting State which is designated as a "Least Developed Country" by the United Nations;
4. Margin of Preference means percentage of tariff by which tariffs are reduced on products imported from one Contracting State to another as a result of preferential treatment;
5. Non-Tariff Measures include any measure, regulation, or practice, other than "tariffs" and "paratariffs";

6. Para-Tariffs mean border charges and fees, other than "tariffs", on foreign trade transactions of a tariff-like effect which are levied solely on imports, but not those indirect taxes and charges, which are levied in the same manner on like domestic products. Import charges corresponding to specific services rendered are not considered as para-tariff measures;
7. Products mean all products including manufactures and commodities in their raw, semi-processed and processed forms;
8. SAPTA means Agreement on SAARC Preferential Trading Arrangement signed in Dhaka on the 11th of April 1993;
9. Serious injury means a significant impairment of the domestic industry of like or directly competitive products due to a surge in preferential imports causing substantial losses in terms of earnings, production or employment unsustainable in the short term;
10. Tariffs mean customs duties included in the national tariff schedules of the Contracting States;
11. Threat of serious injury means a situation in which a substantial increase of preferential imports is of a nature to cause "serious injury" to domestic producers, and that such injury, although not yet existing, is clearly imminent. A determination of threat of serious injury shall be based on facts and not on mere allegation, conjecture, or remote or hypothetical possibility.

Article 2 Establishment

The Contracting States hereby establish the South Asian Free Trade Area (SAFTA) to promote and enhance mutual trade and economic cooperation among the Contracting States, through exchanging concessions in accordance with this Agreement.

Article 3 Objectives and Principles

1. The Objectives of this Agreement are to promote and enhance mutual trade and economic cooperation among Contracting States by, inter-alia:

a) Eliminating barriers to trade in, and facilitating the cross-border movement of goods between the territories of the Contracting States;

b) Promoting conditions of fair competition in the free trade area, and ensuring equitable benefits to all Contracting States, taking into account their respective levels and pattern of economic development;

c) Creating effective mechanism for the implementation and application of this Agreement, for its joint administration and for the resolution of disputes; and

d) Establishing a framework for further regional cooperation to expand and enhance the mutual benefits of this Agreement.

2. SAFTA shall be governed in accordance with the following principles:

a) SAFTA will be governed by the provisions of this Agreement and also by the rules, regulations, decisions, understandings and protocols to be agreed upon within its framework by the Contracting States;

b) The Contracting States affirm their existing rights and obligations with respect to each other under Marrakesh Agreement Establishing the World Trade Organization and other Treaties/Agreements to which such Contracting States are signatories;

c) SAFTA shall be based and applied on the principles of overall reciprocity and mutuality of advantages in such a way as to benefit equitably all Contracting States, taking into account their respective levels of economic and industrial development, the pattern of their external trade and tariff policies and systems;

d) SAFTA shall involve the free movement of goods, between countries through, inter alia, the elimination of tariffs, para tariffs and non-tariff restrictions on the movement of goods, and any other equivalent measures;

e) SAFTA shall entail adoption of trade facilitation and other measures, and the progressive harmonization of legislations by the Contracting States in the relevant areas; and

f) The special needs of the Least Developed Contracting States shall be clearly recognized by adopting concrete preferential measures in their favour on a non-reciprocal basis.

Article 4 Instruments

The SAFTA Agreement will be implemented through the following instruments:-

1. Trade Liberalisation Programme
2. Rules of Origin
3. Institutional Arrangements
4. Consultations and Dispute Settlement Procedures
5. Safeguard Measures
6. Any other instrument that may be agreed upon.

Article 5 National Treatment

Each Contracting State shall accord national treatment to the products of other Contracting States in accordance with the provisions of Article III of GATT 1994.

Article 6 Components

SAFTA may, inter-alia, consist of arrangements relating to:

a) tariffs;

b) para-tariffs;

c) non-tariff measures;

d) direct trade measures.

Article 7 Trade Liberalisation Programme

1. Contracting States agree to the following schedule of tariff reductions:

a) The tariff reduction by the Non-Least Developed Contracting States from existing tariff rates to 20% shall be done within a time frame of 2 years, from the date of coming into force of the Agreement. Contracting States are encouraged to adopt reductions in equal annual installments. If actual tariff rates after the coming into force of the Agreement are below 20%, there shall be an annual reduction on a Margin of Preference basis of 10% on actual tariff rates for each of the two years.

b) The tariff reduction by the Least Developed Contracting States from existing tariff rates will be to 30% within the time frame of 2 years from the date of coming into force of the Agreement. If actual tariff rates on the date of coming into force of the Agreement are below 30%, there will be an annual reduction on a Margin of Preference basis of 5% on actual tariff rates for each of the two years.

c) The subsequent tariff reduction by Non-Least Developed Contracting States from 20% or below to 0-5% shall be done within a second time frame of 5 years, beginning from the third year from the date of coming into force of the Agreement. However, the period of subsequent tariff reduction by Sri Lanka shall be six years. Contracting States are encouraged to adopt reductions in equal annual installments, but not less than 15% annually.

d) The subsequent tariff reduction by the Least Developed Contracting States from 30% or below to 0-5% shall be done within a second time frame of 8 years beginning from the third year from the date of coming into force of the Agreement. The Least Developed Contracting States are encouraged to adopt reductions in equal annual installments, not less than 10% annually.

2. The above schedules of tariff reductions will not prevent Contracting States from immediately reducing their tariffs to 0-5% or from following an accelerated schedule of tariff reduction.

3. a) Contracting States may not apply the Trade Liberalisation Programme as in paragraph 1 above, to the tariff lines included in the Sensitive Lists which shall be negotiated by the Contracting States (for LDCs and Non-LDCs) and incorporated in this Agreement as an integral part. The number of products in the Sensitive Lists shall be subject to maximum ceiling to be mutually agreed among the Contracting States with flexibility to Least Developed Contracting States to seek derogation in respect of the products of their export interest; and

b) The Sensitive List shall be reviewed after every four years or earlier as may be decided by SAFTA Ministerial Council (SMC), established under Article 10, with a view to reducing the number of items in the Sensitive List.

4. The Contracting States shall notify the SAARC Secretariat all non-tariff and para-tariff measures to their trade on an annual basis. The notified measures shall be reviewed by the Committee of Experts, established under Article 10, in its regular meetings to examine their compatibility with relevant WTO provisions. The Committee of Experts shall recommend the elimination or implementation of the measure in the least trade restrictive manner in order to facilitate intra SAARC trade.

5. Contracting Parties shall eliminate all quantitative restrictions, except otherwise permitted under GATT 1994, in respect of products included in the Trade Liberalisation Programme.

6. Notwithstanding the provisions contained in paragraph 1 of this Article, the Non-Least Developed Contracting States shall reduce their tariff to 0-5% for the products of Least Developed Contracting States within a timeframe of three years beginning from the date of coming into force of the Agreement.

Article 8 Additional Measures

Contracting States agree to consider, in addition to the measures set out in Article 7, the adoption of trade facilitation and other measures to support and complement SAFTA for mutual benefit. These may include, among others:

a) harmonization of standards, reciprocal recognition of tests and accreditation of testing laboratories of Contracting States and certification of products;

b) simplification and harmonization of customs clearance procedure;

c) harmonization of national customs classification based on HS coding system;

d) Customs cooperation to resolve dispute at customs entry points;

e) simplification and harmonization of import licensing and registration procedures;

f) simplification of banking procedures for import financing;

g) transit facilities for efficient intra-SAARC trade, especially for the land-locked Contracting States;

h) removal of barriers to intra-SAARC investments;

i) macroeconomic consultations;

j) rules for fair competition and the promotion of venture capital;

k) development of communication systems and transport infrastructure;

l) making exceptions to their foreign exchange restrictions, if any, relating to payments for products under the SAFTA scheme, as well as repatriation of such payments without prejudice to their rights under Article XVIII of the General Agreement on Tariffs and Trade (GATT) and the relevant provisions of Articles of Treaty of the International Monetary Fund (IMF); and

m) Simplification of procedures for business visas.

Article 9 Extension of Negotiated Concessions

Concessions agreed to, other than those made exclusively to the Least Developed Contracting States, shall be extended unconditionally to all Contracting States.

Article 10 Institutional Arrangement

1. The Contracting States hereby establish the SAFTA Ministerial Council (hereinafter referred to as SMC).
2. The SMC shall be the highest decision-making body of SAFTA and shall be responsible for the administration and implementation of this Agreement and all decisions and arrangements made within its legal framework.
3. The SMC shall consist of the Ministers of Commerce/ Trade of the Contracting States.
4. The SMC shall meet at least once every year or more often as and when considered necessary by the Contracting States.

Each Contracting State shall chair the SMC for a period of one year on rotational basis in alphabetical order.

5. The SMC shall be supported by a Committee of Experts (hereinafter referred to as COE), with one nominee from each Contracting State at the level of a Senior Economic Official, with expertise in trade matters.
6. The COE shall monitor, review and facilitate implementation of the provisions of this Agreement and undertake any task assigned to it by the SMC. The COE shall submit its report to SMC every six months.
7. The COE will also act as Dispute Settlement Body under this Agreement.
8. The COE shall meet at least once every six months or more often as and when considered necessary by the Contracting States. Each Contracting State shall chair the COE for a period of one year on rotational basis in alphabetical order.
9. The SAARC Secretariat shall provide secretarial support to the SMC and COE in the discharge of their functions.
10. The SMC and COE will adopt their own rules of procedure.

Article 11 Special and Differential Treatment for the Least Developed Contracting States

In addition to other provisions of this Agreement, all Contracting States shall provide special and more favorable treatment exclusively to the Least Developed Contracting States as set out in the following sub-paragraphs:

a) The Contracting States shall give special regard to the situation of the Least Developed Contracting States when considering the application of anti-dumping and/or countervailing measures. In this regard, the Contracting States shall provide an opportunity to Least Developed Contracting States for consultations. The Contracting States shall, to the extent practical, favourably consider accepting price undertakings offered by exporters from Least Developed Contracting States. These constructive remedies shall be available until the trade liberalisation programme has been completed by all Contracting States.

b) Greater flexibility in continuation of quantitative or other restrictions provisionally and without discrimination in critical circumstances by the Least Developed Contracting States on imports from other Contracting States.

c) Contracting States shall also consider, where practical, taking direct trade measures with a view to enhancing sustainable exports from Least Developed Contracting States, such as long and medium-term contracts containing import and supply commitments in respect of specific products, buy-back arrangements, state trading operations, and government and public procurement.

d) Special consideration shall be given by Contracting States to requests from Least Developed Contracting States for technical assistance and cooperation arrangements designed to assist them in expanding their trade with other Contracting States and in taking advantage of the potential benefits of SAFTA. A list of possible areas for such technical assistance shall be negotiated by the Contracting States and incorporated in this Agreement as an integral part.

e) The Contracting States recognize that the Least Developed Contracting States may face loss of customs revenue due to the implementation of the Trade Liberalisation Programme under this Agreement. Until alternative domestic arrangements are formulated to address this situation, the Contracting States agree to establish an appropriate mechanism to compensate the Least Developed Contracting States for their loss of customs revenue. This mechanism and its rules and regulations shall be established prior to the commencement of the Trade Liberalisation Programme (TLP).

Article 12 Special Provision for Maldives

Notwithstanding the potential or actual graduation of Maldives from the status of a Least Developed Country, it shall be accorded in this Agreement and in any subsequent contractual undertakings thereof treatment no less favourable than that provided for the Least Developed Contracting States.

Article 13 Non-application

Notwithstanding the measures as set out in this Agreement its provisions shall not apply in relation to preferences already granted or to be granted by any Contracting State to other Contracting States outside the framework of this Agreement, and to third countries through bilateral, plurilateral and multilateral trade agreements and similar arrangements.

Article 14 General Exceptions

a) Nothing in this Agreement shall be construed to prevent any Contracting State from taking action and adopting measures which it considers necessary for the protection of its national security.

b) Subject to the requirement that such measures are not applied in a manner which would constitute a means of arbitrary or unjustifiable discrimination between countries where the similar conditions prevail, or a disguised restriction on intra-regional trade, nothing in this Agreement shall be construed to prevent any Contracting State from taking action and adopting measures which it considers necessary for the protection of: (i) public morals; (ii) human, animal or plant life and health; and (iii) articles of artistic, historic and archaeological value.

Article 15 Balance of Payments Measures

1. Notwithstanding the provisions of this Agreement, any Contracting State facing serious balance of payments difficulties may suspend provisionally the concessions extended under this Agreement.
2. Any such measure taken pursuant to paragraph 1 of this Article shall be immediately notified to the Committee of Experts.
3. The Committee of Experts shall periodically review the measures taken pursuant to paragraph 1 of this Article.
4. Any Contracting State which takes action pursuant to paragraph I of this Article shall afford, upon request from any other Contracting State, adequate opportunities for consultations with a view to preserving the stability of concessions under SAFTA.

5. If no satisfactory adjustment is effected between the Contracting States concerned within 30 days of the beginning of such consultations, to be extended by another 30 days through mutual consent, the matter may be referred to the Committee of Experts.
6. Any such measures taken pursuant to paragraph 1 of this Article shall be phased out soon after the Committee of Experts comes to the conclusion that the balance of payments situation of the Contracting State concerned has improved.

Article 16 Safeguard Measures

1. If any product, which is the subject of a concession under this Agreement, is imported into the territory of a Contracting State in such a manner or in such quantities as to cause, or threaten to cause, serious injury to producers of like or directly competitive products in the importing Contracting State, the importing Contracting State may, pursuant to an investigation by the competent authorities of that Contracting State conducted in accordance with the provisions set out in this Article, suspend temporarily the concessions granted under the provisions of this Agreement. The examination of the impact on the domestic industry concerned shall include an evaluation of all other relevant economic factors and indices having a bearing on the state of the domestic industry of the product and a causal relationship must be clearly established between "serious injury" and imports from within the SAARC region, to the exclusion of all such other factors.
2. Such suspension shall only be for such time and to the extent as may be necessary to prevent or remedy such injury and in no case, will such suspension be for duration of more than 3 years.
3. No safeguard measure shall be applied again by a Contracting State to the import of a product which has been subject to such a measure during the period of implementation of Trade Liberalization Programme by the Contracting States, for a period of time equal to that during

which such measure had been previously applied, provided that the period of non-application is at least two years.

4. All investigation procedures for resorting to safeguard measures under this Article shall be consistent with Article XIX of GATT 1994 and WTO Agreement on Safeguards.
5. Safeguard action under this Article shall be non-discriminatory and applicable to the product imported from all other Contracting States subject to the provisions of paragraph 8 of this Article.
6. When safeguard provisions are used in accordance with this Article, the Contracting State invoking such measures shall immediately notify the exporting Contracting State(s) and the Committee of Experts.
7. In critical circumstances where delay would cause damage which it would be difficult to repair, a Contracting State may take a provisional safeguard measure pursuant to a preliminary determination that there is clear evidence that increased imports have caused or are threatening to cause serious injury. The duration of the provisional measure shall not exceed 200 days, during this period the pertinent requirements of this Article shall be met.
8. Notwithstanding any of the provisions of this Article, safeguard measures under this article shall not be applied against a product originating in a Least Developed Contracting State as long as its share of imports of the product concerned in the importing Contracting State does not exceed 5 per cent, provided Least Developed Contracting States with less than 5% import share collectively account for not more than 15% of total imports of the product concerned.

Article 17 Maintenance of the Value of Concessions

Any of the concessions agreed upon under this Agreement shall not be diminished or nullified, by the application of any measures restricting trade by the Contracting States, except under the provisions of other articles of this Agreement.

Article 18 Rules of Origin

Rules of Origin shall be negotiated by the Contracting States and incorporated in this Agreement as an integral part.

Article 19 Consultations

1. Each Contracting State shall accord sympathetic consideration to and will afford adequate opportunity for consultations regarding representations made by another Contracting State with respect to any matter affecting the operation of this Agreement.
2. The Committee of Experts may, at the request of a Contracting State, consult with any Contracting State in respect of any matter for which it has not been possible to find a satisfactory solution through consultations under paragraph 1.

Article 20 Dispute Settlement Mechanism

1. Any dispute that may arise among the Contracting States regarding the interpretation and application of the provisions of this Agreement or any instrument adopted within its framework concerning the rights and obligations of the Contracting States will be amicably settled among the parties concerned through a process initiated by a request for bilateral consultations.
2. Any Contracting State may request consultations in accordance with paragraph 1 of this Article with other Contracting State in writing stating the reasons for the request including identification of the measures at issue. All such requests should be notified to the Committee of Experts, through the SAARC Secretariat with an indication of the legal basis for the complaint.

Article 21 Withdrawal

1. Any Contracting State may withdraw from this Agreement at any time after its entry into force. Such withdrawal shall be effective on expiry of six months from the date on which a written notice thereof is received by the Secretary-General of SAARC, the depositary of this Agreement. That

Contracting State shall simultaneously inform the Committee of Experts of the action it has taken.

2. The rights and obligations of a Contracting State which has withdrawn from this Agreement shall cease to apply as of that effective date.
3. Following the withdrawal by any Contracting State, the Committee shall meet within 30 days to consider action subsequent to withdrawal.

Article 22 Entry into Force

1. This Agreement shall enter into force on 1st January 2006 upon completion of formalities, including ratification by all Contracting States and issuance of a notification thereof by the SAARC Secretariat. This Agreement shall supercede the Agreement on SAARC Preferential Trading Arrangement (SAPTA).
2. Notwithstanding the supercession of SAPTA by this Agreement, the concessions granted under the SAPTA Framework shall remain available to the Contracting States until the completion of the Trade Liberalisation Programme.

Article 23 Reservations

This Agreement shall not be signed with reservations, nor will reservations be admitted at the time of notification to the SAARC Secretariat of the completion of formalities.

Article 24 Amendments

This Agreement may be amended by consensus in the SAFTA Ministerial Council. Any such amendment will become effective upon the deposit of instruments of acceptance with the Secretary General of SAARC by all Contracting States.

6

Birth Pangs of a New Europe

As there are fears in certain political class, largely in Britain, of European Union moving from an economic and monetary Union to the ultimate stage of unity i.e. towards a political Union or a politically unified Europe and the proposed new Constitution likely to give a push towards one single European state to be called Europa or United States of Europe, the debate over the proposed European Constitution is becoming more intense and shrill. The anti-European leaders or the so called eurosceptics voice concerns over losing sovereign rights of a nation state to a new centralised European authority called European Union with its headquarter or should be more appropriately called the Capital in Brussels. As long as there was only a talk of making Europe economically integrated one, there was not much objection to this process but the new Constitution has raised eyebrows in certain European capitals who fear that the national constitutions will be superseded by an European constitution. The fiery speeches against the new emerging European Union with a constitution of its own, in various European capitals and cities, in the run up to the European elections [on 10th June, 2004], may best be described as the birth pangs of a new Europe which would be a force to reckon with in 21st century. This new Europe may emerge as a new superpower, both economically and politically, as the combined military muscle and financial strength of 25 member countries, would catapult Europe in new league of nations in a multipolar world, which may not be a rival but parallel to the American superpower. The South Asians must take note of and get ready to deal with this new emerging geopolitical reality of the 21st century.

Inspite of lot of skepticism among various political groups and citizens at large the leaders of Europe collectively decided on 18 June, 2004, meeting of European Council and perhaps planted a seed for a new politically unified Europe when they all agreed for a new Constitution for a bloc that now embraces most of the continent's people and countries. The Constitution took two years to draft and contains more than three hundred pages determining how the biggest political Union in the world will operate. However all 25 member states with a total population of 450 million must ratify the constitution. This process may take at least three to four years as Britain has won a reprieve till the end of 2006 to go for a national referendum on the Constitution. The new Constitution creates the EU as a legal entity, allowing it to sign treaties in its own right without their having to be ratified by national parliaments and creates a full time President and a foreign minister. The new deal for a constitution strikes a careful balance between keeping national vetoes and introducing majority voting. Thus, the governments can successfully oppose the creation of a European public prosecutor to tackle crimes affecting EU's finances, but once the office is set up and running only a majority decision would be required to extend its powers to investigate other cross border serious crimes. The same principle would be applied on common foreign and security policy issues. The initial strategy decision would be taken by all 25 EU countries, but majority voting would be sufficient for its practical implementation. The EU will now move from unanimity to majority voting in almost 30 policy areas. The most significant of these will cover asylum and immigration policy where EU is playing an increasing role. Described as "faulty" by some, the agreement over the new constitution has proved that the forces pulling Europe together are stronger than the forces pulling apart.

Though the European Union received a big drubbing on the 10th June, 2004, elections for the EU Parliament from its citizens as the voter turnout was not only lowest ever (45%) but the voters also displayed huge vote of no confidence in European institutions. The hostility displayed by millions of citizens in the continent's largest democratic exercises astonished all as the European leaders struggled to come up with a convincing response as the voter turnout of 26% was recorded in 10 new countries who joined EU only 40 days ago. The European Council in its 18th June, 2004, meeting expressed concern at the low voter turnout in June 10, elections to the European Parliament. The Council in a statement said, "It recognizes the need to strengthen a sense among the citizens of Europe of the importance of the work of the Union and its relevance to their daily lives." The European foreign ministers meeting in Luxembourg after the election results described electorates rising apathy and euroscepticism as a "disease" They insisted that the remedy was to demonstrate that the EU works and more intensively educate the public about the Union's benefits. Despite the lowest ever turnout in European elections and record gains by eurosceptic parties, who now control up to a fifth of the European Parliament. The German and French ministers responded by saying," we all know, what is at stake. Europe needs a success." The election results indicated that the eurosceptics will not allow the new European constitution to be adopted in near future.

Though it is officially clarified that the European Constitution would not replace the Constitutions which already exist in most European countries. The new European Constitution will coexist with these constitutions and has its own jurisdiction and its autonomy and it will apply throughout European Union and it defines the context within which European Union is competent to act. The European Constitution would replace the main existing Treaties with a single text. The official documents say that the European Constitution is an important step in the construction of Europe. It is designed to meet the challenges of tomorrow's Europe; a Europe of 25 member states and 450 million inhabitants; a democratic, transparent, efficient Europe working to serve all Europeans.

Political Europe

To meet these challenges the then President of the European Commission Romano Prodi presented a study report in May

2004, commissioned by him, which may add more fuel to the fire. The report entitled "Constructing a political Europe" will reinforce fears in Britain and other countries that Brussels is intent on creating a European Superstate as it calls for a Political Union as the EU's next big project. According to this report the European Union is in crisis and can be saved only by turning it into a fully fledged "political union", with a European tax, minimum wage and pan-European political parties. The report was specifically commissioned as a way of looking at how best to use new decision making powers that the European Constitution is set to give European institutions, and set the path of the EU over the next 20 years. The report states that Europe is at a turning point in its history facing a triple crisis of failing institutions, falling democratic legitimacy and not knowing how far it should expand geographically. The report insists that the solution is to create a "mobilising myth" or "project", for the EU and that only the creation of a "common model society" can give its legitimacy.

The report says that instead of concentrating on healing the divisions of the second world war, the EU should now try to create opportunities for its people. It suggests 50 policies to integrate Europe politically, including a dramatic increase in the EU budget, and the creation of a pan European company tax that is used to fund it. It calls for a European industrial policy to create companies that are "European champions", such as the aircraft maker Airbus, supported by a European Agency for Science and Research, coordinating innovations across Europe. It also calls for panEuropean political parties that would be guaranteed a proportion of places in the European Parliament. To create a sense of belonging to the Union, a European public broadcasting service should be set up, as well as a museum of Europe and European history courses should be taught in schools. Commission officials describe it as a long range document, which is seen as the succession to the big projects— the euro and enlargement.

Decline of British Empire

The proposed new Constitution of European Union is generating much heat in the corridors of powers in many

European capitals and in the media also because of fears of losing sovereign rights of making independent security and foreign policy and other laws of domestic nature. There are serious efforts to stop the drift towards a country called "Europe." With Britain declaring its contentious decision to hold a referendum over the issue of the new Constitution it has raised much eyebrows in the European political circles with fears of stalling the adoption of Constitution and thus preventing the EU to act as a unified body in the field of defence and foreign policy. Just imagine the fate of the glorious British empire of the yesteryears arguing its viewpoint before the collective leadership in Brussels and being compelled to reach a consensus decision with the rest of the Europe. If Britain becomes a fully fledged partner in EU and EU has its way, 21st century will see the decline and ultimate disappearance of the British power and authority as a nation.

For example, the Article III-195 (paragraph-2) on the EU's common foreign and security policy says," The member states shall support the common foreign and security policy actively and unreservedly in a spirit of loyalty and mutual solidarity." Further more, the article 1-27 announces a new position of EU foreign minister. He shall conduct the Union's common foreign and security policy. Now so called eurosceptics (who doubt the rationale of a single European entity taking decisions in the domain of national sovereignty) and often called as narrow-minded nationalists ask, if EU has a foreign minister then who will listen to and take seriously individual foreign ministers of member states of European Union? There are also fears in national diplomatic services in many powerful members that EU Constitution will create a fully fledged rival diplomatic service to run the EU's 128 overseas offices and will speak on behalf of all EU members. The possible appointment of a socalled foreign minister of a united Europe under the new constitution has been seized on by eurosceptics as a sign that the Constitution would give the EU the trappings of a nation state.

The Europeanists point out that there will be no compulsion to accept any ruling on foreign policy by any individual member state since every member state will have a veto power to block the resolution delineating single European policy. They also point out that the wording of the article III-195 is all but identical to Article 11:2 of the Maastricht Treaty, agreed in 1991. Since then as the Iraq war proved so dramatically, member states have openly differed and refused to have a common policy on Iraq. However, the interpretation of the new constitution denies the claim that things have not moved on since Maastricht. Saying so would be misrepresenting the position. For example, several EU members like Germans, Italians and Belgians have been applying heavy pressure to get rid of the veto over foreign policy. The amendment proposed by Italian presidency in 2003 is worrying the eurosceptics. The British, French and few others will not support this when actual negotiation begins. However, as far as the issue of veto is concerned there are provisions in constitution which Britain is prepared to accept, stating that, after a unanimous vote is taken on an overall policy, subsequent decisions on how it is implemented could be taken by majority vote. The British diplomats point out that if a decision was taken to appoint a special representative to a trouble spot, the main decision to do so would be taken unanimously but the subsequent one on who the person might be could be taken by majority vote. The diplomats also insist that a common foreign policy does not mean that a country cannot have own view on certain international issue and cannot pursue own policy in accordance with its thinking. A common foreign policy just means that where you want to act together and there is unanimous agreement that you should, then you can.'

Foreign Minister

The major concern relates to new post of a foreign minister. Right now this job is being undertaken by two authorities, the EU High Representative for foreign and security policy and the EU commissioner for foreign relations. Under the new proposal the two posts are to be merged into a single foreign minister. Concerns are expressed that such a post backed by a large secretariat, is bound to expand beyond the current limit of helping to execute the policy decided by member states and representing the EU as a whole abroad. Critics want to ensure that the foreign minister will be answerable to the Council of Ministers and not the unelected European Commission. As far as European Defence Policy is concerned the British government says that the right to veto a proposal will not be diluted and nothing is being done to undermine NATO. Actually plans to have an independent European Army would not be executed and a Belgian move to set up a permanent European version of NATO's headquarters in Brussels was quashed. The British are firm that nothing will be done to undermine NATO. The British argued that such a center would at best duplicate and at worst complicate NATO. However the British government compromised and agreed for a European planning cell, which will not be a permanent one and will be brought together for specific missions If NATO decides not to get involved in a military operation, this center could be activated. The EU can act only when NATO decides not to move in a given situation. After a unanimous vote any member state if it has requisite military strength can take part in the operation. The member states would contribute the troops. Critics point out that for the first time European military action takes place outside NATO, it is likely to undermine the NATO alliance. Gradually the European planning cell may start ignoring NATO and this is what worries Britain which is a major alliance partner of NATO and the USA. Other allies of the USA in EU would also not like to undermine NATO at the cost of its friendship with the USA.

In fact there is a fierce opposition in Britain for a single constitution in Europe. The British Tory leader Michael Howard said, while addressing an election rally for European Parliament, "Conservatives do not want a European constitution. Countries have constitutions and we do not want to be a part of a country called Europe. I am determined that Britain shall remain a positive and influential member of the European Union. But I do not want an Europe which is a one way street to closer integration to which all must subscribe. Those member states which wish to integrate more closely should be free to do so. But they should not drag Britain and quite possibly some other member states kicking and screaming in their wake."

Warning

The former French President Valery Giscard d'Estang and architect of of the new EU Treaty, issued a veiled warning to

Britain that it would not have to leave the European Union if it voted NO to the proposed EU constitution but Britain would be left on the margins of the EU away from main decision making. Mr Giscard, who headed the convention of European parliamentarians and officials who drew up the draft constitution, said," of course if someone says we do not accept the way that Europe functions it will have to assume the consequences of its own choice. It is up to them then. If this happens in Britain or elsewhere, what will happen in the other countries will matter also. Take the example of the United States, the US constitution or amendments to the US constitution. When two thirds of the people of the United States decide it must be adopted it is adopted. A similar situation could happen to the EU if countries with 300 million out of 455 million of its citizens, backed the constitution, it will mean they will create a situation in which the people, not only government, but the people who want to progress with this functioning of the Union will have to decide how to progress with this functioning by themselves. If by bad luck the British said No and the other Europeans said we want to go, then they would have to find an accommodation. In that case Britain would not be in the core of the system but on the margins. I wouldn't say on the outside but on the edge."[1]

But the defiant Tory leaders of Britain are raising their banners of revolt which would make it difficult for Britain to okay the constitution during the referendum and thus keep Britain away from the center stage of European politics. Mr. Howard launched the Tory campaign for European elections with a ten-point programme for handing greater power to the nation states, in what he described as a "live and let live" approach to EU membership. The proposals include introducing a "red card" system that would require a European Law to be repealed if five or more national parliaments objected to it, and a pledge to put any new European Treaty that transferred significant powers to Brussels to a referendum. Mr Howard described his 10 key proposals as a programme for a 21st century Europe that would make Britain a "positive and influential member of the EU". Some of his proposals are:

1. *The Times*, London, April 30, 2004

1. A 25 % cut in existing European regulations contained in the 80,000 pages of acquis communautaires—the Union's rule book—and "sunset clauses" on new ones to ensure they expire after a given period.
2. Giving member states a right to initiate European legislation, a monopoly currently held by the European Commission.
3. Reforming the rotating EU presidency to create one year joint presidencies shared between a big and a small state to help smaller new members cope with the burden.
4. Appointing a senior minister to be the British representative in Brussels, instead of a diplomat, with a mandate to report back to the Commons and the Lords every fortnight.
5. Mandatory British referendum on all future European treaties that involve a significant shift of powers from Westminster to Brussels.

Reforming the pay and expenses of Member of European Parliaments (MEP) to set them at the same level as MP's, making MEP's pay tax at the same rate as their constituents, and ensuring that MEP's expenses are fully transparent.

Secular Europe

Another issue that is dividing the member States on the Constitution is the religious one. The controversial question of Christianity is haunting the EU members as seven States led by Italy asked the Union to recognise a "historical truth" and refer explicitly to the "Christian roots of Europe" in its new Constitution. The preamble of the current draft Treaty refers only to the "cultural, religious and humanist inheritance of Europe". Specifically mentioning Christianity or God was considered too controversial in the face of furious opposition from secular France and Protestant northerners such as Sweden and Denmark. However largely Catholic States like Italy, Poland, Lithuania, Malta, Portugal, the Czech Republic and Slovakia have submitted a memorandum demanding that a reference to Europe's Christian roots be inserted. However Britain opposed making European Union a "Christian Club" which would complicate negotiations on admitting Muslim Turkey. Opponents argued that it would be wrong to exclude Muslims and Jews and would therefore be better to avoid any religious reference. Spain said, "Spain is a Catholic country, but in the European Constitution our Government is rather secular, and in this sense we want to respect the text as it currently stands." Poland would like a reference based on its own national constitution, which refers to "both those who believe in God as the source of truth, justice, good and beauty, as well as those not sharing such faith but respecting those universal values from other sources." The Vatican made it clear that it wants a reference to Christianity in the Constitution.

However the biggest disagreements are still over voting rights in the EU council of ministers . The Irish proposal says that a decision is taken when supported by 50% of member states representing 60 % of the EU population. But Spain and Poland rejected it as it would mean that Europe's big three—Britain, France and Germany—could form a blocking minority on any decisions they do not like. Spain and Poland want to maintain the overgenerous weighted votes they won in the 2000 Nice Treaty, which gave them almost as much power as Germany, with less than half its population.

Practical Difficulties

No doubt with the enlargement of EU its management would become more and more cumbersome. Giving the chance to each member to run the EU for six months , during which term it assumes the presidency of EU is indeed most democratic and ideal way of running EU but there are practical difficulties which the EU would have to encounter. Just imagine when the turn comes for a country like Cyprus or Malta, having a population only of 400,000 to assume the mantle of EU. These countries just do not have enough resources and expertise to run a huge administration, neither do they have enough manpower to give EU a definite direction and to carry forward the unfinished and ongoing tasks of EU. The country which assumes the Presidency has to play a major role in organising various meetings and conferences and to represent EU in international summit level meetings. This is why the proposal of Mr Howard to give joint responsibilities to a big and small country for running the Presidency for a year has some logic. In view of the enlargement the management system needs to be amended for which the proposed constitution would also have to be altered.

There are serious divisions resulting in mutual acrimony between members on the proposed new constitution. Germany and France openly accused Britain of trying to secure last minute concessions in talks on the EU's controversial new constitution. During a meeting in Brussels when British foreign secretary demanded that safeguards on the charter of fundamental rights be written into the text of the treaty, his German counterpart accused him of employing "salami tactics" to obtain key changes to the Treaty, which is designed to simplify and overhaul procedures for an 25-state EU. Mr Yoschka Fischer was forcefully backed by the French foreign minister, Michel Barnier, amid concerns that Britain might try to use its surprise referendum on the Constitution as an additional means of pressures on its partners. The Franco-German response, a reflection of the close coordination between Paris and Berlin, was apparently designed to warn that a UK referendum could not open "a new credit line" Britain has already declared that it will veto on foreign policy, defence, taxation and criminal justice issues. The charter of the rights issue is sensitive but less important than those. The Constitutional Treaty has to be agreed and ratified unanimously, though it is widely acknowledged that holding a referendum complicates the process hugely. But the pressure for the UK is now domestic than European, with the conservatives and other eurosceptics calling the constitution a "blueprint for tyranny" and a charter for an EU "Superstate". Over the issue of voting rights Poland and Spain fear an outcome that would give a permanent veto to Britain, France and Germany similar to the UN Security Council, thus duplicating something like United Nations of Europe. However Belgium, Germany and France want urgently to move towards greater majority voting to avoid a gridlock in decision making in a Union of 25 states. Paris and Berlin are coordinating their positions closely and have revived proposals that would allow countries cooperating in certain areas to do so without being blocked by non-participants. The British view is that allowing a "two-speed" Europe would be a small price to pay for preserving its own veto in key areas. Tensions between Britain and its European partners were reflected in a jokey exchange about mosquitoes buzzing around in the council of ministers building, with Mr Jack Straw complaining they were "anti-British". The German foreign minister Joschka Fischer retorted that the mosquitoes were actually pro-European.

Superstate

The *Daily Telegraph* in its long editorial (April 30, 2004) raising the fears of the establishment of a sovereign Europe said: "This 'Constitution for Europe' is established by treaty, which has allowed its advocates to claim that it is not a constitution at all, hence cannot create a superstate. True, there is an exit clause (article 59). However the EU as envisaged resembles a federal state: it would have its own executive, legislature, judiciary, police, civil service, currency, central bank, taxes, army, foreign minister, embassies and flag. Above all the EU would have its own legal personality. It would no longer merely be the sum of its parts, but could act in its own right. Our veto is replaced by majority voting in most of the remaining areas of policy left by previous treaties. In foreign and defence policy the text speaks of a common foreign and security policy, which member states would be under pressure to support 'actively and unreservedly in a spirit of loyalty and mutual solidarity'. This policy is to be determined by majority voting and implemented by new bureaucracies led by the new foreign minister, who has the job of bringing refractory member states into line. They are wanted to refrain from any action which is contrary to the interests of the Union. In economic field, virtually all economic, monetary, employment and social policies are 'coordinated' under the constitution, leaving only fiscal policy to the member states Also, the Constitution incorporates the Charter of Fundamental Rights, with incalculable implications for the British legal system. It also embraces the whole area of criminal and civil justice. Common policies on immigration and asylum will be backed by decisions of European courts. The constitution provides for indefinite extension of Union powers. In article 10 it states that the Constitution and EU law, "shall have primacy over the law of the member states." This principle though already established in commerce, is new to the fields such as foreign affairs, defence, criminal justice, transport, environment, energy, health, education and culture. Its effect has been described by an Oxford professor as 'nuclear'. This constitution creates a tyranny that would imperil all that has been achieved since 1945. We should reject it: not just for the sake of Britain, but for the sake of Europe."

Beyond Trade

Countering the eurosceptics apprehensions, columnist Polly Toynbee writes in the *Guardian* (21 May, 04). "The big question remains. What's the EU for, beyond free trade? Old reasons for European unity have gone. Jean Monnet's talk of keeping the peace after a millenium of European war sounds as archaic as gas masks. Once the wall came down there was no common danger to unite against. But the EU always needed a political purpose beyond trade, without that things start to fall apart. Failure to agree a constitution ought to send an electric jolt through the whole Union. It is a warning that once its political purpose is no longer strong enough to overcome day to day irritations, it cannot survive. No doubt anti-Europeans would celebrate. But there is as much need for a strong Europe now as there was in the cold war. Public opinion in Europe sees the issues too: consider the powerful opposition to the Iraq war. But so far their leaders have been too short sighted, wrong headed, weak or politically self interested to seize the right issues to draw the continent together. In a world riven between Muslim and non-Muslim, between the rich north and poor south, where poverty and terrorism go hand in hand, fury against America is a global peril. Madrid felt its hot blast and no doubt we shall too. Europe should be standing at the world's crossroads, trying to mitigate both the wrath of the powerless and recklessness of the overmighty US. The EU will not last long without a galvanising political purpose offering an alternative to the American way."

Voices like this definitely have a majority but a single voice of defiance to the new emerging power center in Brussels would create roadblocks which can only delay the rise of a new politically united Europe with single foreign and security policy in the years to come but ultimately it cannot prevent the EU from acquiring the status of another superpower on this earth, both economically and politically.

The EU Constitution: Salient Features

The Constitution of European Union has established a number of symbols which gives an impression of EU being a sovereign nation state like European flag, the melody, the European motto, the Europe day, etc.

The *European flag* is the symbol not only of the European Union but also of Europe's unity and identity in a wider sense. The circle of gold stars represents solidarity and harmony between the peoples of Europe. The number of stars has nothing to do with the number of member States. There are twelve stars because the number twelve is traditionally the symbol of perfection, completeness and unity. The flag will therefore remain unchanged regardless of future EU enlargements.

The *Melody* comes from the Ninth Symphony composed in 1823 by Ludwig van Beethoven. For the final movement of this symphony, Beethoven set to music the 'ode to joy' written in 1785 by Friedrich von Schiller. This poem expresses Schiller's idealistic vision of humanity in which all men are brothers a vision Beethoven shared.

The *European Motto*, United in Diversity, was chosen through a competition organised by a group of European citizens.

Euro: Also the 12 members of EU have already adopted a common currency Euro which unites the people of Europe more strongly.

The *Europe Day* is celebrated on 9 May, 1950, when the French foreign affairs minister Robert Schuman presented his proposal for the creation of an organised Europe based on the pooling of coal and steel production, chiefly in order to avoid the belligerent countries of Europe from ever going to war with each other again. This proposal, known as the 'Schuman declaration' is considered to be the beginning of the creation of what is now the European Union. The 9th of May is now known as "Europe Day". It is the occasion for activities and festivities that bring Europe closer to its citizens and the peoples of the Union closer to one another.

So European Union has got everything a nation state should have. In accordance with this the European Constitution guarantees a single area of 'freedom, security and justice'. In concrete terms it means that there will be no checks at the European Union's internal borders. All the European citizens may move freely within the borders of the 25 member states (from Helsinki to Lisbon, from Dublin to Tallinn) without being checked or needing to show their passports.

The European Constitution was prepared and adopted through a transparent and democratic process, by a European Convention of 105 representatives (of whom 72 were directly elected members of national parliaments or of the European Parliament). It also has to be ratified by the national parliaments of the 25 member states of the Union (bodies which have likewise been elected by direct universal suffrage), or by referendum.

The Constitution is divided into four parts. Part 1 defines the European Union, its values, its objectives, its powers, its decision making procedures and its institutions. Part II contains the "Charter of Fundamental Rights". Part III describes the policies and functioning of the European Union. Part IV contains the final provisions, including the procedures for adopting and revising the Constitution.

The Constitution also gives the option to any member country to quit the European Union.

European Citizen

The Constitution has a provision of a European citizenship which says that every national of a member State shall be a citizen of the Union. The Constitution offers each citizen the guarantee of respect for certain values and of a model society. Respect for liberty, democracy, equality, the rule of law, human dignity and human rights are enshrined in the Constitution.

It guarantees a society founded on pluralism, tolerance, justice, solidarity and non discrimination. It guarantees free movement of persons, goods, services and capital and no discrimination on grounds of nationality. Only member states which respect these values may become members of the European Union. Moreover, measures can be taken against any member state which fails to respect them. The European citizenship is additional to national citizenship and confers additional right; the right to move and reside freely within the territory of the Union, the right to vote and to stand as a candidate in elections to the European Parliament and in municipal elections, diplomatic and consular protection in third countries, the right to petition the European Parliament, to apply to the European Ombudsman, and to address the institutions and advisory bodies of the Union in any of the languages and obtain a reply in the same language.

In addition a Charter of fundamental rights has been framed which forms an integral part of the Constitution. It applies to the European institutions and to the member states when they are implementing European Union law. It covers not only the civil and political rights enshrined in the 1950 European Convention on Human Rights but also additional areas: workers, social rights, protection of the environment, the right to good administration, etc. The Charter declares total respect for human dignity; the right to life; the prohibition of torture and inhuman or degrading treatment; the right to liberty and security; respect for private and family life; freedom of thought, conscience and religion; freedom of expression and information; the right to education; freedom to conduct a business; the right to property; equality before the law; respect for the cultural, religious and linguistic diversity; equality between men and women; the integration of persons with disabilities; the right to access to justice and to a fair trial; the persecution of innocence and right of defence, etc.

Draft Constitution

It was at Laeken in Belgium that the Heads of State or Government of the 15 member states of the European Union decided to convene a "European Convention", assembling the main parties involved in the debate on the future of Europe. This European Convention was instructed to draw up a document intended to provide a starting point for discussions in an intergovernmental conference to amend the existing European Treaties (the Laeken declaration" of 15 December, 2001). Never before has an amendment of the European treaties been prepared by such a large and open assembly as the European Convention.

The European Convention, chaired by Mr Valery Giscard d'Estaing, began work on 28 February, 2002. It was composed of 105 members (and 102 alternates), comprising one Chairman, 2 Vice-chairman, 2 representatives of the European Commission, 15 representatives of the Heads of State or Government of the member States, 13 representatives of the Heads of State or Government of the candidate States, 30 representatives of the national parliaments of the member states, 26 representatives of the national parliaments of the candidate states and 16 members of the European Parliament. Thus 72 of the Convention members were directly elected members of national parliaments or the European Parliament. After 16 months of work the European Convention reached a consensus on a draft European Constitution (13 June and 10 July, 2003). This draft is under consideration for ratification by various member states.

Areas of Competences

The Constitution clarifies competences, categorising and listing them. It indicates the areas in which the European Union may act alone (exclusive competence), the areas in which the European Union may act along with the member states (shared competence) and the areas in which the European Union may act only in an ancillary capacity (supporting, coordinating or complementary action).

Exclusive Competence: Rules on competition, provisions relating to the Customs Union, common commercial poliy, monetary policy relating to the Euro and conservation of marine biological resources.

Shared Competence: Smooth functioning of the internal market, creation of an area of freedom, security and justice, agriculture and fisheries, transport and trans-European networks, energy, certain aspects of social policy, economic, social and territorial cohesion, environment protection, consumer protection, certain aspects of public health, certain aspects of research, technological development and space, certain aspects of development cooperation and humanitarian aid.

Supporting, coordinating or complimentary action: Industrial policy, protection of human health, education, vocational training, youth, and sport, culture, civil protection.

The Union also has competence to coordinate the economic and employment policies of the member states and to define and implement a common foreign and security policy. It can also—and this is new—promote the framing of a common defence policy.

Principle of conferral of competences: The Union shall act within the limits of the competences conferred upon it by the member states in the Constitution.

Principle of subsidiarity: In areas which do not fall within its exclusive competence the Union shall act only if and in so far as the objectives of the intended action cannot be sufficiently achieved by the member states, either at the central level or at regional level, but can rather, by reason of the scale or effects of the proposed action, be better achieved at Union level.

Principle of proportionality: The concept and form of Union action shall not exceed what is necessary to achieve the objectives of the Constitution.

Review

Review by the Court of Justice: The three principles are subject to judicial review by the Court of Justice and may be subject of proceedings brought before the Court.

The Constitution reinforces the application of the second and third of these principles; from now on, each national Parliament will have the chance to examine whether a Commission proposal respects the principle of subsidiarity, and this could even lead to the Commission revising its proposal.

To enforce transparency of proceedings, henceforth, not only the European Parliament but also the Council of Ministers is obliged to meet in public when examining and adopting a legislative proposal.

Source: Various documents released by European Commission

7

Relations between neighbours

Relations between South Asian neighbours are not only affected by inter state but intra state conflicts also. As intra state conflicts impinge on the inter state relations due to ethno religious overlapping across geographically contiguous border states, there is a tendency to seal the borders between the neighbouring countries affecting free movement of people and trade in the region. These ongoing conflicts, some a recent phenomenon and some few decades old are slowly but surely sapping our energies and worsening the economic condition of our societies and depriving the ordinary masses of a decent livelihood. The north eastern states of India are in the grip of five decades long insurgencies of the tribal communities, thus denying the area an opportunity to grow economically and develop trade linkages with the adjoining states of Myanmar and Bangladesh. The decade old Maoist insurgency in Nepal which has established links with the Indian extremist movements in Bihar and Andhra Pradesh, is not only hampering the growth of tourism industry but also created a constitutional crisis, which has rendered the Nepalese government ineffective. The territorial claims over the state of Jammu and Kashmir has also disturbed the normal life in the region severely and created a permanent conflict situation between India and Pakistan. Bangladesh is also affected with Chakma tribal insurgency and growing fundamentalist tendency. The LTTE led separatist struggle in Sri Lanka has adversely impacted on the growth of Sri Lankan economy. These intra state conflicts in the region have marginalized a huge population, further aggravated by the social and economic divisions of their societies.

As the Tamils of Tamil Nadu and Sri Lanka have mutual affinities, the Bengali culture and language pervades Indian state of West Bengal and adjoining Bangladesh. Similarly the Hindi speaking population of Bihar and Uttar Pradesh (India) have similarities with Hindi speaking Madheshi population of Nepal. These cross border affinities offer huge potentials of a prosperous society, but unfortunately the region due to lack of development, is still languishing in mutual hate relations which deny any economic activity to flourish, as the religious-political-criminal nexus develop their own vested interests to perpetuate their sinister influence. This vicious cycle of economic backwardness, unemployment, insurgency and cross border shelter to insurgent groups is leading to inter state tensions which in turn prevents bilateral trade and cooperation in other areas.

Geography of an area and size of a country cannot be altered but perhaps this is one of the reasons of mutual suspicion, tension and conflicts among South Asian countries. The smaller nations of South Asia allege that India's policies and behaviour are like big brother and hegemonistic and wants to dominate them whereas people complain in India that its smaller neighbours are not sensitive to India's interests and security concerns and are often a cause of domestic tensions. Besides, South Asia and its periphery have been the cradle of Islamic militancy, Jehad and resultant terrorism and which has also been a training place and launch centre of Al- Qaida brand of terrorism which the Western society is now getting a feel of it but this region has been experiencing this menace since long. In fact, a terrorist attack on Indian parliament in December 2001, led to a ten months military standoff between India and Pakistan and the western world feared a nuclear war like probability. In this situation it was, difficult to imagine cooperative economic relations and partnerships in South Asia. However there has been a marked change in the security atmosphere after the then Indian Prime Minister Atal Bihari Vajpayee visited Pakistan to attend the SAARC summit in January 2004. There has been a ceasefire on the India-Pakistan line of control in

Jammu and Kashmir since November 2003, and the leaders of the two countries are once again on talking terms. This on and off relationship between India and Pakistan is mostly responsible for the ups and downs in SAARC history. The crest and trough of SAARC graph has been determined by the dynamics of India-Pakistan relations and in a smaller way by India-Bangladesh and India-Sri Lanka relations though Bangladesh has been much forthcoming in developing better economic relations with India and Sri Lanka has signed a free trade agreement with India and has now developed very cordial diplomatic relations with India after having a rough time in the eighties.

Also there are apprehensions in the minds of smaller countries that India's overwhelming economic strength would cripple their domestic industries. Actually there is a syndrome of asymmetry between India (76% of the total population and 77% of the regional GNP) and its neighbours. This is intensified by the fact that India is situated geographically at the centre of South Asian states, which have no common frontiers. The members of SAARC (except Maldives which is in Indian Ocean) surround Indian borders and have linguistic and ethnic similarity and relations with the adjoining states of India but they live like estranged members of a family. Though people in Indian state of West Bengal and Bangladesh speak the same language and have same culture and both assert their pride in their language and literature, and similarly Tamils in Indian state of Tamil Nadu have across the sea cultural and language affinities and similarities with the Tamils in Sri Lanka. Likewise the people in Indian Punjab and across the border in Lahore in Pakistan also speak similar language and have similar life-style. Even the Nepalese have relatives in Indian state of Bihar and Uttar Pradesh and they send their children for good and higher education to India. But anti-India feeling among all these similar communities living across the border persists. The animosity between the "estranged sisters" is a barrier to regional cooperation. It has isolated the region from other dynamic regions (ASEAN or APEC, for example, who do not wish to import into their structures the decision-blocking South Asian conflicts) and prevented it from setting up other promising group (the Indian Ocean Rim initiative). In addition, geopolitical tension between Pakistan and India has further complicated regional cooperation.

Unstable Region

The animosity between two biggest members had reached to such an extent that Indian subcontinent now known as South Asia is considered a very unstable region as there are now two major rival nuclear powers with medium range missile launching capability. Specially the end of last and beginning of the present century have passed through a very tense phase attracting world's attention and concern. When one talks of the dream of a South Asian Union one cannot ignore the ground realities of the history of political and military tensions between India and Pakistan, the two principal players of the region, and India's not so warm relations with other smaller neighbours. People in western society often wonder how the two ever feuding nations can ever live together in an Union called South Asian Union. But the answer to them is that not very late, in the late seventies and eighties, nuclear missiles of the eastern Communist Europe and western Capitalist Europe were targeted at each other and there were often talks of theatre nuclear war and mutual assured destruction. South Asia has also passed through that phase with Indian and Pakistani leaders threatening each other with total annihilation. The turn of history in Europe was so swift and unexpected that it all looked like a miracle happening with the fall of Berlin wall and disintegration of the Soviet Union and Warsaw pact. Since the symbolic Berlin wall dividing East and West Europe was built on a weak edifice it crumbled within no minute. Similarly the artificial barriers created between India and Pakistan can come crashing down with unexpected turn of events.

It would not be an exaggeration to say that this process has gathered momentum in South Asia as leaders of both the countries have realised that living in a permanent state of tension is not going to solve the problem as both have to accommodate each other's concerns. The common masses cannot be made to suffer for long as military expenditures are mounting day by day with increasing violence and terrorism. If there is peace and stability at the borders then defence budgets of both the countries will also reduce to a substantial extent which will help in diverting the fund towards economic upliftment of the largely poverty ridden society. Peace and stability creates an atmosphere for economic and social development. The peace dividend coming out of India Pakistan rapprochement, as it happened with the end of cold war in Europe, would be enormous. It would not only encourage improved trade between the countries but also attract international investments in various sectors of the economy as South Asian region is considered as the largest and most attractive emerging market in the world. With enormous goodwill prevailing between the peoples of the two countries, as exhibited during the India-Pakistan cricket series in the early 2004, it can very well be assumed that people are simply waiting for their leaders to sign friendship pacts.

Pressure on leaders

The Kargil conflict of 1999, the attack on Indian Parliament on 13 December, 2001, and then the continued military standoff on the India-Pakistan border for ten months raised much hackles around the world. In response to attack on the Indian Parliament the Indian government reacted sharply by suspending air, rail and road links to Pakistan and deploying its army on the border which was accompanied by threats of nuclear attacks from both the sides. However, recent global changes in the geopolitical and economic environment have created more favourable conditions and encouragement for the countries of the region to come together and talk of increased economic cooperation. This has created a pressure on the Indian and Pakistani leadership to talk of more trade. The SAARC agreement on Free Trade Area signed in Islamabad was perhaps a result of those favourable climate in world. They have realised that if they do not live together they would die together. With the continuing ceasefire on line of control in Jammu and Kashmir since 25th November, 2003, and resumption of flights and bus and rail links and no talk of reciprocal nuclear destruction of each side, climate of peace seems to be persisting which is a good augury for South Asia as a whole.

The process kicked off with the then Prime Minister Atal Bihari Vajpayee making his famous speech in Srinagar in April 2003, and the then External Affairs Minister Yashwant Sinha enunciating Indian proposals for resumption of normal relations on 22nd October, 2003. The new steps announced were for resumption of air links with overflight rights over the airspace of each country. Mr Sinha also proposed to resume bus and rail links between Rajasthan and Sindh and between Srinagar and Muzaffarabad, the two capitals of Jammu and Kashmir under the control of India and Pakistan. Sinha also proposed to resume bilateral sporting encounters including cricket also. Links between the coast guards on the pattern of Director General of Military Operations were also proposed. Flag meetings were also proposed in the sea before and after the fishing season. To save the fishermen of both the countries from harassment India proposed that fishermen of both sides should not be arrested within a certain band on the sea. In addition free medical treatment to a second batch of Pakistani children was also proposed. Some of these steps have been implemented and some are under negotiation. After the famous heart surgery of Baby Noor from Pakistan a lot of goodwill was generated for the Indian doctors in Pakistan. These were symbolic measures for confidence and goodwill building between the two countries. Nevertheless the continued terrorist violence in Jammu and Kashmir remained a cause of concern for votaries of Indo-Pakistan friendship as it has the potential of reigniting the war prone region.

Peace Process

The fragile peace process gained momentum with the then Prime Minister Vajpayee attending the SAARC summit in Islamabad where a joint statement was issued after a meeting between Pakistan President Pervez Musharraf and him. After a much publicised failed meeting at Indo-Pakistan Agra summit in June 2001, the two leaders warmed up to the new realities and welcomed the recent steps towards normalisation of relations between the two countries and expressed the hope that the positive trends set by the Confidence Building Measures would be consolidated. According to the joint statement Prime Minister Vajpayee said that in order to take forward and sustain the dialogue process, violence, hostility and terrorism must be prevented. President Musharraf reassured Prime Minister Vajpayee that he will not permit any territory under Pakistan's control to be used to support terrorism in any manner.

President Musharraf emphasized that a sustained and productive dialogue addressing all issues would lead to positive results.

To carry the process of normalisation forward, the President of Pakistan and the Prime Minister of India agreed to commence the process of the composite dialogue in February 2004. With the assumption of new Congress led United Progressive Alliance in India under the command of Manmohan Singh, new hopes have been raised in South Asia for an early rapproachment. The new leaders are confident that the resumption of the composite dialogue will lead to peaceful settlement of all bilateral issues, including Jammu and Kashmir, to the satisfaction of both sides. In Islamabad when PM Vajpayee met President Musharraf both agreed that constructive dialogue would promote progress towards the common objective of peace, security and economic development for our peoples and for future generations. This process is being carried forward by the new regime in India, headed by Prime Minister Manmohan Singh.

It was a pleasant surprise for the observers of SAARC that Pakistan gave its green signal for a free trade area agreement in South Asia starting from 2006 over a period of ten years. It resulted in new warmth and bonhomie during Islamabad summit between Vajpayee and Musharraf. Later on at the February 18, 2004 meeting in Islamabad the two foreign secretaries of India and Pakistan agreed on a roadmap to carry forward the composite dialogue to resolve all their differences. Under this roadmap both countries decided to hold talks on peace and security including confidence building measures and Jammu and Kashmir. This also included Siachen glacier, the highest and coldest battlefield in the world, in Jammu and Kashmir, Wullar barrage/Tulbul navigation project, Sir Creek, terrorism and drug trafficking, economic and commercial cooperation and promotion of friendly exchanges in various fields. In fact, these were issues discussed in 1997 at great length also but the process stopped after the two countries failed to move forward.

Ignore political differences

After years of failed negotiations and tough talking both sides would have to be serious to resolve their differences and simultaneously carry forward the process of peace, economic development and cooperation with all earnestness. In fact, it would not be prudent to assume that the two countries would settle their political differences in a few meetings. For this a proper climate of trust and give and take has to be created to come to a possible resolution of the complex issues that divide the subcontinent. The road to create conducive climate for peace perhaps lies through deeper economic and people to people interaction between the two nuclear neighbours. The business leaders are pushing for this approach to create a positive atmosphere of cooperation in South Asia. Making a fervent appeal to the SAARC leaders to adopt the economic route to resolve political differences the President of SAARC Chamber of Commerce and industry, Mr Macky Hashim, said," we admit that SAARC has an image of a giant who is still sleeping. The painful fact is that after a very promising start and several positive steps in the initial years, the SAARC process had seemed to have come to a virtual standstill. Much to the disappointment of the business community the political differences laid down a major hindrance in the field of trade liberalization. It is crucial for the development of the region to ignore our political differences as when economic advantages become obvious will political support be ensured.[1]

BIMSTEC

However frustrations over lack of progress in SAARC instigated India to look towards non-SAARC neighbours and in consultation with Thailand formed another regional economic cooperation organisation on 6 June, 1997. This new sub-regional grouping called BIST-EC consisted of Bangladesh, India, Sri Lanka, Thailand-Economic cooperation. Later on Myanmar was also incorporated as a full member and the group was renamed as BIMST-EC. Bhutan and Nepal were also given membership of this grouping of south and south east Asian nations. This new Asian grouping led by India and Thailand agreed to create a

1. SAFTA Seminar, New Delhi 3rd March, 2004.

free trade zone encompassing nearly two billion people, but the demands from Bangladesh stopped its march forward towards a free trade zone agreement from 2017, when it asked for compensation in return for abolishing tariffs. However later on excluding Bangladesh India, Myanmar, Sri Lanka and Thailand plus Nepal and Bhutan signed a blueprint agreement for free tarde. It is considered extremely significant for the bridge it establishes between South Asia and South East Asia—two economically dynamic regions of the world. As India is already a signatory to SAARC free trade area agreement and has a stand alone FTA with ASEAN, the BIMST-EC FTA has paved the way for a free trade zone of nearly two billion people. The draft agreement says that import tariffs will be zero on goods by 2012 for trade among India, Thailand and Sri Lanka. These three are categorized as developing countries under the agreement. The least developed countries—Nepal, Bhutan, Myanmar and later when Bangladesh joins—will have up to 2017 to bring their tariffs to zero. This will be a very important link between ASEAN and SAARC. A summit meeting of Heads of States proposed in Phuket, Thailand, in February 2004, could not be held because PM A.B. Vajpayee was unable to attend this due to domestic compulsions. However India's forays in the nearby ASEAN (Association of South East Asian Nations) region has been very successful with which it has signed a free trade area agreement. But these efforts cannot be a real replacement for SAARC as a big regional economy (Pakistan) is left out. However if pursued vigorously this new grouping can act as a growth engine not only for India's north east but the adjoining neighbouring countries also. BIMST-EC can very well run parallel to SAARC and both can complement each other. There would not be any areas of conflicting interests between the two. In fact, if a proposal by a think tank RIS is accepted to convert BIMST-EC into a Bay of Bengal economic energy community, it will reinvigorate SAARC as well. This new Bay of Bengal community will bring together five members of SAARC and two members of ASEAN into a new regional group that will interlink both the organizations and put an end to the artificial separation between South and South East Asia.

The dynamics of relations between India and its other smaller neighbors perhaps is also preventing SAARC to takeoff. As they express fears of India's hegemonistic designs in the region they are on the lookout to forge political and other linkages with powers having rivalry with India to act as a balancing force. India's role in breaking Pakistan in 1971 (the formation of Bangladesh), the merger of Sikkim afterwards, Indian involvement in Sri Lanka's internal affairs in the eighties, helping the LTTE initially but fighting them later on, the suspicions in Nepalese monarchy about India's role in instigating democratic movements, India's role in preventing the coup in Maldives, and the efforts by India to acquire a blue water navy all projected India as a hegemonistic and expansionist country. As Pakistan obtains all sorts of military assistance from China its latest decision to become a major non- NATO ally at the instance of the USA has caused much consternation in India. Though India is also developing a relationship of strategic partnership with the USA, the US decision to grant this extraordinary status to Pakistan has caused concerns in India mainly because it will help Pakistan acquire more weapons which will further add to the unstable environment in India. In fact, the US has always been a factor in India-Pakistan relations. In the eighties the USA ignored Pakistan's nuclear weapons programme mainly because Pakistan was a front line state in war against the Soviet Union. This forced India to change its policy on acquiring nuclear weapons, which India was not doing so inspite of capabilities. The US short term policy in the region also helped in equipping Islam with fundamentalism which later on not only proved to be a destabilising factor in South Asia but also proved to be disastrous for the US interests also. Now that Pakistan is cooperating with the USA in its fight against terror, Indian and Pakistani interests apparently converge at least on this issue. Another matter of concern is that India's neighbourhood remains unstable.

Unstable Neighbours

Nepal is a constitutional monarchy and a multi-party democracy, bordered by China and India. It has maintained a delicate balance in its foreign relations and pursued a policy of nonalignment. Relations with India are characterized by important geographical and cultural links as well as by Nepalese dependence on India for trade in essential commodities and access to the outside world. The ongoing conflict in Nepal between the monarchy and the Maoists has destabilised the Nepalese economy curbing the flow of foreign tourists and economic activities. As the non-Nepalese nationals are being made the target of Maoists attacks it will deter foreign investors specially Indians to go to Nepal. Civil and ethnic strife in Nepal and Sri Lanka remain a matter of acute concern as it is affecting trade and commerce in the region.

However Sri Lanka and India are the two members of SAARC which are now enjoying most robust trade relationship with free trade agreement between them giving a dramatic push to bilateral trade. In Sri Lanka the prospects of peace are not so bright as the Tamil Tigers pose a strong challenge to the authorities in Colombo and this issue has been a major cause of tension between India and Sri Lanka in the eighties. "Bilateral disputes, especially India and Pakistan have been viewed by Sri Lanka as a major hindrance to the success of SAARC. But, it is over generalization to say that Sri Lanka did not use the SAARC for its own political interests. In the 1980's when India and Sri Lanka relations were strained, Colombo used the SAARC meetings successfully to express its reservations on India's policies towards the ethnic issue. It went to the extent of refusing to host the fifth Summit in Colombo unless "foreign troops on its soil" left, and earlier boycotted a Council of Ministers meeting in protest against the IPKF presence. It did not hesitate to gang-up with any of the other members against India."[2]

Bangladesh

Bangladesh also remains a source of concern principally because of rising fundamentalism and anti-India sentiments which has perhaps prevented the government of Bangladesh to sell its huge reserves of natural gas to India which could have changed

---

2. N. Manoharan, Sri Lanka and SAARC: A view from a Small State; *Peace and Conflict*, 2 February, 2004.

Bangladesh economy overnight. However India-Bangla trade has been rising steadily though the balance of trade is heavily in India's favour giving rise to concerns and anti-India feeling of Indian economic dominance. However India is the 10th largest investor in Bangladesh with a total investment registered with the Board of investment of US $330 million. There are 29 Indian joint ventures in Bangladesh and seven wholly owned subsidiaries in such areas as textiles, construction industry, chemicals, information technology and automobiles. Indian companies are also involved in some infrastructure areas in Bangladesh. India has also extended credit line to Bangladesh. India is the largest trading partner of Bangladesh with 14.3% of its imports. Bangladesh exports to India grew from US$50 million to US$84 million, registering a record increase of 67% during 2002-03. Obviously the duty concessions given by India both bilaterally and under SAPTA, are beginning to bear fruits. In fact, it is remarkable that nearly 70 % of Bangladesh's exports to India avail of these trade concessions. Amongst all countries India offers the widest range of trade concessions to Bangladesh. It grants tariff concessions ranging from 50 to 75 % on about 2600 tariff lines and duty free concessions on 79 items. "We are alive to Bangladesh's concern regarding bilateral trade deficit and its desire for expanding its exports to India since the best relationship is one that provides win-win situation for both partners. However, it must be considered that apart from India, Bangladesh has an adverse balance with all SAARC countries (except Maldives) and ASEAN members and a much bigger trade deficit with China".[3]

To improve trade with Bangladesh, India and Bangladesh will soon open six Land Customs Stations (LCSs) including Petrapole, Dawki, Sutarkhandi and Agartala. Both the countries are identifying ways and means to improve the Land Customs Stations on India-Bangladesh border. To sort out the field level problems a Joint Group of Customs of the two countries has been formed.

However a perception persists that India is cornering all the benefits of trade with its neighbours. Indian trade officials point

3. Indian foreign secretary Kanwal Sibbal's address to the Federation of Bangladesh Chambers of Commerce and Industry in Dhaka on 10th March, 2004.

out that actually India is supplying the essential commodities which these countries are not producing themselves, and any way they have to import these from third countries. Importing from India offers them much greater cost advantages. India can only ignore these perceptions at the cost of further improvement in bilateral trade and also the unstable political situation in these countries at the cost of regional stability affecting peace and economic and social development of the area.

As far as Bhutan is concerned India is making a lot of investment in power and other sectors which will greatly boost the revenue of Bhutan government. The diplomatic challenge for India is to develop cordial relations with its neighbours and a viable strategy for stabilisation and peace in the neighbourhood. India will have to play a proactive but discreet role in containing the fallout of this potentially dangerous environment affecting economic development.

In fact, it is the great disparity in population and geography that sometimes creates problem for relations between India and some of its neighbours. So when SAARC was first mooted by President Zia Ur Rahman of Bangladesh in 1980, India was wary. She was not very enthusiastic as India was not enjoying very warm political relations with them. However, perhaps, India realised later on that by joining with them India could check their activities and designs by coming on a common platform. But when India decided to join SAARC wholeheartedly, it was Rajiv Gandhi and senior officials of the ministry of external affairs who gave SAARC a concrete shape which was gladly accepted by other six smaller neighbours as it gave equal status and rights to all the members. The unanimity rule gave confidence to member countries of SAARC that no decision can be imposed on them against their wish and national interests. This helped SAARC take a concrete shape in the initial years but in the beginning of nineties SAARC again floundered due to big power interest in region which badly affected India-Pakistan relations.

ASEAN

Inspite of political differences and territorial disputes the South East Asian countries have formed a very successful and viable, powerful organization called ASEAN. Indonesia was supposed to give leadership to Asean as it was supposed to be Asean centric whereas SAARC was supposed to be India centric. But India was skeptical about the validity of SAARC. It is not true to say that South Asia had territorial disputes to resolve before 'freezing' them through normalisation as implied in the charter of SAARC. Khaled Ahmad[4] makes an interesting observation, "The truth is that three contenders in Southeast Asia, Malaysia, Indonesia and the Philippines, had complex territorial claims on one another which had to be simply buried in favour of engagement in the trading bloc . In South Asia, unresolved disputes assumed a higher priority than a collective response to internal and external challenges. In fact, while India wants members to adhere to the SAARC charter excluding political debate, Pakistan resents the fact that the charter excludes such a debate. India's argument is that SAARC is undermined by the raising of issues disallowed by its charter; Pakistan's argument is that excluding a 'realistic' political debate from the charter hinders the coming together of the members on other issues. There is no such thing as an Asian identity in Southeast Asia. The various member states of ASEAN are not united by any linguistic or cultural commonalty as in South Asia. Although a new commercial ethic is creating a kind of uniformity among them, they don't feel any Asian adhesive in this relationship. On the other hand, in India-centric South Asia, a kind of bond of collective culture is felt by its inhabitants. Could this 'intimacy' be the dividing factor in South Asia?"

Climate of Trust

As the political issues are not going to be resolved soon, considering the extreme conflicting stands of India and Pakistan, a climate of trust and confidence needs to be created between the two countries for peaceful coexistence. For more than five decades there was insistence on politics first economy later but it has not compelled the parties concerned to come to a conclusion. If the same insistence is continued the political issues may not be resolved for many more years, perhaps decades.

4. *South Asia Journal,* Aug-Sept, 2003. Mr Ahmad is a consulting editor of *Friday Times,* Lahore.

Till then economic interests of the ordinary masses cannot be kept hostage to the resolution of political issues. True, the two countries are nuclear armed and situation may flare up any moment if it is allowed to linger on but it all depends on the will power and sanity of the concerned governments to prevent such a situation from developing.

During cold war also the situation in Europe was very tense and nuclear missiles were kept in alert status all the time for any moment to be launched but the two super powers devised certain confidence building measures which prevented the situation to deteriorate. As there are worries in South Asia and in the international community also on the accidental launch of a nuclear missile the two countries need to develop systems like nuclear risk reduction centres (NRRC) that were in place in Europe. According to General V.R.Raghvan[5], the US-Soviet NRRCs demonstrated that despite many issues of ideological and military contention, both sides were partners in a common interest. The determination to avoid a nuclear war was demonstrated in the creation of NRRC's. In fact, it came about by legislative action initiated in the US by Senators Sam Nunn and John Warner. A similar sagacity was demonstrated by Atal Bihari Vajpayee and Nawaz Sharif in 1999 when they signed the Lahore declaration. Then came Kargil which so emphatically changed the political landscape in Pakistan.

The time is now ripe to go beyond the well trodden tracks of diplomacy and put into effect a major nuclear CBM such as NRRC. General Raghvan suggests that it should be manned by scientists, military personnel, missile specialists and bureaucrats from the nuclear related ministries. They would have secure and reliable communication with relevant nuclear nodes such as nuclear power plants, defence services headquarters, Ministries of defence and atomic energy, strategic forces headquarters and with the national security advisor or his equivalent. The NRRC's in Delhi and Islamabad would be linked by reliable and fast communication links for rapid sharing and communicating of critically required crisis management information. The two NRRC's

---

5. Ex-DGMO. Indian Army Nuclear Neighbours (*The Hindu*, 23.12.2003)

would keep a 24-hour watch on developments likely to lead to accidents, misperceptions and rumours. The NRRC would function as part of the National Security setup and not independent of it.

Nuclear CBM

If India and Pakistan remove the possibility of a nuclear war then entire South Asia would be considered a stable one and a place to invest and to do business with. There would be no more advisories by the western governments to their tourists and citizens residing in South Asia to leave the area at once or not to visit South Asia. These kind of advisories affected the economic environment in South Asia during Kargil war and the ten-month military standoff between India and Pakistan during the year 2002.

However in a welcome and very encouraging move, that will instill confidence in the region, the governments of India and Pakistan during the expert level talks on nuclear confidence building measures held in New Delhi from 19-20 June, 2004, committed to each other that they will not conduct any more nuclear tests. The two governments decided to establish a "dedicated and secure" hotline between their foreign secretaries to prevent misunderstandings and reduce nuclear risks and pledged themselves to unilateral moratorium on nuclear tests.

Reaffirming the Lahore declaration on nuclear confidence building measures[6], both sides committed to work towards its implementation. The conciliatory language of the joint statement speaks for itself the new found sincerity among the two nuclear neighbours to live in peace which would be worth presenting here for the readers:

Both sides:

Conscious of the need to promote a stable environment of peace and security between the two countries;

Recognizing that the nuclear capabilities of each other, which are based on their national security imperatives, constitute a factor for stability;

---

6. The memorandum of understanding signed during Prime Minister Atal Behari Vajpayee's historic bus journey to Lahore, with the then Prime Minister Nawaz Sharif from 18-20 February, 1999.

Committed to national measures to reduce the risks of accidental or unauthorized use of nuclear weapons under their respective controls and to adopt bilateral notification measures and mechanisms to prevent misunderstandings and misinterpretations;

Conscious of their obligation to their peoples and the international community;

Committed to work towards strategic stability;

Agreed on the following:

- The existing hotline between the DGMOs[7] would be upgraded, dedicated and secured.
- A dedicated and secure hotline would be established between the two Foreign Secretaries, through their respective Foreign Offices to prevent misunderstandings and reduce risks relevant to nuclear issues.
- Both countries will work towards concluding an Agreement with technical parameters on pre-notification of flight testing of missiles, a draft of which was handed over by the Indian side.
- Each side reaffirmed its unilateral moratorium on conducting further nuclear test explosions unless, in exercise of national sovereignty, it decides that extraordinary events have jeopardized its supreme interests.
- Both countries would continue bilateral discussions and hold further meetings to work towards the implementation of the Lahore MoU of 1999.
- Both countries will continue to engage in bilateral consultations on security and non-proliferation issues within the context of negotiations on these issues in multilateral fora.
- Both countries called for regular working level meetings to be held among all the nuclear powers to discuss issues of common concern.

Hopes

The resolve to live in peace and reduce the risks of a nuclear war raises great hopes in South Asia for a renewed economic engagement

7. Director General Military Operations

on a permanent basis not only between India and Pakistan but among all the SAARC members. As SAARC has the potential to emerge as the most important market and place for investment which will give a new life to the economy of the developed countries also it would be in the interest of the developed world too to extend all possible assistance in making SAARC realize its true potential for which the western powers would have to play a supporting but discreet role in advising the smaller members of SAARC to develop cordial economic relations with India and listen to India's concerns. There is a suspicion in the minds of the Indian leadership that the smaller members of SAARC are playing host to forces inimical to India's security interests. Perhaps under democratic compulsions of vote bank politics and fundamentalist pressures the governments are not able to take measures which seem to develop friendship with India but actually that is in the own interest of the countries. For example in March 2003, a trade fair of Indian goods organised by Confederation of Indian Industries in Dacca was cancelled at the last moment by the Bangladesh government as certain groups had threatened to create havoc in the area, whereas Bangla-deshi industries could organize a trade fair in Kolkata in 2003.

This kind of roadblock India has to encounter in trying to develop deeper economic engagement with the neighbours. On the other hand in March 2004, a Made in Pakistan exhibition organised in New Delhi was a grand success. This raises hopes of a gradual improvement in bilateral economic relations which will have a very positive effect on the SAARC economy as a whole. Though, inspite of WTO obligations, Pakistan should also have extended MFN status to India in response to India extending it in 1996, the SAFTA agreement will extend similar facility to India from 2006 onwards. This will hasten the process of more trade exchanges between the two countries. Inspite of unresolved political issues as Pakistan always insists to solve first the business community in Pakistan is very much excited over the possibility of renewing trade at full scale after five decades. Perhaps this increased business interaction will lead to a better understanding of each other's national interests and concern and lead to a amicable solution of political issues acceptable to both, which will pave the way for SAARC to evolve towards deeper integration and possibly a South Asian Economic Union in a decade or two.

8

SAARC, India and EU

India is the only SAARC member having summit level annual interactions with European Union which signifies India's economic and political importance in the eyes of the European countries. However unlike EU's deep relations with other major trading and economic groupings of the world SAARC does not enjoy such interactions with EU, perhaps because of the fact that SAARC could not emerge as a powerful economic bloc during last two decades of it's existence. The only cooperation programme between EU and SAARC relates to a technical assistance programme. The European Commission took the initiative in 1996 to sign a memorandum of understanding with the SAARC secretariat, offering technical assistance. The MoU was explicitly signed at the political level to overcome the political inertia. Yet, the internal problems of SAARC largely prevented any effective implementation of the MoU. The EU also launched an assistance programme called Assisting SAARC's integration process. Besides this EU has got individual aid and assistance programmes with South Asian countries for trade promotion, poverty eradication and socio-economic development.

However as a group SAARC did enjoy dialogue with the EU ministerial troika from 1994 to 1999. In its dialogue with SAARC the EU has consistently affirmed an interest in strengthening links with SAARC as a regional organisation. This sentiment was equally consistently reciprocated by SAARC. As India is a leading member of the SAARC, EU's relations with India can have equally good impact on it's relationship with SAARC as a whole.

An official document of the EU says that the EU fully realises the difficulties that SAARC has in discussing political issues, and that SAARC member states are not Europe. However, the EU can help consolidate the ongoing integration process through its economic influence in the region, its own historical experience of dealing with diversity, and its interest in crisis prevention. The EU remains convinced that SAARC could play an useful role in regional co-operation and dialogue, although so far SAARC development has been less than breathtaking in the economic and political arena. Economically South Asia accounts for 2% of world's GNP and for 2.2% of EU's external trade. The new Asia invest programme of EU promotes and supports business cooperation between EU member states and SAARC countries. India is a significant investment destination for European countries and with it's own internal diversity has a very modern high tech sector, offering much potential for economic cooperation with Europe.

In SAARC, perhaps only India has got some competence to cooperate with EU on almost equal footing, for example, India's participation in Galileo Satellite project and cooperation in Information and Communication technology and some joint scientific research projects. India-EU relations have been growing at a very fast pace at different levels which can have positive impacts on EU's overall relations with SAARC. EU has developed political and economic relationship with Pakistan also but relations with India go much deeper and have acquired greater relevance in world affairs. With Pakistan EU Troika (Foreign Minister of the presiding country of EU + the incumbent presiding country foreign minister + the EU commissioner for foreign relations) has annual dialogue in which they discuss topics of political developments, improving relations with India, SAARC developments, other regional issues like Afghanistan, international security, nuclear proliferation, etc. EU has signed a trade related technical assistance for Pakistan and aids and grants for other programmes. According to an EU document the EU regards its relationship with Pakistan as very important not only for bilateral interests but because of the contribution that Pakistan can make towards stability of the South Asian region. The EU's relationship with Pakistan is conducted through a cooperation agreement signed in 1986. Since then political dialogue has been upgraded to the Troika level and contacts with Pakistan have been intensified with frequent meetings.The EU is Pakistan's main trading partner representing about 22% of Pakistan's trade. Between 1995 and 2002 EU imports from Pakistan increased by around 50%. The EU has proposed Euro 71 million assistance for Pakistan during 2003-05 period. The EU has also extended Euro 50 million budgetary support programme to Pakistan for the reform of the financial sector.

Poverty Reduction

European Union has been deeply involved in the poverty reduction programmes in Bangladesh and following 1994 EU strategy towards Asia, Bangladesh became a potential beneficiary of a number of regional Asia programmes, the general objective of which was to promote an enhanced economic presence of the European Union in Asia. Bangladesh has always been included in the European Commission's Generalised system of preferences, granting products originating in Bangladesh duty and generally quota free access to the European markets. The garment industry of Bangladesh has thriven on the competitive advantage of a quota free access to the EU market.The reduction of poverty and it's eventual eradication is the main objective of development cooperation between the European Commission and Bangladesh. This cooperation also facilitates the integration of the country as a qualified trading partner into the world trade system. For this the European Commission has signed a cooperation agreement with Bangladesh. The EU is the biggest trade partner of Bangladesh. Presently, among LDCs Bangladesh is the most prominent exporter to the EC representing 20% of the total exports from all LDCs to the European market. Bangladesh principal exports to EU are textile products (75% of the EU imports from Bangladesh). Bangladesh has enjoyed in the last decade a growing trade balance surplus with the EU.

Another least developed member of SAARC, Bhutan also is getting lot of support from EU. The European Commission has prepared its first strategy programme for the period 2002-06.

Under this, the key areas of cooperation include renewable natural resources, health and trade development and export diversification. With Nepal, the European Commission signed a cooperation agreement in 1995 which covered trade, commercial and economic cooperation, development cooperation, joint investment, agriculture, human resource development and many programmes for socio-economic development. EU and Nepal established diplomatic relations in 1975 and an EU-Kingdom of Nepal Cooperation Agreement was signed in June 1998. For the period 2002-2006, EC co-operation strategy for Nepal will be based on the ninth five-year plan which embraces poverty alleviation as the overriding objective. Agricultural production and infrastructure, socio-economic development, institutional strengthening and good governance, alternative renewable rural energy are the most important objectives pursued by this strategy.

Development Policy

With Maldives the European Commission has got no formal cooperation agreement on partnership and development. However EU has got a development policy towards Maldives for which Euro two million have been allocated, the objective of which is to focus on two core objectives (i) Enhancing regional development (social, economic and physical infrastructure) and (ii) enhancing trade capacity and economic development. As a member of the South Asian Association for Regional Co-operation (SAARC) the Maldives benefits from the European Community's Generalised System of Preferences (GSP), subject to compliance with its rules of origin. In 2002, the EU exported goods worth €40 million to the Maldives (mainly machinery). Imports from the Maldives into the EU were worth €38 million, of which textiles accounted for 56% and fish 41%. In 2000, the UN announced that it would graduate the Maldives from the list of Least Developed Countries (LDC) to "become" a Developing Nation. With the graduation from the LDC status the international economic advantages that have contributed to the Maldives' progress will disappear such as preferential market access, development assistance and concessional finance programmes.

With Sri Lanka EU has signed a third generation cooperation agreement which is being implemented since 1995. It focuses on partnership and cooperation, respect for human rights and democratic principles, development and diversification of trade and investment, building Sri Lanka's economic capability to interact more effectively with EU. The EC has allocated Euro 61.32 million for Sri Lanka for the year 2003-04. EU is one of the Sri Lanka's major trading partners. In 2001, it accounted for Sri Lanka's 27.1% exports, second only to the US which accounted for 41.9%. The EU was also Sri Lanka's largest source of imports, accounting for 15.7% of the total in 2001. The EU has identified economic cooperation in its relations with Sri Lanka as a priority area. The promotion of trade and development is not only central to addressing the underlying problems of economic development, but also to sustain its peace process. Co-operation between the EU and Sri Lanka dates back to 1975 when a Commercial Co-operation Agreement was signed. The present agreement entered into force on 1 April, 1995.

India

As far as historical relations between India and European countries are concerned the main SAARC region of today which is mostly loosely federated India of ancient days has very interesting and deep rooted interactions. An official document of EU says," The relationship between India and Europe pre dates history. Europe owes most of its linguistic heritage to India—and much of its cultural base. Nor is this now just a historical irrelevancy. In July 1987, *Forbes* magazine published the results of scientific research, which concluded that Sanskrit is the mother of all the European languages (and) the most suitable language for computer software. This symbolises the relationship between India and the EU, which is at one and the same time very old, yet dynamic and entirely modern. Besides the political, economic and trade dialogues which tend to dominate the vision of EU-India cooperation, there is a strong supporting cultural and social relationship encompassing many sectors and levels of both societies. Europe and India have a relationship that stretches back thousands of years, but in their present incarnations they are both of the same, post-second world war generations. India famously achieved freedom 'at the stroke of midnight hour' on 15 August,1947, Europe began its own 'tryst with destiny' four years later, with the 1951 Treaty of Paris that founded the European Coal and Steel Community, subsequently strengthened by the 1957 Treaty of Rome and successive treaties.

It is not surprising therefore, that India and EU have so much in common. Both the societies are founded on democratic values that are firmly anchored in their respective constitutional frameworks. The EU-India relations go back to the early 1960's: India was amongst the first countries to set up diplomatic relations with EEC. More bilateral agreements were signed in 1973 and 1981. Both partners are signatories of the UN declaration on universal human rights, a fact which is reflected in the cooperation agreement between the EU and India signed on 20 December,1993, which stipulates that 'respect for human rights is the basis for cooperation' Called third generation agreement it goes much beyond trade and economic cooperation. The institutional basis for EU-India political dialogue is a joint political statement signed simultaneously with the third generation cooperation agreement. It fixed annual ministerial meetings and opened the door to a broad political dialogue. The EU-India enhanced partnership agreement of June 1996, was a leap forward and contributed to put the commission in the driver's seat of EU-India relations. The European Parliament has endorsed this agreement. The 1994 cooperation agreement provides for an EC-India Joint Commission as the central guardian mechanism to oversee and inspire the entire range of cooperation activities between India and the European Commission. Three separate Sub-Commissions on Trade, Economic Cooperation and Development Cooperation, cover a more detailed agenda and report directly to the Joint Commission. All of this is set against a backdrop of enormous cultural diversity, in both partners. With over one billion inhabitants, India is one of the world's ethnically and linguistically diverse nations, with 18 official languages. The EU, meanwhile, consists of 25 member states, with a population of 450 million and 20 official languages. In this background there is a clear need to reinforce and promote ongoing and up-to-date discussions at as many levels of society as possible. This has been the focus of much thought and reflection over recent years, with the result that there are now a number of fora and initiatives that bring Indian and EU citizens together.

Besides the many meetings at political and official levels, the EU-India round table brings together leading members of Indian and EU civil societies on a regular basis. Indian and European scientists cooperate together on joint research projects, under the EU's research framework programmes and now also under the 2001 EU-India Science and Technology agreement. Civil society is encouraged to cooperate and exchange views through the economic cross-cultural programme, the future EU-India think tank network programme and the small projects facility. Thus dialogue between India and EU, so old in many respects, is vibrant today, providing testimony to the everlasting and evolving cultural relationship between the two partners. The EU-India summit declarations have underlined the importance of enhancing contact between civil societies as a means of fostering greater mutual understanding.

Economic Relations

The European Union is the worlds biggest economic bloc and India the world's second most populous nation. Trade and economic relations between the two are therefore of paramount importance to both sides. The EU is both the biggest foreign investor in India and the nation's biggest trading partner. However actual FDI from EU was less than Euro one billion per year. Though India is the world's fifth largest economy measured in terms of purchasing power parity but it ranks as EU's 18th biggest trading partner taking in just 1.3% of what EU exports. EU sources 21.4% of India's imports and takes 23.2% of exports (2002). In 2002, EU exported goods worth Euro 14 billion and imported roughly same from India. Germany and the UK continue to be India's biggest trade and investment partners within the EU. A document of EU says that India has a dynamic economy that has experienced strong, regular growth in recent years and it is emerging as a world leader in key economic sectors such as ICT. The two share many economic philosophies and objectives. Forging an economic alliance is therefore vital to both: the relationship strengthens the economies of both sides and enhances their positions on the world stage. To that end, India and the EU are successfully pursuing joint initiatives to promote cooperation in a number of important areas such as civil aviation, maritime transport, science and technology, space industry, information technology and telecommunications, etc.

For over three decades, European Union support for India's development programmes has been a central pillar of the EU-India relationship. A fine example of this cooperation is Operation Flood, which helped India to become the world's leading milk producer. An early flagship cooperation project running from 1970-96, and involving the Indian government, the European Commission and the World Bank. Operation Flood was the world's largest food and development programme which is considered to be greatly successful. Since 1976, European Commission has committed Euro 2 billion to India in development assistance. The European Commission cooperation with India involves an expenditure of roughly Euro 100 million (Rs 5,000 crores) per year. The EC is the largest donor of grant funds to India. However, the main emphasis of the EU's development cooperation with India will move increasingly from support for centrally sponsored schemes towards strategic antipoverty partnerships with reform minded states, on the basis of good governance. This new development strategy was outlined in the European Commission's country strategy paper for India, which covers the period 2002-06.

India and European Union are committed to an equal and dynamic dialogue on all subjects of interest and concern to them as major entities in their own regions, and as a global actors on the world stage. EU-India relations entered a new phase with the first EU-India summit in Lisbon in 2000. Its now a routine annual feature in which EU and India express their commitment for a strengthened bilateral cooperative relations and for a peaceful stable world.

Strategic Partnership

Building on this solid foundation of harmonious cooperative relations the European Commission proposed a new strategic partnership between the EU and India. The European Commission adopted a communication on 16th June, 2004. The communication examines the many facets of EU-India relations in the light of India's role as an emerging global player and a major regional actor. It proposes a series of concrete steps to strengthen co-operation in five key areas: International cooperation through multilateralism with a focus on conflict prevention, the fight against terrorism, non-proliferation and human rights; Strengthening of economic partnerships through sectoral and regulatory policy dialogues; Cooperation in development policies in order to help India meet the Millennium Development Goals; Fostering intellectual and cultural exchanges and Improvement of the institutional architecture of EU-India relations.

Improving International Cooperation: the EU and India should reinforce their strategic alliance for the promotion of an effective multilateral approach, promoting peace, security, human rights and democracy in the world. They should co-ordinate positions in the preparation, negotiation and implementation of major multilateral conventions in the UN. They also should strengthen their co-operation on conflict prevention and post-conflict reconstruction, addressing global concerns such as non-proliferation, terrorism and organised crime. Their human rights dialogue should be enhanced, both bilaterally and internationally.

Strengthening the Economic Partnership : The Communication defines a coherent economic strategy in order to raise volumes of trade and investment. The EU and India should develop a dialogue on cross-cutting issues such as industrial policy, good governance, competition and environment and on strategic sectors such as information society, transport, energy, biotechnology or space cooperation (where the EU and India intend to cooperate closely through Galileo).

Development Cooperation: The EU should support India's determination to meet the United Nations Millennium

Development Goals and support its objective to reduce social inequalities and regional disparity. A special attention should be given to improved governance and environmental sustainability.

Mutual understanding: The EU and India should boost intellectual and cultural ties through the development of parliamentary and academic exchanges as well as cultural projects.

Institutional Architecture: The EU and India should streamline and make more effective the framework of their relationship.

To benefit SAARC

It is expected that EU's strong engagement with India will pave the way for deeper inroads in South Asia and its markets. SAARC-EU relations can get much strength from EU-India strategic partnerships from which other SAARC members can also benefit immensely.

Statements and figures sourced from European Commission documents.

9

Common Policy

European Union over the decades has evolved in such a way that all the member countries take a common decision on common issues and problems. They frame a common Europewide policy to give shape to those decisions and through this it has not only been able to improve the life of its people but also protect the interests of not only its common citizens but communities like farmers, fishermen and biotechnologists, etc. They also take a common stand in International trade bodies like WTO, where EU sends its top representative as a single voice of the Europe. The EU has framed joint policies like common agricultural policy, fisheries policy, biotechnology policy, environment policy, European trade policy, common justice and home affairs policy, common aviation policy etc. To protect the continent's interests in various sectors of economy in world fora, the EU is represented by its trade commissioner.

SAARC also needs to emulate the European experience in protecting collectively the interests of its farmer, business and other communities, as South Asia is predominantly an agrarian economy. The collective action is making EU the most important agent of change in contemporary government and policy making. Jacques Delors, the then President of the European Commission, claimed in 1988 that about 80 percent of the socio-economic legislation in the EU member states was framed by treaty commitments, policy rules and legislations agreed through the institutions of the EU. Whether or not the percentage is precisely accurate does not matter. What matters is the acknowledgement that EU agreements pervade the policy making activities of individual countries, both the member states and their neighbours.[1]

Governance

Through this policy route, people in Europe now a days talk of governance through policy rather than government whereas in South Asia the government leaders and the bureaucracy are concerned less and less about governance. Bihar and some other Eastern states in India would be the extreme example of lack of governance and the union government can't intervene in most of the cases. So it would be a far cry to talk of transnational governance in South Asian countries for the common good of the masses. Similar is the case in other South Asian countries as lack of governance is perhaps responsible for the continued misery of the people, whereas there are some policy sectors in which the European Union has powers as extensive as those normally associated with country level governance, while in other sectors the EU has much lighter and more fragile regimes. The most important policy initiatives were in the field of single market which marked a turning point in the European integration. The advantages of a single market policy has drawn other European countries towards EU membership and changed the context in which many other policies are shaped. In fact, after the concept of free trade area is implemented in SAARC according to the Islamabad declaration of 2004, South Asia would also evolve towards a single market regime. In Europe single market was a major turning point in transnational policy making in many other sectors of the economy like the agriculture, fisheries, etc. The aim to establish a single market started with the treaty of Rome. This set targets for creating a customs union and the progressive approximation of legislation, as well as for establishing the "four freedoms" of movements of goods, services, capital and labour, all within a single regime of competition rules. The harmonization of national legislation, especially for standards and market management, was one important policy instrument for moving towards the

1. *Policy making in the European Union* by Helen Wallace and William Wallace (Oxford University Press)

common market goal. According to Helen Wallace, the principal instrument of the original European Economic Community for advancing the four freedoms was the directive, in principle, setting the essential framework of policy at the European level and leaving the scope and method to the member states. In fact, an EU document claims that in last one decade the EU single market has provided 2,500,000 extra jobs to its people and Euro 877,000,000,000 in extra prosperity.

A common South Asian market with harmonised policies would be the biggest single block where the multinational companies would like to invest in creation of infrastructure and in production of goods. But South Asian countries have different rules, standards and legislations which prove difficult for transnational operations by the multinational companies. Huge investments of billions of dollars would be attracted in the creation of roads, airports, ports and railway infrastructure to tap the single and harmonised market of South Asia. An investment boom would create opportunities for large employment and wealth generation which in turn would help reduce social and economic imbalance in South Asia. In the 1960's the members of EEC had different national standards which were proving to be a barrier in improved trade exchanges among them. Therefore harmonization measures were drafted by the European Commission in cooperation with the working groups, one for each Industrial sector, composed of experts nominated by member governments. However the single market was not complete by the 1992 deadline. Although much of the legislative agenda was in place, crucial elements like taxation and corporate law were missing. These issues were successfully taken care of in the years to come creating ideal environment for increased trade and investment in European countries.

Agriculture

The Common Agricultural Policy (CAP) in the 1960's represented a striking example of the evolution of European policy. In the early years of EU the distinctive features of the CAP were seen as laying the ground for intensified European integration. The creation of the European Common market was based on the elimination of national barriers, but in the case of agriculture this required the coordination and the fusion of six highly developed systems of state intervention.[2] Supranational organizations and agencies replaced most of the national systems of agricultural support, thereby establishing direct links between the farming population of the member states and the EU. The Common Agricultural Policy is seen as a politically driven and defensive strategy to modernize European agriculture against both the internal threat of the industrrial society and the external threat of American trade competition. According to Helen Wallace: Like the welfare state institutions that deal with labour, the CAP is both an economic and a political mechanism; it seeks to integrate the national farming population into both the transnational and the national polity. Agricultural protectionism, reflected in domestic food prices often more than twice as high as world prices, is its basic instrument. Inspite of the conflicting interests of Germany in the Industrial sector and agricultural interests of France the Common Agricultural policy was a compromise formula which is working to the advantage of the European farmers as a whole and Europe was able to tackle the threat from the protectionist policies of the USA.

As far as social policy formulation is concerned EU can directly intervene in the social policies of the member states in two ways: by enacting significant policy initiatives of its own, and by striking down features of national systems that are deemed incompatible with the development of the single market. In addition the process of European integration also has less direct, but nonetheless significant effects, on member state's social policies, as both the economic policies of the EU and the responses of the social actors to those policies put pressures on the national welfare states.

Environmental policy is now one of the major policy areas in which Brussels plays a major role. No matter whether a member state (such as the UK) has clearly struggled to adapt to EU laws or whether it has traditionally played a leadership role in setting the EU's environment agenda (Germany for

2. *Policy making in the EU* by Helen and William Wallace.

example), the impact of the EU on that member state's domestic policy is significant. At the international level the EU is now widely recognised as a leader, especially in the crucial climate change negotiations. Although the EU, like many individual countries, often has problems implementing international agreements once ratified, the impact of the EU as a negotiating bloc within the global system has grown. The EU is now asserting a collective position in global regime building. The Montreal protocol was the first strong instance of this. EU's role in Kyoto protocol is also one of the shining example which safeguarded EU's competitiveness. Thus it is evident that the EU's policy process is capable of making binding decisions, which most federal systems would find extraordinarily challenging. The EU is now engaged in developing environmental policy at three main levels: global, EU and national.

Biotechnology

Biotechnology policy is relatively new policy field which cuts across existing categories of policy management and involves several sectors such as agriculture, medicine, pharmaceuticals, chemicals, and processed foods. This requires a degree of horizontal policy coordination and communication for which there are few precedents. Few policy debates have been economically as important or politically as explosive as the recent debates on regulating biotechnologies in the EU. Similarly the biotechnology issues generate much heat in India also. Biotechnology regulatory policy will have a critical impact on the technology trajectories of many European industries and on the political economy of the EU as a whole. The EU is enunciating a Europewide policy in order to achieve a true internal market, and it is coordinating the positions of the member governments in international policy arenas as well. Since India is developing as a major research and development centre in the field of bio- technology and applications of biotechnology in food and human life are growing very fast it should take initiative in formulating a biotechnology policy for the SAARC also.

Fishery

Since South Asian countries are a major fishing community they need to look at the EU policy on fishing, which has a meager population of only 300,000 involved in fishing. In the seventies the European countries were at loggerheads over fishing rights in the sea. In 1971 the government of Iceland unilaterally declared that it was henceforth sovereign over the waters up to 50 nautical miles from its coasts. This triggered a "Cod war" with British fishermen, who were excluded, without further ado, from a traditional fishing area. In 1975, Iceland followed by Norway and Canada, extended its national fishing control up to 200 hundred nautical miles, just as the third conference of the United Nations on the Law of the sea, launched in 1973, seemed to legitimise this measure. The impact of this 'nationalisation' of the seas on the UK, Ireland and Denmark—the new members of the EU—was considerable. Accustomed to operating in Norwegian and Icelandic waters for generations, British fishermen particularly suffered from this exclusion, which was exacerbated by a severe increase in oil prices and made it more expensive to redeploy vessels to new fishing areas. To sort out this kind of issue the fisheries ministers from the member countries now meet three times a year and also to discuss the Common Fishery policy of the EU. In fact, the various wings of European Union are most of the time busy on the fish business which is a lesson for SAARC also as fishermen from SAARC countries often face harassment and arrest for months from the authorities of the other countries for fishing in their waters, though inadvertently. In European Union the Council of Fisheries Ministers is the place where the main decisions over the Common Fishery Policy are discussed and finally adopted. Issues like depleting stocks of fishes are discussed and measures to regulate their exploitation are decided and all the countries adhere to it. The SAARC ministers responsible for fishery can also meet from time to time to sort out the issues amicably and issue common guidelines for the fishermen of all the SAARC countries. Facilities like forecasting of coastal storms, and when the fishermen should not go out in the sea, etc., can be made available from Indian satellites to all the fishermen of the region.

Health

The European Union has entered the health sector also where they are going to adopt common courses and procedures for medical practitioners so that the Europeans of one region and language do not have to face problems while getting treatment. It is specially more important because the medical colleges and hospitals of the former East European countries had a very different clinical procedures and systems So the European Commission is feeling the urgent need to harmonise all these practices and procedures. The Commission has started issuing from mid 2004 a health card to all the people living in the member countries of Europe. It will now be much easier to access healthcare for a EU citizen when travelling in another EU country. Thanks to the EU health insurance card that will have all the personal health details of the person. EU officials say that it will be another piece of European identity in the pockets of Europeans giving them a sense of being an European citizen.

Combating Crime

One of the major concerns of South Asian countries is combating the transnational crime, terrorism, illegal immigration and asylum and managing the borders. If the various regimes of the region are honest and transparent in their intentions to seriously deal with these issues they can cooperate in a constructive and systematic manner to create not only a climate of trust and confidence among themselves but also to create an atmosphere conducive to conducting interstate business so as to allow the free movement of business people without any fear from one state to another. For this cooperation among national agencies dealing with the above issues is very much required. The European Union has a very rich experience of dealing with these issues for which they developed policy network among national law enforcement agencies. In fact, in the late nineteen nineties it became the most active field for meetings convened under the council of ministers. No doubt, the Maastricht Treaty on European Union (TEU) negotiations were marked by frequent disputes about the role of the EU institutions on these issues and had to do many delicate compromises. Nevertheless the Amsterdam treaty incorporated the Schengen agreements on the abolition of internal border controls into the EU treaty framework and transferred migration and asylum policy from the third pillar to the first. Since then cooperation has gathered momentum. The European Union decided to constitute an European police force called Europol which became operational in 1999.

The Maastricht Treaty formalized the network of intergovernmental cooperation among national ministries of justice and the interior, and among related national agencies into a "third pillar". It dealt with rules on external border controls, immigration policy and rules for third country nationals within EU, combating drug addiction and international fraud, judicial cooperation in civil and in criminal matters, customs cooperation and police cooperation for the purposes of preventing and combating terrorism, unlawful drug trafficking and other forms of serious international crimes. Considering the present political and security atmosphere in South Asia cooperation at this level among member states seems improbable but when a free trade regime starts in SAARC and the people start interacting with each other on a massive scale, as tourists and as businessmen, there would be demand from various quarters to deal with these crimes effectively so as to make their movement across the nations more safe, comfortable and free of fear. The pressure on the governments to act and cooperate together will perhaps result in similar cooperation from SAARC members in future as we are witnessing in the European Union today.

Common Civil Law

As citizens of member states of European Union very often reside in mother country, work in another country and marry with a third country citizen, their children may grow up and find job in another country and lead a retired life in a country of their choice which may be a fourth country, it raises jurisdictional problems for civil law. This increasing interaction and interdependence among the citizens has created many inter state legal issues. To deal with these issues the idea of a European Judicial Space had first been floated by French President Giscard d'Estaing and Spanish Prime Minister Felipe Gonzalez in the 1970's within the framework of the council of

Europe,[3] both as a new initiative in European integration and as a means of resolving jurisdictional problems in criminal and civil justice. Many of the issues at stake, however, touch on sensitive issues of social order and national tradition. It took for example five years to negotiate the Convention on Jurisdiction and the Recognition and Enforcement of Judgements in matrimonial matters (the Brussels II convention, signed in May 1998) which deal with issues such as custody of children and the division of property on the break up of cross border marriages. The pursuit of common rules for extradition was complicated by French and Belgian reluctance to end political asylum for Basque terrorists, who had been welcomed during General Franco's authoritarian regime, even after democratic Spain had joined the EU. South Asia is also facing similar issues where terrorist and extremist elements find shelter in neighboring countries and the governments do not cooperate in extraditing them. Now the Europeans have a common extradition law. Adopting this law in South Asia is the need of the hour but it requires commitment from all the members of SAARC that they will not interfere in each other's affairs. With the gradual integration of the economy there would be large movements of businessmen and the tourists but along with them the criminal and terrorist elements would also be moving and there is a need to deter them from committing any illegal activity.

If and when a common market develops in South Asia, people would start working in another country, get married there and may purchase properties also as it is happening in Europe now a days. Similar kind of jurisdictional problems will arise in South Asia too in the years to come which may force the South Asian countries also to adopt a common civil and criminal law and also a common extradition law to deal with all transnational crimes. In fact a common market would lead to adoption of not only common trade procedures but also common legal practices also for which the South Asians should get mentally prepared for the next generation.

---

3. *Policy making in the EU* by Helen and William Wallace.

Aviation Policy

The common aviation policy of European Union would herald a new era in air travel for the European citizens. It's a lesson for South Asian countries as how to manage their airspace jointly. The European Union's plans for improving the management of the growing air traffic in its crowded skies finally got the green signal from the European Parliament in January 2004. The single European sky programme came into effect at the end of the year. The key aims of the new regulatory framework include: decreasing flight delays, making air traffic control more efficient and stepping up safety measures, with the goal of achieving a unified European airspace in 2005. The Single European Sky programme allows for a much needed reorganisation of Europe's air traffic control system. This initiative will ultimately benefit the air passengers by improving safety, reducing flight times and delays as well as decreasing fuel consumption. The proposals also include closer cooperation between civil and military airspace authorities involved in the work of the Single Sky Committee, which will oversee the closer coordination of national air traffic control systems. The South Asian countries need to study this experience as they have been very often subjected to overflight bans, resulting in longer flight duration and extra use of fuel, etc. The way the Europeans have involved the civil and military authorities of all the member countries in managing the airspace all over Europe jointly is worth emulating in South Asia as it will generate confidence among the people that they will no longer face the war like situation as it will render the air forces of the rival countries under one unified civilian command of SAARC aviation officials. Perhaps this will remain a dream for the South Asians for years to come.

10

A Common Currency

As Europe has successfully introduced a common currency called EURO and as it has made life easier for the common European people and businessmen there is a talk of introducing common currency for the South Asian people also. It may be a distant or a nonrealisable dream for some but financial experts, businessmen and diplomats have already started describing it as a probability. Since the SAARC members have not yet started a SAARC free trade zone the reality of a common currency seems to be a far cry but experts agree that given the direction in which the SAARC members are likely to move in the next few years or decades the grand vision of a common currency may start taking shape as the EURO will continue to inspire the South Asian businessman and the economists.

However unless the South Asian Free Trade Agreement is implemented a monetary union will remain just a dream. Experts are now talking of creating a South Asian Regional Fund (SARF) on the lines of European Central Bank. SARF can introduce a parallel currency called SAR or RUPA (various names are being proposed) which will not replace the existing currencies but coexist with them and will be freely convertible. SAR can be made mandatory for countries to use SAR for all business transactions within the region. Experts also suggest to back SAR by a corpus. Ten percent of the regions reserve—more than $10 b can be used to create the fund and all countries have to be a part of this. Experts also suggest that SAR should be used for funding infrastructure projects and research and development. This initiative will promote trade and help create an understanding of the common unit. The less developed countries can use it to tide over their balance of payment problems. SAARC Finance, a body consisting of central bank governors of SAARC countries which already exists, needs to be strengthened.

Parallel Currency

Nobel Laureate Robert Mundell,[1] sometimes referred as Father of Euro, argued at a lecture at Asian Development Bank that while Asia may not be ready for a common currency it might be for a parallel currency. The same goes for South Asia. We can start immediately with a parallel currency which can be a currency composite of South Asian currencies and may perhaps be called SAR (South Asian Rupia). Parallel currency[2] can facilitate regional integration by funding provision of regional public goods in the area of transport and communication, energy, information technology and capacity building, biotechnology, food security, tourism and advanced science and technology. The parallel currency of SAARC will be fully convertible into any international currency and will be fully backed by a reserve fund. It will be legal tender for cross country transactions within South Asia and will be increasingly used as a unit of account for trade and investment transactions within the region. For effective progress in regional currency reforms, it is important to make a distinction between parallel currency and common currency. Common currency means that individual countries do not have their own currency and whole task of currency creation and monetary expansion. Parallel currency on the other hand requires no such surrender of sovereignty. It requires little more than what is being achieved even at the global level through creation of special drawing rights (SDR) under the International Monetary Fund. Individual countries will retain control of their currencies and monetary policies. But in addition there will be a currency created jointly according to certain rules allocated among the member countries. In the context of European integration process the first stage was introduction of European Currency Unit (ECU), a composite monetary unit consisting of a basket of

1. RIS Policy Brief (Dec., 2003)
2. Dr. Ram Gopal Agarwal, Sr. Advisor, R.I.S., New Delhi.

European Communities currencies and the process of consolidation under European Monetary Union (EMU) before gradual evolution to the single currency.

As single currency can only be the final stage of the economic union, the South Asian countries have to think of first giving shape to a parallel currency. A single currency will eliminate exchange rate risk from intra-SAARC zone trade. Though the SAARC single currency will still be prone to fluctuations against other major currencies of the world like Euro, Dollar, Yen etc., the benefits to member states will depend on the proportion of the trade undertaken with the SAARC rather than third countries. The greater the ratio of intra-SAARC to extra-SAARC trade, the greater the potential gains from membership of the SAARC monetary Union.

India's Proposal

The proposal for a common currency was first of all officially proposed by the Indian Prime Minister and later repeated by the Indian foreign minister during Islamabad SAARC summit for establishing a SAARC economic Union on the lines of European Monetary Union but Pakistan reacted to it by saying that immediate focus should be on conflict resolution. Mr Yashwant Sinha while addressing the SAARC Chamber symposium on regional cooperation in Islamabad during the Islamabad SAARC summit had said that South Asia with one currency, one tariff regime and free movement of goods was well within the realm of possibility. The Pakistani foreign ministry however did not reject the proposal outright and said that Indian proposal was a good long term objective, but emphasised that the right atmosphere has to be created by removing conflicts in the region. The Pakistani spokesman Masood Khan said that the proposal even though not premature could be a long term goal but it was an idea that required a 'step by step' approach.

India's leading daily *The Times of India* was so excited by the possibilities of a common currency, as enunciated by the Indian Prime Minister Vajpayee, that it front paged a lead item quoting experts how to make the common currency a viable proposition for which the central banks would have to start coordinating their policies so that the process of economic integration is achieved. For this there should be agreements for the FDI in the region and allowing temporary movement of professionals within the region. Agreements on stabilising the exchange rates, creating a common customs union with common uniform external tariff, removal of restrictions on capital flows, interest rate parity etc., have to be achieved as the European Union has done. As a final step the practical aspects of designing the currency, naming it, printing sufficient quantities and fixing a date for introduction would follow. According to experts at this stage local currencies can be abolished. As far as the location of the SARF office is concerned it can be in a mutually agreed city like Karachi, Mumbai or Kathmandu. It should be run by a board of directors based on statutory guidelines. Initially it can give out a credit on account to the central banks. Later a paper currency can be introduced. As for printing it should be done in proportion to the contribution to the reserve fund. It is interesting to find the kind of discussion which has already started in the media on a common currency for SAARC.

The Director General of India's leading Confederation Of Indian Industry (CII) Tarun Das writing in the *Hindustan Times* said, "Prime Minister Vajpayee's call for a common currency for South Asia is another typically visionary initiative. It has the potential to help more than 1.3 billion residents of South Asia (more than China) by bringing them closer to each other. Equally importantly it will bring South Asian businesses much closer to each other, kickstarting closer economic ties. This is bold for two reasons. First it is a new way to solve our many problems. Few people have talked about a common currency for South Asia, believing that our political differences were too deep to have any meaningful economic cooperation. Rather, Vajpayee is going about this the other way by using economic cooperation to bridge political differences. Second it is an inspirational statement. Something that all of us can relate to: a tribal in Baluchistan, a farmer in Bihar and a trader in Bangladesh can all understand the importance of a single currency. They know that this is something specific, something practical and something that will make everyone's life simpler. Thirdly this is eminently achievable. From the macro economic side, we meet all the tests: our economies are in the similar stages of development, facing similar problems and carrying out broadly similar economic reforms. Foreign exchange reserves are rising everywhere, so we can build up a sufficient chest to deal with future problems. Also there are two more reasons why this is doable. Most South Asians already use a currency called the "rupee". Sri Lanka, Nepal, Pakistan and India have a currency called the rupee. Bhutan has both the Indian Rupee and the Ngultrum as legal tender. Maldives currency is the Rufiya. Only Bangladesh has the Taka (Interestingly people in Indian state of West Bengal call the Rupee as Taka). So it would be easy to get a popular consensus for a unified currency."

According to Mr Das, there is a historical background for a common currency. As part of the British Empire, we all had a common currency, which extended not just to South Asia, but even to Middle East and to South East Asia. The withdrawal of British empire created new countries but there is a force of globalisation and freer trade which is taking South Asia back to its history at least in economic terms. It will cut the transaction costs for domestic business as they start to increasingly trade with each other. Similarly a common currency for 1.3 billion will make South Asia an even bigger market for foreigners to invest in. Companies will be able to raise funds in different markets. It will also help tourists as they travel across the region by removing the hassle of having to change currency frequently.

It will be too early to calculate the quantum of the "dividend" but there will be a dividend that every country can bank on greater investment, in greater movement of people and in greater economic stability. So, we must start work now. Just as we conceived SAARC in the mid-fifties, but are now moving to a SAFTA, so now we must move from a SAFTA to a South Asian Currency Union concept and vision. Fortunately we know how Europe entered into a common currency; we can learn from them. First the European countries set up something called the European Monetary Union, then they stabilised foreign exchange rates, finally, they created a shadow currency, called the ECU (European Currency Unit) that was a basket of all the currencies.

For us the most important practical step is for the Governors of the Central Banks of each country to meet and work out the timetable to a currency union, which will be at least four and maybe six years. Europe too took eight years from the time it decided to have a common currency after the Maastricht Treaty in 1992, till the January 2001, introduction of EURO but South Asia must be more ambitious in regard to the timeframe.

Pak Response

The view from Pakistan is no less enthusiastic but full of doubts. According to a report in *Islamabad News* by Ibrahim Khan, Indian Prime Minister Atal Bihari Vajpayee's feeler on single currency tastes sweet and sour, beneficial economically but baneful politically in the diversified systems of governments in seven countries of SAARC. The newspaper quoting the analysts said that the feeler, if implemented with a popular will of the peace loving people and cooperation of various governments in not a distant future, could be helpful to the Pakistani farmers producing fresh and dry fruits, but would hurt the industry including the automobiles, which are unable to compete with Indian products. On the other hand the President of the Federation of Pakistan Chambers of Commerce and Industry (FPCCI) told *The News,* "This was to be implemented ultimately in 10, 12 or 15 years. It is possible, but the private sector and business community should be involved in the interaction." A former Chairman of Karachi Stock Exchange Yasin Lakhani said, "The EURO is the model before us for introducing a single currency in the SAARC region. There is every likelihood of introduction of a single currency in 10 or 20 years on the pattern of the European Union if the process of peace continued in an honest way." The Chairman of Banking, Credit and Finance committee of FPCCI Dr Mirza Baig said, "It is premature. It is too early to think about it given the present political scenario between the two great South Asian nations." One member of the Karachi Chamber of Commerce and Industry said the European Union had adopted the single currency unit of the EURO, which was now gaining strength day by day against the powerful dollar of the United States.

Good for Farmers

Another group of people, belonging to the farming community, which consists of more than 70 % of the Pakistan's 150 million people, believes that its farm produce would fetch better price in India, where there was a great demand for grapes, kino, oranges, apples, pomegranates, mango, dates, almond, pistachio and carpets, etc. A free trade under single currency can boost the income of the Pakistani farmers and orchard keepers while it can also ruin the emerging industrial base producing cars, trucks, jeeps, tractors, auto spare parts, light machinery, etc. Those who favour the currency feeler say that it would dismantle the barriers, promote industrialisation and the farmers will get better returns. In the open market the 100 Indian rupees are traded at 128/133 Pakistani rupees compared with 100 or 90 Pakistani rupees some 25 years ago.

According to a Karachi based economist and social analyst S. Akbar Zaidi, Vajpayee's common currency proposals needs to be seen in the light of current India-Pakistan economic relations, in light of which it seems quite astonishing. Europe has emerged as a common currency economic zone after fifty years following the end of hostilities in 1945. It emerged from an agreement on reducing tariffs on steel in the 1950's, to the entities it has become now. It has taken half a century of political, economic and social negotiations, continuous and difficult, for it to become a union. In contrast India and Pakistan since December 2000, had not been talking to each other. Pakistan and India have been trading for all but nine of the last 56 years, yet this trade has been miniscule, by any comparison. In last decade, official trade between the two countries has been less than half a percentage point of either country's imports or exports. In terms of trade within South Asia, both India and Pakistan export a mere five percent of their total exports to the region. Yet, the fact there is huge unknown potential is recognised by all businessmen and by economists. If we assume that investors and traders from both countries be treated like those from any other, there is no limit to what is possible. With low transport costs, common cultural and economic profiles, easy access to raw materials and markets, the sky is the limit. Greater trade and economic relations can change the future of South Asia, interlocking both economies into a regional trading block, countering the negative impact of the globalisation. Yet this is all a pipedream until India takes the lead. Mr Zaidi advises that if India has any vision for South Asia, whether it is in the form of a Federation or having a common currency, the first giant step towards that goal, will undoubtedly have to come from India itself.

But critics in India point out that India extended the MFN status to Pakistan way back in 1996 and inspite of no reciprocal facility India has not complained to the World Trade Organisation as Pakistan is bound to extend similar status under WTO rules. No other SAARC member has in fact denied this facility to India which is in fact a commitment for all the WTO members to extend this facility on mutual basis. Lack of will from Pakistan has in fact hindered improved trade exchanges but the positive attitude shown by Pakistan during the last SAARC summit In Islamabad (4-6 January, 2004) promises smooth road ahead. It is worth noting that Indian Rupee is very much prevalent in Nepalese and Bhutanese markets.

Birth of Euro

As interesting media discussion begins in South Asia on the remote but exciting possibility of a common currency the birth of the idea of Euro had also a similar start when in 1970, the Werner report[3] named after the then Prime Minister of Luxemburg proposed a convergence between the economies and currencies of the six EEC countries. However the first step in this direction was not taken until March 1979, when the European Monetary System (EMS) was set up. The EMS was designed to reduce the variations in the exchange rates between the currencies of the member states. It allowed them fluctuation margins of between 2.25% and 6%. But its mechanism were weakened by a series of crises caused by the instability of US Dollar and the weakness of some currencies that became prey to speculators, especially at times of international tension. At the height of cold war it was quite natural as we are witnessing

3. Nigel M. Healy, *Reforming European Union*, Longman.

today in South Asia where there are lot of mistrust still prevailing among member states. But the need for an era of monetary stability was felt increasingly as Europe made progress in completing the single market. The next important step was taken when the Single European Act was signed in February 1986, which logically implied convergence between European economies and the need to limit fluctuations in the exchange rates between their currencies. European financial experts always asked: how could a single market, based on the free movement of people, goods and capital, be expected to work properly if the currencies involved could be devalued? Devaluing a currency would give it an unfair competitive advantage and lead to distortions in trade.

When the European Council met in Madrid in June 1989, the Commission President Jacques Delors put forward a plan and a timetable for bringing about economic and monetary union (EMU).[4] This plan was later enshrined in the Treaty signed at Maastricht in February 1992. The treaty laid down a set of criteria to be met by the member states if they were to qualify for EMU. These criteria were all about economic and financial discipline. The member states were expected to curb inflation, cut interest rates , reduce budget deficits to a maximum of 3% of GDP, limit public borrowing to a maximum of 60% of GDP and stabilise the currency's exchange rate. However Denmark and the United Kingdom reserved the right not to move the third stage of EMU (i.e. adoption of the Euro) even if they met the criteria. This was called the 'opting out'. Denmark conducted a referendum on this issue and announced that it did not intend to adopt the Euro. Sweden too expressed reservations. Britain has also not taken any decision to join Euro.

Stability

Inspite of the major economies, decision to keep themselves out, the role of Euro in providing stability to the currencies has attracted world's attention. The member states have found

---

4. Report on economic and monetary union in the European Community, 1989.

a way to ensure the stability of the single currency. As the inflation makes the economy less competitive, it undermines peoples confidence and reduces their purchasing power. To deal with the issue an independent European Central Bank (ECB) was set up in Frankfurt. The ECB was tasked to determine interest rates to maintain the value of the Euro. To maintain strict financial and fiscal discipline the European Council adopted two important resolutions in Amsterdam in June 1997. The first was known as the 'Stability and Growth Pact'. This pact committed the member countries to maintain their budgetary discipline. They would have to keep a regular watch on one another and not allow any of them to run up excessive deficits. The second resolution committed the member states to make sure that employment remained at the top of the agenda of the European Union.

Further in December 1997, the European Council met in Luxembourg and adopted a resolution on coordinating economic policies of the participating states. Thus the political leaders of Europe opened the way for a deep interaction between the Euro countries and which went beyond the monetary union to embrace financial, budgetary, social and fiscal policies of the member states. The Euro has in fact now become the world's second most important currency. The Euro is now being used for international payments and as a reserve currency, alongside the US Dollar. According to an European expert, Pascal Fontaine, inspite of the turbulent world situation (with stock market crises, terrorist attacks and the war in Iraq) the Euro area has enjoyed the kind of stability and predictability that investors and consumers need. European's citizens confidence in the Euro was boosted by the successful and unexpectedly swift introduction of coins and bank notes during the first half of 2002.

EURO : The success story*

Treaty of Maastricht—the treaty on European Union (EU) and Economic and Monetary Union (EMU) was signed in February 1992, and came into force in November 1993. The

* *Source:* European Commission documents

treaty was agreed in Maastricht in December 1991. Under this treaty the member states agreed to replace their national currencies with a single European currency provided the participating states meet the required economic criteria like budget deficit not to exceed 3% of GDP for more than a short period. Also public borrowing should not exceed 60% of GDP.

European Monetary Institute: In January, 1994, the EMI was set up and new procedures were introduced for monitoring EU countries economy and encouraging convergence between them.

Stability and Growth Pact: In June 1997, the European Council meeting at Amsterdam agreed to have a stability and growth pact and the new exchange rate mechanism (a reborn EMS) designed to ensure stable exchange rates between the Euro and the currencies of the EU countries that remain outside the Euro area. In this meeting a design was also agreed for the 'European' side of the Euro coins.

Criteria for Euro: The European Union's political leaders met in Brussels from 1 to 3 May, 1998, and agreed that 11 EU countries meet the requirements for the membership of the area. They announced the definitive exchange rates between the participating currencies.

Euro is born: On 11 January, 1999, the 11 currencies of the participating countries disappeared and were replaced by the Euro. Thus Euro became the shared currency of Austria, Belgium, Finland, France, Germany, Iceland, Italy, Luxembourg, the Netherlands, Portugal and Spain. (Greece joined them on 1 Jan, 2001). From this point onwards the European Central Bank took over from the EMI and became responsible for a monetary policy, which is defined and implemented in Euro. Exchange operations in Euro began on 4 January, 1999, at a rate of about Euro 1 to 1.18 US dollars. This was the start of the transitional period that lasted till 31 December, 2001.

Euro coins: On 1 January, 2002, Euro-denominated notes and coins were introduced and put into circulation. This was the start of the period during which national currency notes and coins were withdrawn from the circulation. This period ended on 28 February, 2002. Thereafter, only the Euro became legal tender in the Euro member countries.

11

Common Foreign and Security Policy

After successfully integrating their economies the members of European Union now wants to increase the level of its integration to political front and increase its clout in world affairs. Similarly an united South Asia can also be a force to reckon with in 21st century. To increase its say in international affairs, some member states would like the EU to have its common foreign and security policy as they are fed up with continued silence and inaction over important international crises. It is an irony that Brussels which hosts the headquarters of EU is not able to get out of the shadow of North Atlantic Treaty Organisation which also has its headquarters in Brussels. The overpowering military influence of NATO is visible in the headquarters of European Commission where the officials sidetrack the contentious issues like Iraq and UN reform that divide the major European powers. Though European Union as a whole is allowed to be represented by one authority called Trade Commissioner in international trade and economic issues, especially in WTO talks, the European Union was only able to develop a consensus on the appointment of a common foreign minister in the European Council meeting of the Heads of States on 18th June, 2004. Perhaps with majority members on his side the EU foreign minister would be able to present single view of Europe on major issues. The frustration of the President of European Commission Romano Prodi on foreign

1. *The Times*, London; 17 May, 2004

and security policy front was evident in his speech in an Italian town lambasting the Italian support for a "mistaken war in Iraq". Romano Prodi said that the mismanagement of Iraq could only be "laid at the door of the United States" and post war construction could only be carried out if the UN had an" absolute dominant role".

European Security Strategy

Earlier in December 2003, the High Representative of European Union Javier Solana referred to the need for Europe to share the responsibility for global security and in building a better world. In his proposal on ***European Security Strategy*** Mr Solana said," As a Union of 25 member states with over 450 million people producing a quarter of the world's Gross National Product (GNP), and with a range of instruments at its disposal, the European Union is inevitably a global player. In the last decade European forces have been deployed abroad to places as distant as Afghanistan, East Timor and Democratic Republic of Congo. The increasing convergence of European interests and the strengthening of mutual solidarity of the EU makes us a more credible and effective actor. Europe should be ready for this role."

Relevance for South Asia

The document titled ***"A secure Europe in a better world: European Security Strategy"*** prepared by Javier Solana was adopted by the Heads of State and Government at the European Council in Brussels on 12 December, 2003. This document has much relevance for policy planners in South Asia as it would be relevant to discuss this along with the evolving foreign and security policy directions and ambitions of European Union. This document says that the post Cold War environment is one of increasingly open borders in which the internal and external aspects of security are absolutely linked. Flows of trade and investment, the development of technology and the spread of democracy have brought freedom and prosperity to many people. Others have perceived globalisation as a cause of frustration and injustice. These developments have also increased the scope for non-state groups to play a part in international affairs. And they have increased European dependence and so vulnerability on an interconnected infrastructure in transport, energy, information and other fields.

Since 1990 almost 4 million people have died in wars, 90% of them civilians. Over 18 million people worldwide have left their homes as a result of conflict. In much of the developing world, poverty and disease cause untold suffering and give rise to pressing security concerns. Almost 3 billion people, half the world's population, live on less than 2 Euros a day. About 45 million die every year of hunger and malnutrition. AIDS is now one of the most devastating pandemics in human history and contributes to the breakdown of societies. New diseases can spread rapidly and become global threats. Sub-Saharan Africa is poorer now than it was 10 years ago. In many cases, economic failure is linked to political problems and violent conflict.

Security is a precondition of development. Conflict not only destroys infrastructure, including social infrastructure, it also encourages criminality, deters investment and makes normal economic activity impossible. A number of countries and regions are caught in a cycle of conflict, insecurity and poverty.

Competition for natural resources—notably water—which will be aggravated by global warming over the next decades, is likely to create further turbulence and migratory movements in various regions. Energy dependence is a special concern for Europe. Europe is the world's largest importer of oil and gas. Imports accọunt for about 50% of energy consumption today. This will rise to 70% in 2030. Most energy imports come from the Gulf, Russia and North Africa.

Terrorism: Key Threat

Large-scale aggression against and between any member state is now improbable. Instead, Europe faces new threats which are more diverse, less visible and less predictable. This strategy paper was followed up in the 18th June, 2004, EU council meeting where the Heads of States welcomed the report by the Secretary General/High Representative on integrating in the council secretariat an intelligence capacity on all aspects of the terrorist threat. Probably this will mean setting up of an intelligence wing for the

EU. The council requested the High Representative to implement such arrangements as soon as possible. On practical operation front, the European Union Council welcomed the reestablishment of the counter terrorism task force within Europol to which the flow of criminal and operational intelligence will occur. The heads of the security forces of the member states would meet regularly in the counter terrorist group format. The EU council reaffirmed its determination to confront the terrorist threat relentlessly and comprehensively for which a decision was taken to appoint an EU counter terrorism coordinator. The council recognized the danger that Europe is both a target and a base for terrorism: European countries are targets and have been attacked. Logistical bases for Al Qaeda cells have been uncovered in the UK, Italy, Germany, Spain and Belgium. Concerted European action is indispensable.

According to the strategy paper proliferation of weapons of mass destruction (WMD) is potentially the greatest threat to our security. The international treaty regimes and export control arrangements have slowed the spread of WMD and delivery systems. We are now, however, entering a new and dangerous period that raises the possibility of a WMD arms race, especially in the Middle East. Advances in the biological sciences may increase the potency of biological weapons in the coming years; attacks with chemical and radiological materials are also a serious possibility. The spread of missile technology adds a further element of instability and could put Europe at increasing risk. The most frightening scenario is one in which terrorist groups acquire weapons of mass destruction. In this event, a small group would be able to inflict damage on a scale previously possible only for states and armies.

Concern on Kashmir

Talking of regional conflicts, the paper says that problems such as those in Kashmir, the Great Lakes Region and the Korean Peninsula impact on European interests directly and indirectly, as do conflicts nearer to home, above all in the Middle East. Violent or frozen conflicts, which also persist on our borders, threaten regional stability. They destroy human lives and social and physical infrastructures; they threaten minorities, fundamental freedoms and human rights. Conflict can lead to extremism, terrorism and state failure; it provides opportunities for organised crime. Regional insecurity can fuel the demand for WMD. The most practical way to tackle the often elusive new threats will sometimes be to deal with the older problems of regional conflict.

State Failure: Bad governance—corruption, abuse of power, weak institutions and lack of accountability—and civil conflict corrode states from within. In some cases, this has brought about the collapse of state institutions. Somalia, Liberia and Afghanistan (under the Taliban) are the best known recent examples. Collapse of the state can be associated with obvious threats, such as organised crime or terrorism. State failure is an alarming phenomenon, that undermines global governance, and adds to regional instability.

Organised Crime: Europe is a prime target for organised crime. This internal threat to security has an important external dimension: cross-border trafficking in drugs, women, illegal migrants and weapons accounts for a large part of the activities of criminal gangs. It can have links with terrorism. Such criminal activities are often associated with weak or failing states. Revenues from drugs have fuelled the weakening of state structures in several drug-producing countries. Revenues from trade in gemstones, timber and small arms, fuel conflict in other parts of the world. All these activities undermine both the rule of law and social order itself. In extreme cases, organised crime can come to dominate the state. Nearly 90% of the heroin in Europe comes from poppies grown in Afghanistan—where the drugs trade pays for private armies. Most of it is distributed through Balkan criminal networks which are also responsible for some 200,000 of the 700,000 women victims of the sex trade world-wide. A new dimension to organised crime which will merit further attention is the growth in maritime piracy. Taking these different elements together—terrorism committed to maximum violence, the availability of weapons of mass destruction, organised crime, the weakening of the state system and the privatisation of force—we could be confronted with a very radical threat indeed.

STRATEGIC OBJECTIVES

We live in a world that holds brighter prospects but also greater threats than we have known. The future will depend partly on our actions. We need both to think globally and to act locally. To defend its security and to promote its values, the EU has three strategic objectives:

Addressing the Threats: The European Union has been active in tackling the key threats.

- It has responded after 11 September with measures that included the adoption of a European Arrest Warrant, steps to attack terrorist financing and an agreement on mutual legal assistance with the U.S.A. The EU continues to develop cooperation in this area and to improve its defences.
- It has pursued policies against proliferation over many years. The Union has just agreed a further programme of action which foresees steps to strengthen the International Atomic Energy Agency, measures to tighten export controls and to deal with illegal shipments and illicit procurement. The EU is committed to achieving universal adherence to multilateral treaty regimes, as well as to strengthening the treaties and their verification provisions.

Nuclear Risks in South Asia

The European Union and Member States have intervened to help deal with regional conflicts and to put failed states back on their feet, including in the Balkans, Afghanistan, and in the Democratic Republic of Congo. Restoring good government to the Balkans, fostering democracy and enabling the authorities there to tackle organised crime is one of the most effective ways of dealing with organised crime within the EU. In an era of globalisation, distant threats may be as much a concern as those that are near at hand. Nuclear activities in North Korea, nuclear risks in South Asia, and proliferation in the Middle East are all of concern to Europe. Terrorists and criminals are now able to operate world-wide: their activities in central or southeast Asia may be a threat to European countries or their citizens. Meanwhile, global communication increases awareness in Europe of regional conflicts or humanitarian tragedies anywhere in the world. Our traditional concept of self-defence upto and including the Cold War—was based on the threat of invasion. With the new threats, the first line of defence will often be abroad. The new threats are dynamic. The risks of proliferation grow over time; left alone, terrorist networks will become ever more dangerous. State failure and organised crime spread if they are neglected—as we have seen in West Africa. This implies that we should be ready to act before a crisis occurs. Conflict prevention and threat prevention cannot start too early. In contrast to the massive visible threat in the Cold War, none of the new threats is purely military; nor can any be tackled by purely military means. Each requires a mixture of instruments. Proliferation may be contained through export controls and attacked through political, economic and other pressures while the underlying political causes are also tackled. Dealing with terrorism may require a mixture of intelligence, police, judicial, military and other means. In failed states, military instruments may be needed to restore order, humanitarian means to tackle the immediate crisis. Regional conflicts need political solutions but military assets and effective policing may be needed in the post conflict phase. Economic instruments serve reconstruction, and civilian crisis management helps restore civil government. The European Union is particularly well equipped to respond to such multi-faceted situations.

Building Security in Neighbourhood: Even in an era of globalisation, geography is still important. It is in the European interest that countries on our borders are well-governed. Neighbours who are engaged in violent conflict, weak states where organised crime flourishes, dysfunctional societies or exploding population growth on its borders all pose problems for Europe.

The integration of acceding states increases our security but also brings the EU closer to troubled areas. Our task is to promote a ring of well governed countries to the east of the European Union and on the borders of the Mediterranean with whom we can enjoy close and cooperative relations. The importance of this is best illustrated in the Balkans. Through our concerted efforts with the US, Russia, NATO and other international partners, the stability of the region is no longer threatened by the outbreak of major conflict. The credibility of our foreign policy depends on the consolidation of our achievements there. The European perspective offers both a strategic objective and an incentive for reform.

It is not in our interest that enlargement should create new dividing lines in Europe. We need to extend the benefits of economic and political cooperation to our neighbours in the east while tackling political problems there. We should now take a stronger and more active interest in the problems of the Southern Caucasus, which will in due course also be a neighbouring region. Resolution of the Arab/Israeli conflict is a strategic priority for Europe. Without this, there will be little chance of dealing with other problems in the Middle East. The European Union must remain engaged and ready to commit resources to the problem until it is solved. The two state solution—which Europe has long supported—is now widely accepted. Implementing it will require a united and cooperative effort by the European Union, the United States, the United Nations and Russia, and the countries of the region, but above all by the Israelis and the Palestinians themselves. The Mediterranean area generally continues to undergo serious problems of economic stagnation, social unrest and unresolved conflicts. The European Union's interests require a continued engagement with Mediterranean partners, through more effective economic, security and cultural cooperation in the framework of the Barcelona Process. A broader engagement with the Arab world should also be considered.

Policy Implications for Europe

The European Union has made progress towards a coherent foreign policy and effective crisis management. We have instruments in place that can be used effectively, as we have demonstrated in the Balkans and beyond. But if we are to make a contribution that matches our potential, we need to be more active, more coherent and more capable. And we need to work with others. More active in pursuing our strategic objectives. This applies to the full spectrum of instruments for crisis management and conflict prevention at our disposal, including political, diplomatic, military and civilian, trade and development activities. Active policies are needed to counter the new dynamic threats. We need to develop a strategic culture that fosters early, rapid, and when necessary, robust intervention. As a Union of 25 members, spending more than 160 billion Euros on defence, we should be able to sustain several operations simultaneously. We could add particular value by developing operations involving both military and civilian capabilities. The EU should support the United Nations as it responds to threats to international peace and security. The EU is committed to reinforcing its cooperation with the UN to assist countries emerging from conflicts, and to enhancing its support for the UN in short-term crisis management situations. We need to be able to act before countries around us deteriorate, when signs of proliferation are detected, and before humanitarian emergencies arise. Preventive engagement can avoid more serious problems in the future. A European Union which takes greater responsibility and which is more active will be one which carries greater political weight.

More Capable: A more capable Europe is within our grasp, though it will take time to realise our full potential. Actions underway—notably the establishment of a defence agency—take us in the right direction. To transform our militaries into more flexible, mobile forces, and to enable them to address the new threats, more resources for defence and more effective use of resources are necessary. Systematic use of pooled and shared assets would reduce duplications, overheads and, in the medium-term, increase capabilities. In almost every major intervention, military efficiency has been followed by civilian chaos. We need greater capacity to bring all necessary civilian resources to bear in crisis and post crisis situations.

Stronger diplomatic capability: We need a system that combines the resources of Member States with those of EU institutions. Dealing with problems that are more distant and more foreign requires better understanding and communication. Common threat assessments are the best basis for common actions. This requires improved sharing of intelligence among Member States and with partners. As we increase capabilities in the different areas, we should think in terms of a wider spectrum of missions. This might include joint disarmament operations, support for third countries in combating terrorism and security sector reform. The last of these would be part of broader institution building. The EU-NATO permanent arrangements, in particular Berlin Plus, enhance the operational capability of the EU and provide the framework for the strategic partnership between the two organisations in crisis management. This reflects our common determination to tackle the challenges of the new century.

Defence Policy

More Coherent: The point of the Common Foreign and Security Policy (CFSP) and European Security and Defence Policy (ESDP) is that we are stronger when we act together. Over recent years we have created a number of different instruments, each of which has its own structure and rationale. The challenge now is to bring together the different instruments and capabilities like European assistance programmes and the European Development Fund, military and civilian capabilities from Member States and other instruments. All of these can have an impact on our security and on that of third countries. Security is the first condition for development. Diplomatic efforts, development, trade and environmental policies, should follow the same agenda. In a crisis there is no substitute for unity of command. Better co-ordination between external action and Justice and Home Affairs policies is crucial in the fight both against terrorism and organised crime. Greater coherence is needed not only among EU instruments but also embracing the external activities of the individual member states.

Coherent policies are also needed regionally, especially in dealing with conflict. Problems are rarely solved on a single country basis, or without regional support, as in different ways experience in both the Balkans and West Africa shows.

There are few if any problems we can deal with on our own. The threats described above are common threats, shared with all our closest partners. International cooperation is a necessity. We need to pursue our objectives both through multilateral cooperation in international organisations and through partnerships with key actors. The transatlantic relationship is irreplaceable. Acting together, the European Union and the United States can be a formidable force for good in the world. Our aim should be an effective and balanced partnership with the USA. This is an additional reason for the EU to build up further its capabilities and increase its coherence. We should continue to work for closer relations with Russia, a major factor in our security and prosperity. Respect for common values will reinforce progress towards a strategic partnership. Our history, geography and cultural ties give us links with every part of the world: our neighbours in the Middle East, our partners in Africa, in Latin America, and in Asia. These relationships are an important asset to build on. In particular we should look to develop strategic partnerships, with Japan, China, Canada and India as well as with all those who share our goals and values, and are prepared to act in their support.

A Capable EU

The strategy paper concludes by saying, "this is a world of new dangers but also of new opportunities. The European Union has the potential to make a major contribution, both in dealing with the threats and in helping realise the opportunities. An active and capable European Union would make an impact on a global scale. In doing so, it would contribute to an effective multilateral system leading to a fairer, safer and more united world."

Welcoming the report of the Secretary General/High Representative on 15 June, 2004, on the progress in taking forward the proposals in the document "European Defence: NATO/EU Consultations", the European Council reaffirmed the importance of the proposed measures coming into force as soon as possible and of the necessary resources being provided as a matter of priority. Accordingly the European Council agreed to take forward work on the establishment of a civil/military cell within EU military Staff, as set out in the above mentioned report, and agreed that the cell should begin its work at the latest by the end of 2004.

The European Council also agreed to take forward work on establishing an operations center and its functioning should start by 1st January, 2006. The Council reaffirmed the importance of the parameters for this capacity as set out in the Presidency paper endorsed by it, in particular that this will not be a standing HQ, that the main option for autonomous military operations remains national HQs and that a decision to draw on the collective capacity of the EUMS would be taken, upon the advice of the Military Committee, in particular where a joint civil/military response is required and where no national HQ is identified. The European Council declared that concrete progress is being achieved towards enhancing EU capabilities. The Council endorsed the Headline Goal 2010 and the Action Plan for Civilian Crisis Management and welcomes the steps taken to further improve EU capacity to undertake military rapid response operations for crisis management. It also endorsed the elaboration of the modalities under which the EU could provide military capabilities in support of United Nations. The European Council also welcomed the agreement on the Joint Action providing for the establishment of the European Defence Agency. The Council also welcomed the important progress made on European Defence: NATO/EU consultations, planning and operations.

European Security and Defence Policy

The European Security and Defence Policy (ESDP) is an integral part of the CFSP and aims to make the CFSP more effective, more coherent and more visible so that Member States can carry out a range of humanitarian, peacekeeping and crisis management tasks, known as "Petersberg Tasks". The resulting ESDP is designed to reinforce the EU's external action through a crisis management capability that includes both military and non-military aspects, while fully respecting the principles of the United Nations Charter. Three inter-connected focal points to ESDP are:

- military crisis management;
- civilian crisis management;
- conflict prevention.

ESDP has now entered an operational phase, which has already seen the launch of four EU-led missions. Two EU police missions—EUPM in Bosnia-Herzegovina and Operation Proxima in the former Yugoslav Republic of Macedonia are ongoing. Operation Concordia, a military monitoring/stabilization mission in the former Yugoslav Republic of Macedonia, and Operation Artemis, a temporary stabilisation force in the Democratic Republic of Congo, have successfully concluded.

Cooperation with other international organisations, such as the UN, the OSCE and NATO, is an important aspect of the EU's approach. The EU and UN have cooperated closely in the contexts of the above mentioned EUPM and Artemis operations. The signing, on 24 September, 2003, in New York, of a Joint Declaration on EU-UN cooperation in crisis management provides a basis for the further strengthening of practical cooperation between the two organisations.

A role for NATO in relation to ESDP arises from the need for the EU, which is not a military organisation, to have access to certain capabilities and resources such as transportation, headquarters and planning facilities which will be required for substantial crisis management missions. These arrangements are often referred to as the 'Berlin Plus' arrangements. EU-NATO relations are underpinned by principles agreed at European Council level, including full respect for the autonomy of EU decision-making, recognition of the different nature of the EU and NATO, and non-discrimination against any of the Member States.

Further to adoption of the EU Programme for the Prevention of Violent Conflicts at the Gothenburg European Council in June 2001, efforts are ongoing towards explicit 'mainstreaming' of conflict prevention throughout all areas of the EU's CFSP, including ESDP.

The Political and Security Committee

The Political and Security Committee (PSC) plays a central role in the development and implementation of the CFSP and the ESDP. It prepares recommendations on the future functioning of the CFSP, including ESDP, and deals with the day-to-day running of these issues, including preparation of CFSP aspects of GAERC meetings. The PSC is also authorised to take decisions under delegated authority from the Council during periods of crisis management. This includes both civilian and military aspects of crisis management. The PSC consists of representation at ambassador level from the Member States and the Commission.

As stated in the "Presidency Conclusions" of the Helsinki summit, "The Union will contribute to international peace and security in accordance with the principles of the United Nations Charter. The Union recognises the primary responsibility of the United Nations Security Council for the maintenance of international peace and security. The European Council underlines its determination to develop an autonomous capacity to take decisions and, where NATO as a whole is not engaged, to launch and conduct EU-led military operations in response to international crises. This process will avoid unnecessary duplication and does not imply the creation of a European army."

"It is obvious that the Euopean Union while maintaining its independent line on foreign and defence policy does not want to antagonise and undermine the importance of NATO and wants to work in collaboration to deal with the conflict and crisis situation in various parts of the world. In other words it reserves its right to act as a policeman of the world but only in collaboration with NATO. But as far as other measures are required to punish the erring parties the EU can also impose sanctions as economic measures independently to assert its role and as a referee in important international issues.

12

The Parliament

To say that the SAARC members should also have a common Parliament of its own as it is functioning and evolving in Europe, would be asking too much considering the present state of relations between South Asian countries. However it would be interesting to understand how European countries are discussing their problems and framing a common policy on a single central legislative platform giving the impression of a federal Parliament like India has in its federal capital New Delhi and all the legislative bodies of European countries behaving like Indian provincial assemblies situated in the state capitals. Though there are deep divisions over EU's plan to have a common foreign and security policy and a common foreign minister answerable to the European Parliament and Council of European Union, the day is not far off when EU will ultimately get the right to propound its own foreign and security policy and in that case the Parliaments of member states of Europe will be reduced to the status of Indian state assemblies. The European Parliament based in Brussels and Strasbourg have alternate sessions like Indian state of Maharashtra has its Assemblies in Nagpur and Mumbai, and Jammu & Kashmir in Jammu and Srinagar.

However, the European Parliament inspired the academics in India also as perhaps only India has an excellent track record of a strong parliamentary system of governance whereas the other South Asian neighbours like Sri Lanka and Bangladesh can be said to have intermittent periods of strong parliament. Bhutan has been a monarchy and Maldives is an authoritarian regime whereas Nepal has a limping Assembly (Panchayat). The Pakistani parliamentary system has been undermined by the overpowering influence of the military. Parliament has rarely functioned as a supreme decision making institution especially in the management of foreign policy and defence. In this background it is difficult to think of a common parliament for South Asia. However as we move along the path of deeper economic integration, peoples interaction in all walks of life will increase very much, which will result in greater aspirations for a democratic way of governance in their own country followed by a desire for a common parliament, which will collectively think and try to evolve a common solution for their common problems, as we are witnessing in Europe these days where they discuss their issues from health and agriculture to foreign and defence policies. Though they have not been able to evolve a common European stand on international issues, they have been able to chalk out a plan of co-operative and united Europewide policy and action on issues of domestic nature. The European Parliament is gradually evolving towards a supreme decision making body for the member states of EU, having similar impact on all the EU citizens. It is expected that when the new Constitution of the EU is accepted by all the 25 members and implemented the EU will be able to take a united, common decision on all international issues.

The discussion in academic circles on a South Asian Parliament started in early nineties and the then Chairman of the Indian Council of Social Science Research M L Sondhi organised India Pakistan social scientists forum which issued a call to establish a South Asian Regional Parliament. Perhaps the idea was picked up officially by India when the then Indian Prime Minister P V Narshimha Rao on Dec 8, 1995 proposed the setting up of a South Asian Parliament in his inaugural address during the deliberations of SAARC ministerial meeting to celebrate the 10th anniversary of SAARC and in response to this proposal the Bangladesh foreign minister Mustafizur Rahman endorsed the idea in the form of a non-legislative South Asian Parliament. Recently in December, 2003, during a conference on peace and development in South Asia, Congress leader Sonia

Gandhi commented," overtime why can't we for instance conceive a South Asian Parliament as a permanent deliberative body on issues of regional concern and importance".

However, considering the political nature of the present regimes in South Asia and their attitudes towards democratic governance, the idea of a South Asian Parliament seems to be a distant dream. If South Asian countries are ever to emerge into an integrated economy, then this idea may gain ground, which may take a few decades to materialise as we have seen in Europe where most of the Eastern and some of the western members of EU were once authoritarian regimes. However last decade saw a dramatic new wave of democracy sweeping all over Eastern Europe, which ultimately inspired them to join European Parliament by sending democratically elected representatives from their countries to sit in Brussels and Strasbourg.

Considering the huge varied population in South Asian countries, the smaller countries would not like a Parliament dominated by India on the basis of its huge population, so a formula has to be evolved to give a proper balance to all the countries from a population of 200,000 (Maldives) to over one billion (India), as the EU Parliament has devised for small and big member nations of EU. The South Asian Parliament may initially discuss issues of peoples concern like environment, health, agriculture etc., and pass resolutions and as Bangladesh foreign minister proposed in 1995, the South Asian Parliament may have non legislative character, it may issue advisories on various issues which might prove to be a moral responsibility of the member states to accept and implement in their countries.

The European Parliament initially was a non legislative body, which has today developed into a powerful European institution of governance. The European Parliament represents, in the words of the 1957 Treaty of Rome,' the peoples of the state brought together in the European Community'. Some 450 million European citizens in European community in 25 countries are now involved in the process of European integration through their 732 representatives in European Parliament. The first direct elections to the European Parliament were held in June 1979, when 34 years after the end of second world war, the peoples of the European nations, once torn apart by war, went to the polls to elect the members of a single parliament. Europeans could have devised no more powerful symbol of reconciliation. The European Parliament, which derives its legitimacy from direct universal suffrage and is elected every five years, has steadily acquired greater influence and power through a series of treaties. These treaties, particularly the 1992 Maastricht Treaty and the 1997 Amsterdam Treaty, have transformed the European Parliament from a purely consultative assembly into a legislative parliament, exercising powers similar to those of the national parliaments. Today the European Parliament, as an equal partner with the Council of Ministers, passes the majority of European laws—laws that affect the lives of Europe's citizens. Members of the European Parliament (MEPs) have been elected by direct universal suffrage since 1979 and at subsequent five year intervals. They are elected under a system of proportional representation. Elections are held either on a regional basis, as for example in the United Kingdom, Italy and Belgium, on a national basis, as in France, Spain, and Denmark, or under a mixed system as in Germany. In Belgium, Greece and Luxembourg voting is compulsory. A common code of democratic rules applies everywhere: these include the right to vote at 18, equality of men and women, and the principle of the secret ballot. Since the Maastricht Treaty came into force in 1993 every citizen of an EU member state who lives in another country of the Union may vote or stand for election in their country of residence.

No National Bloc

The European Parliament is the only Community institution that meets and debates in public. Members sit in political groups in the chamber, not in national delegations. Parliament currently has seven political groups, as well as 'non-attached' members. They also sit on parliamentary committees and delegations, as either full or substitute members. Members of Parliament do not form any national blocs but discuss issues in Europe-wide political groups that bring together all the main political parties operating in the EU member states.

Members spend one week each month at a plenary session in Strasbourg, when Parliament meets in full session. Additional two-day sittings are held in Brussels. Parliament's secretariat is located in Luxembourg. When sessions alternate between Brussels and Strasbourg millions of Euros are spent on transferring documents on contracted lorries as it happens between Jammu and Srinagar and Mumbai and Nagpur in India. The European Parliament, whose seat is in Strasbourg, has three places of work: Strasbourg, Brussels and Luxembourg. The reasons for this are historical: these are the places where the main European institutions have had their headquarters since they were established. Strasbourg, symbol of Franco-German reconciliation, was chosen as the seat of the Council of Europe, and since 1952 the European Parliament has also held most of its part-sessions there.

Seats

A protocol annexed to the 1997 Amsterdam Treaty states that: 'The European Parliament shall have its seat in Strasbourg where the 12 periods of monthly plenary sessions, including the budget session, shall be held. The periods of additional plenary sessions shall be held in Brussels. The committees of the European Parliament shall meet in Brussels. The General Secretariat of the European Parliament and its departments shall remain in Luxembourg.' For practical reasons, however, a number of officials and the staff of the European Parliament's political groups work in Brussels. Two weeks in every month are set aside for meetings of Parliament's committees in Brussels. The remaining week is devoted to meetings of the political groups. With the assistance of its translators and interpreters, Parliament works in the 20 official languages of the Union:

The European Parliament has three main roles:

1. It shares with the council the power to legislate. The fact that it is a directly elected body helps guarantee the democratic legitimacy of European Law. The most common procedure for passing a EU legislation is "co-

decision". This places the European Parliament and the Council on an equal footing and the laws passed using this procedure are joint acts of the Council and Parliament. It applies to legislation in a wide range of fields. On a range of other proposals Parliament must be consulted, and its approval is required for certain important political or institutional decisions. Parliament also provides impetus for new legislation by examining the commission's annual work programme, considering what new laws would be appropriate and asking the commission to put forward proposals.

2. It exercises democratic supervision over all EU institutions, and in particular the commission. It has the power to approve or reject the nomination of commissioners, and it has the right to censure the commission as a whole. The European Commission is politically answerable to the parliament. The members of the commission attend plenary sessions of Parliament and meetings of the Parliamentary committees, maintaining a continuous dialogue between the two institutions. Parliament also monitors the work of the council: Parliament members regularly ask the council written and oral questions, and the President of the Council attends the plenary sessions and takes part in important debates. Parliament also works closely with the council in certain areas, such as common foreign and security policy and judicial cooperation, as well as on some issues of common interest such as asylum and immigration policy and measures to combat drug abuse, fraud and international crime. The Council Presidency keeps Parliament informed on all these subjects.

3. It shares with the council authority over the EU budget and can therefore influence EU spending. At the end of the procedure, it adopts or can reject the budget in entirety. The EU's annual budget is decided jointly by Parliament and the Council of the European Union. Parliament debates it and it does not come into force until it has been signed by the President of Parliament.

Division of Work

Parliament's work is divided into two main stages: Preparing for the plenary session:

1. This is done by the MEP's in the various parliamentary committees that specialise in particular areas of EU activity. The issues for debate are also discussed by the political groups.
2. The plenary session itself. Plenary sessions , attended by all MEP's, are normally held in Strasbourg (one week per month) and sometimes in Brussels (2 days), At these sessions, Parliament examines proposed legislation and votes on amendments before coming to a decision on the text as a whole. Other items on the agenda may include questions about what is going on in the European Union or the world.

Composition of the European Parliament

The number of members per state is laid down by the Treaties. In the chamber, members sit in political groups, not in national delegations. These political groups include members from over one hundred national political parties.

Political groups	
PPE-DE	Group of the European People's Party (Christian Democrats) and European Democrats
PSE	Group of the Party of European Socialists
ELDR	Group of the European Liberal, Democrat and Reform Party
Verts/ALE	Group of the Greens/European Free Alliance
GUE/NGL	Confederal Group of the European United Left/Nordic Green Left
UEN	Union for Europe of the Nations Group
EDD	Group for a Europe of Democracies and Diversities
NI	Non-attached

Political Groups

The vast majority of MEPs belong to one or other of the political groups. Members who do not belong to any of the groups are known as 'non-attached Members'. A political group must include MEPs from more than one member state and have a minimum number of members. There are currently seven political groups in the European Parliament. The groups draw on more than a hundred national parties. Several of the political groups have links to parties at European level, recognised by the Treaty as 'a factor for integration within the European Union which contributes to forming a European awareness and to expressing the political will of the citizens'. Each political group has a chairman, a bureau and a secretariat.

MEPs do not sit in national delegations in the Parliament, but in multinational political groups. The centre-right European People's Party (EPP) and European Democrats group, which includes British Conservatives, is the largest political group. British Labour MEPs belong to the Party of European Socialists, the second biggest group.

The European Liberal Group, where the largest national contingent is from the UK, is third biggest, closely followed by the Green/European Free Alliance which has brought together Green MEPs from 13 countries, including Britain's two Green members, and nationalist parties, including Plaid Cymru and SNP members.

Two British members elected for the United Kingdom Independence Party (UKIP) joined The Europe of Democracies and Diversities Group. The other groups are the European United Left / Nordic Green Left, which brings together Left and Green members from a number of countries including France, Greece and Italy; and the Union for Europe of the Nations. There are also a small number of UK MEPs who sit as independents.

The European Parliament's budget for the year 2004 is £1,231 million. This covers staff costs, buildings, MEPs' travel allowance and expenses. The Parliament employs about 4200 people, of whom about 1300 work in the linguistic services covering a total of 20 working languages. Salaries of MEPs are the same as national MPs in their own countries. EU leaders have been asked by Parliament to agree to a standard EU-wide salary for MEPs as part of a package for reforming pay and expenses.

Committees

Before votes in plenary sessions, the groups consider reports from Parliament's committees in the light of their political views and often table amendments to them. They also play an important part in deciding on the agendas for plenary sessions and choosing the topical issues to be placed on these agendas.

The President oversees all the activities of Parliament and its constituent bodies. He or she presides over its plenary sittings and chairs the meetings of the Bureau and Conference of Presidents. He or she represents Parliament in all external relations, particularly international relations. The committees: Parliament's standing committees, of which there are seventeen, do the preparatory work for Parliament's plenary sessions. Each committee appoints a chairman, three vice-chairmen and has a secretariat. The committees draw up and adopt reports on legislative proposals and own-initiative reports. They also prepare opinions for other standing committees. In addition to these standing committees, Parliament can set up temporary committees and committees of inquiry. The joint parliamentary committees maintain relations with the applicant country parliaments, the inter-parliamentary delegations with parliaments in other non-EU states.

The Secretariat: Under the authority of a Secretary-General some 3,500 officials, recruited by competition from all the countries of the Union, work in the service of the European Parliament. The political groups have their own staff and members their own assistants.

The European Parliament has to work within the constraints of multilingualism—which accounts for about one third of its staff and the fact of having three places of work namely Strasbourg, Brussels and Luxembourg. Running the European Parliament costs €2.5 per year per EU inhabitant (the equivalent of 1.08% of the Union's total budget).

Parliament's role in European and world politics has been growing very fast. Actually, co-decision on legislation has enhanced the European Parliament's political clout. This influence is ever more evident in key areas of European Union activity, from the Common Foreign and Security Policy and co-operation in police and judicial matters, to EMU, the Charter of Fundamental Rights and the Convention on the Future of Europe.

The Common Foreign and Security Policy

The aim of European political cooperation, which started in the early 1970s, was to go beyond the economic and social framework set up by the Community treaties to achieve a genuinely common strategy in the field of foreign policy. The Treaty on European Union incorporated the security dimension into foreign policy: one of its sections is entitled 'Provisions on a common foreign and security policy (CFSP)'. The setting up of the European Rapid Reaction Force has, for the first time in its history, given the European Union a foreign and security policy identity of its own. The council consults Parliament on major foreign policy decisions. Parliament puts questions to the council, and can make recommendations. Through its Committee on Foreign Affairs, Human Rights, Common Security and Defence Policy in particular, Parliament is in regular contact with the Union's High Representative for the Common Foreign and Security Policy. International events are the subject of regular debates concluding with the adoption of resolutions urging a particular approach to the European Union's foreign policy. Any accession of a state to the European Union and most international agreements require the assent—i.e. the approval of the European Parliament. In the case of an international agreement or an accession treaty the European Parliament must be kept fully informed of the mandate and the state of negotiations. It can ask for its recommendations to be taken into account at any time.

An international forum: The influence wielded by Parliament through its work on foreign policy and external relations has given it the status of an international forum. In recent years the European Parliament has been addressed by the UN Secretary-

General, the President of the United States, the heads of state of Mexico, Chile and Colombia, and the King of Jordan, to name only a few.

Citizenship

Citizenship of the Union, which exists by virtue of the Treaty, is conferred on everyone who is a national of an EU member state. EU citizenship complements, and does not replace, national citizenship. Election by universal suffrage gives the European Parliament full legitimacy. By voting in its elections the citizens of Europe enhance its status and influence.

European citizenship gives EU citizens the right of free movement and residence in the territory of the Member States, the right to vote and stand for election in European and local elections, the right to diplomatic protection in third countries, as well as:

- the right to petition the European Parliament;
- the right to bring complaints before the European Ombudsman; and
- the right to address any of the Union's institutions or bodies in one of the official languages and to receive an answer in the same language.

13

Structure of European Union

If twentieth century can be called the century of wars, cold and hot, and the resultant divisions and political blocks it can also be called the century of economic groupings. During the last few decades the world saw the emergence of several major economic groups like ASEAN, NAFTA, and APEC and smaller groups like MERCOSUR, SADEC, SAARC. But none of them can be compared to European Union, which was also formed with the prime objective of improving the economic lot of the European people and giving them a collective voice. The latter half of 20th century produced one of the history's greatest amalgamation of nation states surrendering their right of governance in most of the areas to a single authority called European Union headquartered in Brussels, the capital of Belgium, which is now better known as the power centre or the capital of European Union. In just half a century of existence, the European Union has achieved remarkable things. It has delivered peace between its members and prosperity for its citizens. It has created a single European currency (the Euro) and a frontier free 'single market' where goods, services and capital move around freely. The EU has grown from six to 25 countries and it is preparing to embrace a few more.

The way the EU has evolved over the years it gives the shape of a federation like the United States. In order to assert their sovereignty most of the EU members repeatedly say that it will not be allowed to become like that. The official publications of European Union describe it as a family of democratic European countries, committed to working together for peace and prosperity. It is not a state intended to replace existing states, but it is more than any other international organisation. The EU is, infact, unique. Its member states have set up common institutions to which they delegate some of their sovereingty so that decisions on specific matters of joint interest can be made democratically at European level. This pooling of sovereignty is also called "European integration". The historical roots of European Union lies in the second world war. The idea of European integration was to prevent such killing and destruction from ever happening again. It was first officially proposed by the French foreign minister Robert Schuman in a speech on 9th May, 1950. This day, the birthday of what is now the EU, is celebrated annually as Europe Day. The success of European Union owes a lot to its unique nature and the way it works. The EU authorities clarify that it cannot be called United States of Europe. At the same time it is also not an organisation of cooperation between the governments, like the United Nations. The countries that make up the EU (called member states) remain independent sovereign nations but they pool their sovereignty in order to gain strength and world influence none of them could have on its own. Smaller countries from Malta (population 400,000) to Slovenia to Ireland are all proud to be its members now as they will be respected on world stage as members of the European Union. Pooling sovereignty means, in practice, that the member states delegate some of their decision making powers to European institutions they have created, so that decisions on specific matters of joint interest can be made democratically at the European level. The three main decision-making institutions are:

European Parliament: It represents the EU's citizens and is directly elected by them.

Council of the European Union: It represents the individual member states.

European Commission: Its job is to uphold the interests of the Union as a whole. It is the executive arm of the EU.

This institutional triangle forms the European Union. which produces the policies and laws (directives, regulations and decisions) that apply throughout the EU. The rules and procedures that the institutions must follow are laid down in the treaties, which are agreed by the member states presidents and prime ministers and ratified by their parliaments. In principle, it is the commission that proposes new EU laws, but it is the Parliament and council that adopts them. In fact the commission is like ministries in the government that manages functioning of various departments and proposes laws, runs programmes, frames policies, etc.

The Court of Justice upholds the rule of European Law, and the court of Auditors checks the functioning of the Union's activities.

Five other bodies complete the system:

1. **European Economic and Social Committee:** It represents civil society and the industry.
2. **Committee of the Regions:** It represents regional and local authorities.
3. **European Central Bank:** It is responsible for European monetary policy.
4. **European Investment Bank**: It finances European investment projects.
5. **European Ombudsman:** It guards EU citizens and organisations against maladministration.

To handle certain technical, scientific or management tasks specialised agencies have been set up.

Treaties and decision-making process in EU

The EU is founded on four treaties:

1. The Treaty establishing the European Coal and Steel Community (ECSC). It was signed on 18 April, 1951, in Paris and came into force on 23 July, 1952, and expired on 23 July, 2002.
2. The Treaty establishing the European Economic Community (EEC), which was signed on 25 March, 1957, in Rome and came into force on 1 January, 1958.
3. The Treaty establishing the European Atomic Energy Committee (Euratom), which was signed in Rome along

with the EEC treaty. These two treaties are often referred to as the Treaties of Rome. When the term 'Treaty of Rome' is used, only the EEC treaty is meant.

4. The Treaty on European Union (EU) was signed in Maastricht on 7 February, 1992, and came into force on 1 November, 1993.

The first three of above treaties created the three 'European Communities' i.e., the system of joint decision-making on coal, steel, nuclear power and other major sectors of the member states economies. The Community institutions set up to manage this system were merged in 1967, resulting in a single Commission and a single Council.

The EEC, in addition to its economic role, gradually took on a wide range of responsibilities including social, environmental and regional policies. Since it was no longer a purely economic community, the fourth Treaty (Maastricht) renamed it simply 'The European Community' (EC).

The Maastricht Treaty also introduced new forms of cooperation between the member state governments for example on defence and in the areas of 'justice and home affairs '. By adding this intergovernmental cooperation to the existing Community system, the Maastricht Treaty created a new structure with three 'pillars' which is political as well as economic. Thus the European Union has three pillars which stands on the foundation of The Treaties. The three pillars are:

1. Community domain (most of the common policy areas),
2. Common Foreign and Security Policy, and
3. Police and judicial cooperation in criminal matters. Thus the European Union is founded on its treaties. Its three pillars represent different policy areas with different decision-making systems. The treaties are the foundations for everything the European Union does. Whenever the treaties have to be reviewed and amended, this is done by a special conference of the EU's national governments (an intergovernmental conference or the 'IGC').

The treaties have been amended each time new member states have joined. Moreover, every decade or so, the treaties have been amended to reform the institutions and give them new areas of responsibility.

- The Single European Act (SEA) was signed in February 1986, and came into force on 1 July, 1987. It amended the EEC Treaty and paved the way for completing the Single Market.
- The Treaty of Amsterdam was signed into force on 1 May, 1999. It amended the EU and EC treaties, giving numbers (instead of letters) to the EU Treaty articles.
- The Treaty of Nice, signed on 26 February, 2001, entered into force on 1 February, 2003. It further amends the other Treaties streamlining the EU's institutional system

Decision-making

Decision-making at European level involves various European institutions, in particular;

1. The European Commission
2. The European Parliament
3. The Council of the European Union

There are three Councils in European Union:

- **The European Council:** This means the Heads of State and government of all EU countries, plus the President of the European commission. It is the highest level policy making body in the European Union, which is why its meetings are often called 'Summits'. The European Council meets in principle four times a year to agree on overall EU policy and to review its progress.
- **The Council of the European Union:** Formerly known as the Council of Ministers, this institution consists of government ministers from all the EU countries. The council meets regularly to take detailed decisions and to pass European Laws.
- **The Council of Europe:** This is not an EU institution at all. It is an intergovernmental organisation which aims (among other things) to protect human rights, to promote Europe's cultural diversity and to combat social problems such as racial prejudice and intolerance. It was set up in

1949 and one of its early achievements was to draw up the European Convention on Human Rights. The Council of Europe has 44 member states including the 25 European countries. and is based at Strasbourg (France).

The Council of the European Union is the main decision-making body. Like the European Parliament, the council was set up by the founding treaties in the 1950's. It represents the member states , and its meetings are attended by one minister from each of the EU's national governments. Which minister attends which meeting depends on the agenda. If, for example, the council is to discuss environmental issues, the meeting will be attended by the environment minister from each EU country and it will be known as the environmental council. The EU's relations with the rest of the world are dealt with by the General Affairs and External Relations Council. Altogether there are nine different council configurations. The council's work are managed in Brussels. Here, each member state has a permanent team (representation') that represents it and defends its national interests at the EU level. The head of each representation is in effect, his or her country's ambassador to the EU. These ambassadors (known as permanent representatives meet weekly within the Permanent Representatives Committee (Coreper). The role of this committee is to prepare the work of the council, with the exception of agricultural issues, which are handled by the Special Committee on Agriculture.

The presidency of the council rotates every six months. In other words each EU country in turn takes charge of the council agenda and chairs all the meetings for a six month period., promoting legislative and political decisions and brokering compromises between the member states. Ireland was the President of the Council. in first half of 2004, in the second half the Netherlands took charge and the first half of 2005 will be headed by Luxembourg, and then the UK will take over.

Decisions in the council are taken by vote. The bigger the country's population the more votes it has. But the number is not strictly proportional: it is adjusted in favour of the less populous countries. After the accession of 10 new member states in the EU the number of votes each country can cast is as follows.

•	Germany, France, Italy and UK	29
•	Spain and Poland	27
•	The Netherlands	13
•	Belgium, Czech Republic, Greece,	
•	Hungary, and Portugal	12
•	Austria and Sweden	10
•	Denmark, Ireland, Lithuania, Slovakia and Finland	7
•	Cyprus, Estonia, Latvia,	4
•	Malta	3
	Total	321

Qualified Majority Voting

The most common voting procedure in the council is 'qualified majority voting' (QMV). This means that, for a proposal to be adopted, it needs the support of a specified minimum number of votes. However, in some particularly sensitive areas such as Common Foreign and Security Policy, taxation, asylum and immigration policy, council decisions have to be majority or unanimous. In other words each member state has the power of veto in these areas.

The European Commission proposes new legislation, but it is the Council and Parliament that passes the laws. Other institutions also have role to play in specific areas. The commission is the politically independent institution that represents and upholds the interests of the EU as a whole. It is the driving force within the EU's institutional system; it proposes legislations, policies and programmes of action and it is responsible for implementing the decisions of the Parliament and the council. Like the Parliament and the council the European Commission was set up in the 1950's under the EU's founding treaties. The term 'commission' is used in two senses. First, it refers to the 'Members of the Commission'—i.e. the team of 20 men and women appointed by the member states and Parliament to run the institution and takes its decisions. Second, the term 'Commission' refers to the institution itself and to its staff. Informally the members of the commission are known as 'Commissioners'. As members of the commission they are committed to act in the interests of the Union as a whole and not taking instructions from their national governments. A new commission is appointed every five years. The commission remains politically answerable to the Parliament, which has the power to dismiss it by adopting a motion of censure. The commission attends all the sessions of the Parliament, where it must clarify and justify its policies. The day to day work of the commission is done by its administrative officials, experts, translators, interpreters and secretarial staff. There are approximately 24,000 of these European civil servants. Commission bureaucrats are selected from every EU country through competitive examinations. The seat of the commission is in Brussels, but it also has offices in Luxembourg, representations in all EU countries and delegations in many capital cities around the world.

The rules and procedures for EU decision-making are laid down in the treaties. Every European law is based on a specific treaty article, referred to as the 'legal basis' of the legislation.

There are three main procedures for enacting new EU laws:

- Consultation
- assent
- co-decision

The main difference between them is the way Parliament interacts with the council. Under the consultation procedure, Parliament merely gives its opinion under the co-decision procedure. Parliament genuinely shares power with the council. The European Commission, when proposing a new law , must choose which procedure to follow. The choice will, in principle, depend on the 'legal basis' of the proposal- in other words which Treaty article it is based on.

The Court of Justice

The Court of Justice of the European Communities was set up under the ECSC Treaty in 1952. Its job is to ensure that EU legislations (technically known as Community Law) are interpreted and applied in the same way in each member state. The court has the power to settle legal disputes between member states, EU institutions, businesses and individuals. The court is composed of one judge per member state, so that all the EU's national legal systems are represented. The court is assisted by eight 'advocate generals'. Their role is to present reasoned opinions on the cases brought before the court. They must do so publicly and impartially. The judges and advocate generals are either former members of the highest national courts or highly competent lawyers appointed for a term of six years. To help the Court of Justice cope with the thousands of cases brought before it and to other citizens better legal protection, a 'Court of First Instance' was created in 1989. This court is attached to the Court of Justice and is responsible for giving rulings on certain kinds of cases, particularly actions brought by private individuals and cases relating to unfair competition between businesses.

The court gives ruling on cases brought before it. The four most common types of cases are:

1. Requests for a preliminary hearing
2. Proceedings for failure to fulfil an obligation
3. Proceedings for annulment
4. Proceedings for failure to act.

The courts in each country are responsible for ensuring that EU law is properly applied in that country. But there is a risk that courts in different countries might interpret EU law in different ways. To prevent this happening there is a 'preliminary ruling procedure'. This means that if a national court is in any doubt about the interpretation or validity of an EU law it may, and sometimes must, ask the Court of Justice for advice. This advice is given in the form of a preliminary ruling.

Also if the commission has reasons to believe that a member state is failing to fulfil its obligations under EU law the commission can initiate proceedings against that member. The court investigates the allegations and gives its judgements. The accused member state, if it is indeed found to be at fault, must set things at right at once. Judgements of the court are decided by a majority and pronounced at a public hearing. Dissenting opinions are not expressed.

Court of Auditors

The European Court Of Auditors checks that all the Union's revenue has been received and all its expenditures incurred in a lawful and regular manner and the EU budget has been managed soundly. The court was established in 1977. The court has one member from each country, appointed by the council for a period of six years. The court's main role is to check that the EU budget is correctly implemented—in other words, that the EU income and expenditure is legal and above board and to ensure sound financial management. So its work helps guarantee that the EU system operates efficiently and openly. The Court of Auditors has no legal powers of its own. If auditors discover fraud or irregularities they pass the information as quickly as possible to the EU bodies responsible, so that they can take appropriate action.

European Central Bank

Twelve of the EU's 25 members now share a single currency, the Euro. Euro bank notes and coins came into circulation on 1 January, 2002.

The European Central Bank was set up in 1998, under the treaty on European Union, to introduce and manage the new currency Euro and to conduct foreign exchange operations and ensuring the smooth operation of payment systems. The ECB is also responsible for framing and implementing the EU's economic and monetary policy. To carry out this role, the ECB works with the' European system of central banks which covers all 25 countries. However only 12 of these countries have so far adopted the Euro. The 12 collectively make up the euro area and their central banks, together with the European Central Bank, make up what is called the 'Eurosystem'.

The European Central Bank works in complete independence. Neither the ECB, the central banks of the Eurosystem, nor any member of their decision making bodies can ask or accept instructions from any other body. The EU institutions and member state governments must respect this principle and must not seek to influence the ECB or the national central banks. The ECB, working closely with the national central banks, prepares and implements the decisions taken by the Eurosystem's decision making bodies—the Governing Council, Executive Board and the General Council.

One of the main tasks of ECB is to maintain price stability in the euro area, preserving the Euro's purchasing power. That means keeping inflation under strict control. The ECB aims to ensure that the year-on-year increase in consumer prices is less than 2%. The ECB goes about this in two ways:

1. By controlling the money supply If it is excessive compared to the supply of goods and services, inflation will result.
2. Second, by monitoring price trends and assessing the risk they pose to price stability in the euro area. Controlling the money supply involves, amongst other things, setting interest rates throughout the euro area. This is the perhaps Bank's best known activity.

To finance development projects in member states the European Investment bank was set up in 1958 by the Treaty of Rome. It helps achieve the Union's objective by financing certain types of investment projects. The projects selected are the ones that promote European integration, balanced development, economic and social cohesion and an innovative knowledge based economy.

The European Economic and Social Committee

This is the voice of the civil society. Founded in 1957 under the Treaty of Rome, the European Economic and Social Committee (EESC) is an advisory body representing employers, trade unions, farmers, consumers and the other interest groups that collectively make up the 'organised civil society'. It presents their views and defends their interests in policy discussions with the commission, the Council and the European parliament. So the EESC is the bridge between the Union and its citizens, promoting a more participatory, more inclusive and therefore more democratic society in Europe. The committee is an integral part of the EU's decision-making process: it must be consulted before decisions are taken on economic and social policy. On its own initiative it may also give opinions on other matters it considers important. The committee will have a total of 344 members after the enlarged EU of 25 members. The members are nominated by the EU governments but they work in complete political independence. They are appointed for four years. Working mostly in their countries of origin, the members of the committee form three groups that represent employers, workers and various economic and social interests.

Committee of the Regions

Set up in 1994 under the Treaty on European Union (Maastricht), the Committee of the Regions (COR) is an advisory body composed of representatives of Europe's regional and local authorities. It is called the voice of the local government. It ensures that these authorities have a say in European Union policy making and that regional and local identities and prerogatives are respected. The committee has to be constituted on matters that concern local and regional government, such as regional policy, the environment, education and transport. The 25 member EU will have 344 members. The members of the committee are elected municipal or regional politicians, representing the entire range of local and regional government activities in the European Union. They may be regional presidents, regional parliamentarians, town councillors, mayors of large cities, etc. They are nominated by EU governments but they work in complete political independence. The Council of the European Union appoints them for four years, and they may be reappointed. The Committee of the Regions appoints a President from among its members, for a term of two years.

The role of the Committee of the Regions is to put forward the local and regional points of view on EU legislation. It does so by issuing opinions on commission proposals. The commission and the council must consult the committee of the regions on topics of direct relevance to local and regional authorities, but they can also consult the committee whenever they wish. For its part the committee can adopt opinions on its own initiative and present them to the Commission, Council and Parliament.

The European Ombudsman

Under the Treaty of European Union (Maastricht) the position of European Ombudsman was created. The ombudsman acts as an intermediary between the citizens and the EU authorities. He is entitled to receive and investigate complaints from EU citizens, businesses and institutions and from anyone residing or having their legal domicile in an EU country. The ombudsman is elected by European Parliament for a renewable term of five years, which corresponds to Parliaments legislative term.

The ombudsman helps to uncover 'maladministration' in the European institutions and other EU bodies. Maladministration means poor or failed administration—in other words, an EU institution fails to do something it should have done, or does it the wrong way, or does something that ought not to be done. Examples of maladministration: unfairness, discrimination, abuse of power, lack or refusal of information, unnecessary delay, incorrect procedures. The ombudsman can make recommendations to the EU institutions and may refer a matter to the European Parliament so that it can take whatever political action is necessary.

Europol

The European Police office called the Europol was set up in 1992 to handle Europewide criminal intelligence. It is based in the Hague, the Netherlands, and its staff includes representatives of the national law enforcement agencies (police, customs, immigration services, etc.)

Europol's aim is to help the EU member states cooperate more closely and effectively in preventing and combating organised international crime, in particular: Drug trafficking, immigration networks, vehicle trafficking in human beings including child pornography, forgery of money and other means of payment, trafficking in radioactive and nuclear substances and terrorism.

Source: European documentation series.

Members of European Union: A Brief Outline

Country	Capital	Size in Sq km	Population	Language	Religion	Currency	GDP
Austria	Vienna	88,858	8 m	German	Roman Catholic 78% Protestant (5%), Muslim and others 17%	Euro	Per capita purchasing power E-22,800
Belgium	Brussels	30,510	10.4 m	Walloon(French) 60%, Flemish(Dutch) 40%	Roman Catholic 75% Protestant and other 25%	Euro	PPP E-23,800
Cyprus	Nicosia	9,250 of which 3,335 in Turkish area	777,000	Greek, Turkish, English	Greek Orthodox 78% Muslim 18%	Cyprito Pound (Greek area) Turkish Lira (Turkish area)	PPPGreek area: E-12,400 Turkish a: E-5000
Czech Republic	Prague	78,866	10.2 m	Czech(Cestina)	Roman Catholic 39.2% Protestant 4.6%, Orthodox 3% Others 13.4% Atheist 39.8%	Czech Koruna	PPP E-12,600

(Contd.)

Country	Capital	Size in Sq km	Population	Language	Religion	Currency	GDP
Denmark	Copenha-gen	43,094	5.4 m	Danish, Faroese, Greenlandic, German, English	Evangelical Lutheran 95%, other Protestant and Roman Catholic 3%, Muslim 2%	Danish Crone	PPP E-23,800
Estonia	Talinn	45,226	1.4 m	Estonian, Russian Ukranian, Finnish	Evangelical Lutheran, Russian Orthodox, Estonian Orthodox, Baptist, Methodist, Seventh Day Adventist, Roman Catholic, Pentecostal, world of life, Jewish	Estonian Kroon	PPP E-9,000
Finland	Helsinki	337,030	5.2 m	Finnish 93.4% Swedish 5.9% plus small Sami and Russian speaking	Evangelical Lutheran 89% Russian Orthodox 1%, none 9% Others 1%	Euro	PPP E-21,500
France	Paris	547,030	60 m	French with regional dialects (Provencal, Breton, Alsatian, Basque, Flemish	Roman Catholic 83% Protestant 2%, Jewish 1%, Muslim 5-10%, Unaffiliated 4% Other Christian 1.0%	Euro	PPP E-21,200

(Contd.)

Country	Capital	Size in Sq km	Population	Language	Religion	Currency	GDP
Germany	Berlin	357,021	83 m	German(Deutsch)	Protestant34%, Roman Catholic 34%, Muslim 3.7%, Unaffiliated or Others 28.3%	Euro	PPP E-21,700
Greece	Athens	131,940	11 m	Greek (99%) English, French	Greek Orthodox 98%, Muslim1.3% Other 0.7%	Euro	PPP E-15,000
Hungary	Budapest	93,030	10.1	Hungarian(Magyar) 98.2% Others 1.8%	Roman Catholic 67% Calvinist 20%, Lutheran 5%, Atheist and Others 7.5%	Forint	PPP
Ireland	Dublin	70,280	4 m	English 90%, Irish (Gaelige) 10%	Roman Catholic 88.4% Church of Ireland 2.5%	Euro	PPP E-25,100
Italy	Rome	301,230	57.5 m	Italian with small German, French and Slovenia minorities	Mainly Roman Catholic with mature Protestant and Jewish communities and a growing Muslim immigrant community	Euro	PPP E-20,100
Latvia	Riga	64,589	2.3 m	Latvian, Lithuanian Russian other	Lutheran, Roman Russian Orthodox	Latvian Lat	PPP E-6,800

(Contd.)

Country	Capital	Size in Sq km	Population	Language	Religion	Currency	GDP
Lithuania	Vinius	65,200	3.4 m	Lithuanian	Roman Catholic (Primarily Lutheran, Russian Orthodox, Protestant, Evangelical Christian Baptist, Muslim, Jewish	Litas	PPP E-21,700
Luxem-bourg	Luxem bourg	2,586	450,000	Luxembourgish (National Lang.), German (admini-strative language	Roman Catholic 86%, Protestant 13%, plus Jewish and Muslim minorities	Euro	PPP E-36,200
Malta	Valleta	316	400,000	Maltese, English	Roman Catholic 98%	Maltese Lira	PPP E-14,000
The Netherlands	The Hague	44,526	16.2 m	Dutch, Frisian	Roman Catholic 31% Protestant 21%, Muslim and unaffiliated 40%	Euro	PPP E-22,100
Poland	Warsaw	312,685	38.5 m	Police (Polski)	Roman Catholic 95% (about 75% Practising) Eastern Orthodox, Protestant and Others 5%	Zloty	PPP E-7,800

(Contd.)

Country	Capital	Size in	Population Sq km	Language	Religion	Currency	GDP
Slovakia	Brastislava	48,845	5.4 m	Slovak, Hungarian	Roman Catholic 60.3% Atheist 9.7%, Protestant 8.4%, Orthodox 4.1%, Others 17.5%	Slovak Koruna	PPP E-10,000
Portugal	Lisbon	92,391	10.5 m	Portugese	Roman Catholic 94% Portestant and Others 6%	Euro	PPP E-14,800
Slovenia	Ljubljana	20,273	2 m	Slovenian 91%, Serbo-Croat 6% Others 3%	Roman Catholic 70.8%, Lutheran 1%, Muslim 1%, Atheist 4.3% Others 22.9%	Tolar	PPP E-14,800
Spain	Madrid	504,482	41 m	Castilian Spanish 74%, Catalan	Roman Catholic 94%, Others 6%	Euro	PPP E-17,000
Sweden	Stockhom	449,964	9 m	Swedish plus small Sami	Lutheran, 87%, Roman Catholic, Orthodox, Baptist, Muslim, Jewish, Buddhist	Swedish	PPP E-21,000
United Kingdom	London	244,820	60 m	English, Welsh, Scots Gaelic	Church of England/ Anglican 30%, Roman Catholic 9%, other Christian16.2%, Muslim 2%, None 39	British Pound	PPP E-14,800

14

Europe and South Asia

Similarities

The European Union of today is multicultural, multiethnic, multilingual, multireligious group of nations. The member states have undergone the agony of mutually suspicious relations as nuclear missiles were targeted between East European and West European countries for more than two decades. The two dominant ideologies of Communism and Capitalism guided the political regimes of the adversarial eastern and western states. Similarly South Asia also has too many languages, cultures, religions and traditions. The countries of South Asia still live under mutual hatred, and an atmosphere of cold war persists between two major countries of South Asia resulting in arms race with India and Pakistan acquiring missile and nuclear capability and trying to undermine each other's interests most of the time at any international forum. After a bloody conflict in Kargil (Jammu and Kashmir) in 1999 and ten months military standoff in 2002 the two countries have relaunched peace negotiations. The hopes of a rapproachment between the two biggest South Asian countries have raised the possibilities of a deeper economic cooperation in the region with gradual opening of markets and borders for trade and travel. As the end of cold war in early nineties has facilitated the conducive atmosphere for integration of European economies and enlargement of European Union to 25 member countries, South Asia also holds similar promises of at least developing a common market in next two decades if not in near future.

Though the culture of democracy has not evenly spread all over South Asia, India being the exception as a shining example of the largest functioning democracy in the world, the Europe of today has witnessed unprecedented new phase of democratisation in the last one decade and also with respect to human rights and values. In South Asia, Sri Lanka and Bangladesh also qualifies as democratic states but Pakistan, Nepal, Maldives and Bhutan have mixed forms of democracies with military rulers and kings dominating the political scene. The Europe in the last half of 20th century was divided between authoritarian and democratic regimes but the end of cold war in the beginning of last decade of 20th century has facilitated the democratisation of mostly Communist dictatorships and their final integration in European Union. In fact in the early seventies Spain was also ruled by a military dictatorship. In 1973 and 1974 there were many military coups in Greece, Portugal and Cyprus.

Unity in Diversity

The basic prerequisites of joining the European Union for East European countries was to have a democratic form of governance and after the East European countries quickly got themselves rid of the authoritarian yoke they soon got themselves included in the new European society of which they were the original members in the early and middle part of the last century. Similarly the people of South Asia also strongly desire to have democratic governance in their lands but the authoritarian rulers are powerful enough to deny them this political luxury. However with the advent of free market economy and more trade and economic interactions among the South Asian countries the other South Asian countries will soon be attracted towards the aroma of democracy and thus creating a condition similar to Europe for a unified South Asia at least in the economic arena.

There are many similarities between Europe and South Asia especially India. Both are ancient civilisations and modern political formations, though partly in South Asia. Both are geographic entities of continental proportions with similar land area and vast range of landscapes and climates—from snow clad peaks to undulating plains to verdant river valleys to vast coastlines. Both

Europe and India celebrate diversity in its richest forms in all walks of life: religions, customs and traditions, values and beliefs, art and architecture, music and culture, literature and languages. The European Union has 20 official languages while India has 18. Both India and EU are home to many of the greatest civilisations and religions in the world. The local dialect changes every few kilometres in the Indian hinterland, just as the accent of the speaker of any European language changes with the native place. Yet at the core of this manifest diversity, there is a unity that weaves it all together into a coherent whole. So that while somebody may hail from Punjab or Karnataka, Maharashtra or Assam he is essentially an Indian. Similar consciousness about being a European citizen in addition to being a French, German or Italian citizen is beginning to firm up amongst the people of European Union. However the idea of Europeanness is as difficult to define as Indianness. This concept of Indianness can't be applied across South Asia though they mostly belong to the greater area called Indian subcontinent, the South Asian countries can at least begin to think in terms of a common heritage and giving a wider name to all the South Asians. However as European Union India is also committed to preserve its cultural diversity. Unity in diversity is the principal characteristics of Indian republic. Similarly, European Union with members belonging to various language and cultural background, have also adopted the same slogan 'United in Diversity' in its constitution.

As members of SAARC have huge differences of size and population from one billion in India to a few hundred thousands in Maldives the European Union also have a country like Germany of 80 million to a country like Malta of 400,000. By integrating their economies some of the bigger European economies have to sacrifice some gains for the economic upliftment of the poorer East Europeans. India also being the top five economies of the world has to coexist and adjust to the economic requirements of smaller neighbouring countries so as to live in a harmonious manner and to let the other smaller countries also have opportunities to flourish. Though many south Asians are fearful of India's dominance in the political and economic field in an integrated South Asia like European Union there are certain unchangeable and inescapable regional realities.

As aptly described by the former foreign minister of Sri Lanka, Mr Lakshman Kadirgamar, India has a preponderant position over all others in South Asia, based on size, resources, development and power, allied to influence. A second factor is India's unique centrality. No two others among the South Asian countries can interact directly with each other without touching or crossing Indian land, sea or airspace. Also with each of its neighbours, India has special ties—whether of ethnicity, language culture, kinship, common historical experience or shared access to and dependence upon vital natural resources—of a character and to a degree of intensity not shared by any two others. A third reality is the coterminality of the national borders of regional border states with those great natural physical barriers which encompass South Asia—the Himalayas and the Indian Ocean. Probably no other region in the world presents such an integral security zone. Consider the analogy of a wheel. At its hub lies regionally preponderant India. Radiating as spokes are India's neighbours with each of whom India shares land or maritime boundaries, but no two others are thus joined without at the same time touching India also. Binding those spokes to that hub are the physical barriers that I mentioned. Recognition of this characteristic of the security of the region being an integer, a thing complete in itself, was central to the administration of the British Raj. Given its preponderance and centrality within the region it would not be surprising, indeed it would be wholly logical, if India regards its security along similar lines. In my view India may justifiably regard any alien presence or influence within those natural security borders, without its consent, as a potential threat to its national security.[1]

Considering the tensions in the South Asian region people especially the westerners question the idea of replicating the successes of European Union. But to the sceptics it is enough to say that European countries in last few decades have also passed

1. Securing South Asia (*The Hindu*: 29.12.2003)

through the worst phase of relations. No body could have imagined the dream of the Congress of Europe held in 1948 would ever come true. Similarly if the South Asian countries decide to live together peacefully and move towards solution of disputes without any military tensions, as they very often claim that they wish to do so, then cooperation in economic and other fields will be very easy. As the then foreign Minister I.K.Gujral[2] in a speech on India's foreign policy objectives referred to the commitment of political will on the part of India to mitigate the impact of the asymmetries that the smaller South Asian countries often complain about and express fears that how their economy will be crushed under the heavy weight of giant Indian economy. Mr Gujral referred to India's neighbourhood policy which stands on five basic principles. First with the neighbours such as Nepal, Bangladesh, Bhutan, Maldives and Sri Lanka, India does not ask for reciprocity but gives all that it can in good faith and trust. Secondly no South Asian country should allow its territory to be used against the interest of another country of the region. Thirdly none should interfere in the internal affairs of another country. Fourthly, all South Asians must respect other's territorial integrity and sovereignty. And finally they should settle all their disputes through peaceful bilateral negotiations. He felt that these five principles scrupulously observed would recast South Asia's regional relationships, including the tormented relationship between India and Pakistan, in a friendly, cooperative mould.

Peace Dividend

There is continuity and further refinement in India's neighbourhood policy, and the present Indian regime also endorses the same principles of living together. As the European countries are reaping the peace dividends and showing to the entire world the advantages of living together harmoniously, the then Prime Minister Atal Bihari Vajpayee also talking of peace dividend for South Asia[3] said that it is the creation of a new hope and opportunity for its billion and a half people. We need

---

2. Speech at Royal Institute of International Affairs, London, may 1996.
3. Address at the *Hindustan Times* peace seminar, 12 Dec, 2003.

no stronger justification for peace than this simple statement. The investment inputs required to reap this dividend are pragmatic policies, rational economics and popular participation. "There can be no argument about our inherent advantages, common interests and complementary strengths, which present a tremendous opportunity for our region to realize its full potential:

- First and foremost, our rich and varied human resources. Our citizens have created waves around the world with their technical, financial and managerial expertise. Their energies and talents can find greater application in regional cooperative enterprises.
- Second, our populations are younger than the world average and will therefore constitute an increasing proportion of the global workforce in the future.
- Third, our technological advances have put us at the vanguard of today's Knowledge Economy enabling us to accelerate our development processes.
- Fourth, the size and increasing purchasing power of our collective market create economies of scale for cost effective production.
- Fifth, efficient exploitation of our synergies can vastly enhance intra regional trade, even as we work towards a rule based international trading regime.
- Sixth, the region has massive untapped capacities for hydropower and unexploited hydrocarbons, which can more than meet its huge energy deficit.
- Seventh, the rich diversity of our bio resources - in the Himalayan region and elsewhere—are yet to be exploited for our common benefit.
- Eighth, our combined political weight and economic strength can give us considerable leverage in pursuing our shared objective for a cooperative multipolar world order.

The peace dividend lies in converting this exciting potential into vibrant reality. Our region is heir to a centuries old tradition of tolerance, pluralism and creative interaction. We need to recapture this ethos in the modern context. In the post-cold war world of globalisation, countries around the world are increasingly focusing on regional economies. Political disputes have been resolved diplomatically or quietly deferred for tackling at a more opportune time. Conflict has given way to cooperation; dialogue moderates differences. There is clear recognition that hostility only stunts economies, inhibits trade and retards progress.

This realization has dawned not only in the developed world, but also in developing regions that have experienced bitter differences and violent conflicts in the past. It encompasses Mercosur and the Andean Pact, COMESA and SADC, NAFTA and APEC. Nearer home, we have the outstanding example of ASEAN. South Asia needs the wisdom to heed these lessons. By most estimates trade within regions accounts for nearly three fourths of global trade. Yet inspite of our geographical proximity, shared economic characteristics and similar development infrastructure intra south Asia trade is under five percent of our total foreign trade. We must discard the myth that because of asymmetries in our economies, the smaller countries do not benefit from closer economic integration within South Asia. Our free trade agreements with Nepal and Sri Lanka have resulted in narrowing the trade deficit of both these countries with India. In fact the success of the India-Sri Lanka Free Trade Agreement has inspired us to expand its scope to cover services and investment in a comprehensive economic partnership agreement."

"As we develop greater economic stakes in each other, we can put aside mistrust and dispel unwarranted suspicions. We will also develop mutual sensitivity to each other's concerns and promote more of our common interests. If we provide legitimate avenues of free commercial interaction, we can eradicate the black market and underground trade, money laundering and other transnational crimes, which today flourish in our region because of our mutual rivalries and inadequate coordination. Once we reach that stage, we would not be far from mutual security cooperation, open borders and even a single currency."

This vision of then Indian Prime Minister Atal Behari Vajpayee is also shared by other SAARC nations. The need of the hour is to understand the cooperative relationships that are developing in other parts of the world among a group of nations situated in a continent and to emulate those examples for the benefit of millions of poverty ridden hungry population. The conference of SAARC heads of state in Islamabad in January 2004, gave affirmations to this commitment. There is lot of desire among other south Asian countries to start this process as soon as possible and it was a welcome relief for the observers of the South Asian geopolitics to find the South Asian leaders talking the need of a unified economy and even having a common currency during the Islamabad SAARC summit in January 2004, as the European nations have achieved.

Union of States

The South Asia which consists largely of India, Pakistan and Bangladesh were brought under one political entity though under British rule and when the Britishers left India and Pakistan were formed and later on Bangladesh was created out of Pakistan in 1972. But the point to mention here is the fact that over five hundred princely states of various cultural and ethnic background decided to live together in an Union of states called Republic of India after partition of Indian subcontinent in 1947 chiefly because the visionary leaders of Indian freedom movement decided to have a secular, democratic system respecting equality to all. The European Union of today is promising similar guarantees to all. In India with 28 states living under a federal system with common foreign, security and economic policy rights delegated to the New Delhi the states enjoy much autonomy in framing their legislations. Similar experiments are now being repeated in Europe but with an important difference. The states in Europe which are trying to pool their resources together are sovereign states with different backgrounds and strains of foreign, security and economic policy. Now most of them are agreeing to the need for a common foreign and security policy. The states in European Union though will remain sovereign entities their rights and responsibilities will be reduced to more or less similar of Indian federal states. As the provinces in India elect their own assemblies to run their affairs the member states of European Union will also retain their national

Parliaments mainly to discuss issues like law and order, municipal administration, education etc., of their own states whereas issues of foreign and security policies will increasingly be taken care of by the authorities in Brussels which will be governed by a Council of Europe consisting of the Heads of State of all the member countries which in turn will be guided by a rotating troika of three Presidents on a six-month term thus giving opportunities to all the member countries to sit over the regime in Brussels.

Susane Hoeber Rudolph and Lloyd I. Rudolph[4] makes an interesting observation, "In thinking about something with which to compare India's federalism, the multilingual European Union seems more appropriate than does the United States. Much like the English and the Italians, the Hindi speakers of Bihar state in the shadow of the Himalayas and the Tamil speakers of Tamil Nadu at the subcontinent's southern tip speak quite distinct languages. They share little history and few points of contacts. Their traditional rulers, legends and folk cultures are distinct from one another. Their socio-economic profiles are as different as those of Sweden and Portugal. Bihar is poor and mostly illiterate. Tamil Nadu is prosperous and advanced. No contrast between any two of the US states comes anywhere close. Forty years ago, there seemed good reason to fear that Selig Harrison was right to warn that India's "fissiparous tendencies", particularly its linguistic differences, would soon lead to balkanization or dictatorship. Today such worries seem unpersuasive. The federal system has helped India to live peacefully with its marked difference.

Federal State

"How anomalous is a multinational federal state? India reminds us that the nation state as we know it is a relative historical newcomer, with roots in post-revolutionary, post-Napoleonic Europe of the nineteenth century, the Nation State reached its apogee after the two world wars. Before 1914, the numbers of people and extent of territory ruled by nation-states were dwarfed by those which lay under the sway of

---

4. University of Chicago, South Asia face the future (*Journal of Democracy*, January 2002).

multinational entities such as the Habsburg, Ottoman and Romanov empires, or the maritime dominions of Britain and other European colonial powers. After 1945, the working out of Woodrow Wilson's doctrine of self determination had seemingly conferred sovereignty on enough aspiring "nations" to bring the era of the multinational state to a decisive end. The nation state, said many scholars, stood revealed as the natural end toward which the history of state formation had been tending.

This claim was soon belied, however, by the formation of the European Community and its successor, the European Union. On 1 May 2001, the *New York Times* reported the proposal by German Chancellor Gerhard Schroeder's Social Democratic Party of "a far reaching plan......to turn the European Union into a more centralized federal system." The EU was becoming more like the sovereignty sharing Holy Roman Empire than the warring nation states of the first world war. Had the Holy Roman Empire become the dominant polity in the twelfth century, the process of state formation in Europe would have conformed more closely to the world norm. The path that marks the rise of India's federal, multinational state since 1947 also tracks the emergence of an alternative to the increasingly outmoded nation-state.

By promoting peace among their constituent parts, both the EU and the vast republic that is India are saving the world from a great deal of trouble and strife. If it has done nothing else, the EU, the creation of a Europe—bloodied, exhausted and chastened by two gigantic and terrible wars, has radically reduced the prospect of conflict among its member states. Something similar is true of India. Each of its 28 federal states could well be a nation-state unto itself. The largest, Uttar Pradesh, has more people than Germany and France combined, and is nearly as populous as Russia. If Uttar Pradesh and its neighbours were two sovereign nation-states there would be that many more countries living in the Hobbesian world of anarchy and self-help. Instead of ending in domestic arbitration, the dispute between Tamil Nadu and Karnataka over Krishna River water rights could have led to war. The internal conflicts within Punjab and Assam, like the civil wars that roiled Congo-Kinshasa during the 1990s could have been made worse by outside forces seeking strategic gain. As it is, the international community has quite enough to occupy it as a result of the longstanding dispute between India and Pakistan over the fate of Kashmir, India's northernmost and only Muslim majority state.

Living as family

Had the Indian subcontinent which is called South Asia now been one entity, the big powers would not have got the opportunity to play their dirty geopolitical game of pretending to help India and Pakistan resolve their disputes over Jammu and Kashmir? Now the same geographic area having three nation states are having strained relations and much of their resources are being frittered away on the weapon systems purchased from the same powers to prevent one former member of the family from attacking the other. It is time now to learn the lessons from European states who were once bitter enemies for four decades but are now living as a family sharing their bread together but maintaining distinct sovereign status but planning and managing the well being of their masses together. Now the million dollar question is, can the sovereign states of South Asia come together on a single platform leaving behind the animosities of the last five decades? As the then Prime Minister of India Atal Bihari Vajpayee, aptly commented[5] "those who think that this goal seems unrealistic and utopian were, perhaps being unnecessarily cynical. Let us remember that the world did not anticipate the sudden end to the Cold War or the collapse of the Berlin wall. No one thought that apartheid South Africa could be transformed bloodlessly into Mandela's rainbow country. Each one of these developments flowed from objective factors in the global environment, but actually occurred because of some enlightened and responsible decisions" by people at the helm of affairs.

No doubt the South Asian countries are trying to wriggle out of this strained atmosphere and making serious efforts to

---

5. Address at a peace seminar (*Hindustan Times* leadership initiative 12 December, 2003.

give a push to the South Asian Association for Regional Cooperation (SAARC) formed in 1985. For two decades the SAARC remained embroiled in mutual suspicions. Trade and economic exchanges have moved at snail's pace. Now the big issue today is can the leaders of South Asian countries coexist in amity for the benefit of their people as the visionary leaders of Europe have shown the way to the rest of the world? Can South Asia also ever think of open borders and a common currency? Before 1947 they were all one with open borders and common currency. Can the wheels of history be turned back? Not for surrendering sovereignty, as there are fears among European countries due to the formation of European Union, but opening their borders as it existed in 1947? In fact minus Pakistan and Bangladesh in South Asia India became a multicultural, multireligious, multilingual and multiethnic union of states long before the European Union. In terms of cultural, religious and linguistic variations India that was created in 1947 could be compared to European Union of today but the Indian Union never realised its true economic potential and remained prisoner to cold war tensions. The two-nation theory propounded by Pakistan in the name of religion also affected the growth of conducive environment for economic prosperity in the region. With the end of prolonged period of cold war the European nations have decided to put aside their differences of ideologies, religion, language and culture but the animosity that was introduced on the basis of the two-nation theory and the resultant clash of Islamic and Hindu civilisations is still being sustained. The jehadi culture in South Asia is affecting the peace and stability of the region. The rising Hindu fundamentalism is also a cause of concern. The south Asian leaders have to learn a lesson from European countries who have cast aside their differences and put together a grand alliance of nations even surrendering most of their sovereign rights in decision making.

Political Differences

With the addition of ten new member states mostly eastern and central European countries a new chapter in world history has been written as the final act of the purging of Europe's 20th century horrors. Can the South Asian countries also move towards resolution of their political differences and think of implementing agreed measures for having a similar common market where goods and services can flow easily? As more and more European countries join European Union the more and more they are going to trade among themselves. The trade and services are freely flowing among themselves even at the cost of the economy and employment in some of the richest European countries. Consequently they will be trading less with the non-European countries which has an implication for countries of South Asia. In most of the sectors the south Asian countries will have less opportunities to export to the European markets. It is therefore a warning for the south Asian countries to get their house in order and start interacting more with each other, otherwise on the one hand they will not only lose export markets but they will also remain a market for European products as before.

Once the south Asian economies make their products and services competitive through mutual cooperation the benefits of EU enlargement will start accruing to south Asian countries especially India. As the enlarged European Union offers a simplified and enhanced access to the newly acceded countries' markets the South Asian countries can take advantage of this. According to the Ambassador of the delegation of the European Commission to India, Mr Francisco Da Camara Gomes[6], the enlargement would mean even larger market than before for the third countries like India with a population of almost 455 million and GDP of around 9712 billion Euros. In case of services the third countries services providers will benefit from the implementation of the single market in the acceding countries, where they will get the same treatment as in the rest of the EU. The third countries will receive enhanced levels of intellectual property rights (IPR) protection in the acceding countries due to their adoption of EU directives in this field upon accession. As the new member states subsidies will be brought within EU rules, which are in line with OECD and WTO disciplines this will

6. Speech at a CII seminar.

benefit third countries. The impact of enlargement on trade policy would also be beneficial for third countries. For trade in goods, the new member states will have to adopt the Community Common Customs Tariff (CCT) upon accession. The average weighted industrial tariffs of the acceding countries are in general higher than the 3.6 percent average for the EU. And as far as farm products are concerned most acceding countries have a lower average rate, though the biggest agricultural economies such as Poland and Hungary have rates that are higher than the average tariff for EU imports of farm goods. Thus in most cases, according to Mr Gomes, third countries business will benefit from lower tariffs in their trade with new member states.

Thus the European unification is going to present attractive opportunities for the South Asian countries. Similar unification of South Asian economy can also present equally attractive opportunities for the European countries. With huge middle class population, which would be more than half of the enlarged EU population, having similar lifestyle, the South Asia can be a magnet for European investors provided the South Asian countries arrange their house in order. The SAARC and EU can have complementary roles to help each other in improving the lives of their people.

15

Brief Profile of SAARC Members

Bangladesh

Bangladesh emerged as an independent country on 16 December, 1971. Its official name is the 'People's Republic of Bangladesh'. Dhaka is the capital of the Republic and Bangla is the state language. The Independence and National Day of Bangladesh is 26 March.

The population of the country currently stands at around 126 million. About 80 percent of the people live in rural areas. Sixty percent of the people depend on agriculture for their livelihood.

The four major religions in the country are Islam, Hinduism, Buddhism and Christianity. The Muslims constitute about 88% of the population and Hindus about 10%. The constitution guarantees religious and cultural freedom to all citizens of Bangladesh.

Bangladesh is a unitary, independent and sovereign republic comprising three basic organs: the Executive, the Legislature and the Judiciary. The President is the Head of State and is elected by the members of Parliament. The President acts in accordance with the advice of the Prime Minister.

Bangladesh has primarily an agrarian economy. Agriculture is the single largest sector in the economy producing about 30% of the country's GDP and employing around 60% of the total labour force. The country has a considerable number of large, medium and small-sized industries in both the public and private sectors based on both indigenous and imported raw materials.

Among them are jute, cotton, textiles, fertilizer, engineering, shipbuilding, steel, oil-refinery, paper, newsprint, sugar, chemicals, cement and leather.

Bhutan

The Bhutanese call their country Druk-yul, the land of the Drukpas (the people) and of the Druk (Thunder Dragon as in the national flag of Bhutan). The ancient history of the kingdom remains shrouded in mystery. Since the 8th century A.D., however, it is clear that Buddhism has played a large part in shaping the course of Bhutan's history. Although Bhutan was unified under a central authority in the 17th century, evidence strongly suggests that it had existed as an independent entity from very early times.

Bhutan's population currently stands at 638,000 people. The people of Bhutan may be divided into two main groups – the Drukpas, who are of Mongoloid origin and are Buddhists, and the Lhotsampas, or the southerners, of Nepali origin, mainly Hindus.

Bhutan is a monarchy, ruled by the Wangchuck dynasty, which was founded in 1907 by King Ugyen Wangchuck. Over the years, the monarchs of Bhutan have been the fountainhead of far-reaching and often dramatic changes in the legislative, judicial and administrative systems in the country.

With over 80% of the people dependent on subsistence farming, the Bhutanese economy is predominantly rural. The share of the agriculture sector in the gross domestic product has dropped to less than 50% with the increase in the contribution of hydroelectric power generation and sale which now accounts for over 30 percent. The country has the potential to generate 30,000 MW of power from its rivers. Besides electricity, Bhutan exports calcium carbide, wood products and cement.

India

The roots of Indian civilization stretch back in time to pre-recorded history. The earliest human activity in the Indian subcontinent can be traced back to the Early, Middle and Late Stone Ages. India gained independence from the British on 15

August, 1947. The freedom struggle was led by Mohandas Karamchand Gandhi, also known as the Mahatma, who is revered as the Father of the Nation.

India has one of the world's most diverse populations, with most of the màjor races represented. Today, India has over one billion people. There are fifteen languages recognized by the Indian Constitution and 1600 dialects. Hindi, the widely spoken language in the world, is the language of 30% of the population and the official language of India.

The Constitution of India, which envisages a parliamentary form of government, is federal in structure with unitary features. The President of India is the Constitutional Head of the Executive of the Union. The Constitution provides that there shall be a Council of Ministers with the Prime Minister as head, to aid and advise the President, who shall in exercise of his functions, act in accordance with such advice. Real executive power, thus, vests in the Council of Ministers with the Prime Minister as head. The Legislature of the Union is called the Parliament, and consists of the President and two Houses, known as the Council of States (Rajya Sabha) and the House of the People (Lok Sabha).

India ranks among the top ten industrial nations of the world and has an increasingly powerful middle class. The Indian economy is potentially very strong with its large industrial output, technological knowledge and extensive reservoir of skilled manpower. Major exports include cotton goods, iron, raw jute and jute products, coffee, electrical goods, leather, handicrafts, diamonds, chemicals and software. The major imports are machinery, petroleum, chemicals, cereals, copper, and zinc.

The majority of Indians (64%) earn their livelihood from the land with agriculture accounting for about 35 % of national income.

Maldives

The civilization of Maldives as far as can be estimated, dates back more than 2000 years. Archaeological findings from many ancient sites in Maldives show ruins of old Buddhist structures, some dating back to 3rd and 4th centuries. The evidence shows that at the time of conversion to Islam in 1153 A.D. the population of Maldives was mainly Buddhist.

Throughout its history, Maldives has remained independent, although the Portuguese occupied the country for 15 years in the 16th century. From 1887, Maldives was a British protectorate until it became fully independent on 26 July, 1965.

The archipelago of the Republic of Maldives is made up of a chain of 1190 small and low-lying islands, stretching over 800 kms from north to south. Out of them only 198 islands are inhabited.

The population of Maldives is 270,101 (2000 census). Maldivians comprise a mixed race, unified through sharing a common history, language and religion. Dhivehi is the official language. Islam is the strength and backbone of the country, permeating the entire fabric of the Maldivian culture, polity and civil society.

The Maldives political system is a unique blend of its history, traditions, Islamic faith and modern democratic principles. It has evolved over a period of many years, the first written constitution having been proclaimed in 1932, though unwritten constitutional principles had been in existence long before then. A republican form of government in 1968 replaced the constitutional monarchy, with an Executive President as the Head of State. A new Constitution, that is more comprehensive and in tune with the country's democratic principles was adopted by the country on 1 January, 1998.

The mainstay of the Maldives economy today comprises fisheries and tourism. Nearly 19% of the labour force is engaged in the fisheries sector, which accounts for over 6% of the GDP. Tourism, which became a major industry since the mid-eighties accounts for 33% of the GDP. Industrial activity consists of a traditional and modern sectors. The traditional sector consists of boat building, mat-weaving, rope making, black-smithing, handicrafts and other cottage industries. The activities in the modern sector include fish canning, manufacture of garments, construction of fiberglass boats, production of cleaning fluids, and bottling of aerated water.

Nepal

The documented history of Nepal begins with the Changu Narayan temple inscription of King Manadeva I (464 A.D.)

followed by Malla rulers among other important ones. Before Nepal's emergence as a unified nation in the latter half of the eighteenth century, the designation of Nepal was applied only to the Kathmandu Valley. Nepal had been segmented into more than 52 small principalities. Prithvi Narayan Shah, the Great King of Gorkha, was the maker of modern Nepal who united the country by 1769 by conquering Kathmandu Valley and making it the capital.

Nepal has a population of about 23.9 million made up of over 61 ethnic groups living in different regions speaking 70 languages and dialects. Nepali is the national language. Hinduism is the official religion of Nepal and Hindus constitute over 85% of the population. Buddha, the founder of Buddhism, was born in Nepal about 563 B.C. and Buddhists account for 7.8% of the population. A small minority of Nepalese adheres to Islam and Christianity.

After 1951, Nepal has exercised multi-party democracy except during the period of about three decades from 1961 to 1990 when a party-less panchayat system existed. But again, following the democratic movement of 1990, Nepal restored a multiparty system with a constitutional monarchy. His Majesty the King is the Head of State and the Prime Minister serves as Head of Government. Constitutionally, there are two houses of parliament namely Pratinidhi Sabha (House of Representatives) and Rastriya Sabha (National Assembly). The House of Representatives consists of 205 members elected by the people for a five-year term. The National Assembly comprises 60 members, 10 of whom are nominated by His Majesty the King while remaining 50 are elected, 35 by members of the Pratinidhi Sabha and 15 by members of local bodies.

The mainstay of the Nepalese economy is agriculture, which accounts for 41% of the GDP with more than 80% of the people dependent on it. The main crops grown are paddy, maize and wheat. Manufacturing, trade and tourism follow farming as the main economic activities of the country. Hand knitted woolen carpets and readymade garments are flourishing industries in the country whose total share in the exports figures is almost 32 percent. Petroleum products, chemicals and drugs, food and live animals, vehicles, machinery and equipment are the major imports of Nepal.

Pakistan

The Islamic Republic of Pakistan appeared on the world map on 14 August, 1947, under the leadership of Muhammad Ali Jinnah, Quaid-e-Azam (the Great Leader), who is revered as the Father of the Nation. Pakistan is divided into four provinces: Sindh, Baluchistan, Punjab and the North-West Frontier Province. Islamabad is the capital of the country.

The population of Pakistan (1998 estimate) is 130.58 million. The national language is Urdu, while the official language is English. The leading religion of Pakistan is Islam, which is the faith of about 95 percent of the people. Hinduism and Christianity form the leading minority religions. Other religious groups include the Sikhs, the Parsis and a small number of Buddhists.

Pakistan has a federal structure. The Parliament consists of the Lower House (National Assembly) and the Upper House (Senate). The new administration consists of the President, the National Security Council headed by the Chief Executive, and the Cabinet. Governors are appointed in all the four Provinces.

Agriculture and related activities engage 46.1 percent of the workforce and provide 25 percent of GDP. The main exports include cotton textiles, cotton yarn and thread, clothing, raw cotton, rice, carpets and rugs, leather, fish and petroleum products. The main imports include machinery, electrical equipment, petroleum products, transportation equipment, metal and metal products, fertilizer and foodstuffs.

Sri Lanka

Lanka means "resplendent" (from the Pali "alankara"). Stone-age implements found on the island date back at least ten millennia, while evidence is available that the domestication of plants may have taken place around 15,000 B.C. Given Sri Lanka's central location on the trade routes of the ancient world and the attraction then of her "products"—pearls, timber, gems and ivory, and later spices, the island had become a center of East-West commerce well before the Christian era.

The direct influence of European maritime powers was felt beginning from the 16th century with the arrival of the Portugues Dutch and later British. Sri Lanka gained independence from the British on 4 February, 1948.

The population of Sri Lanka (1998 estimate) is 18.77 million. The country is a multi-ethnic nation. The Sinhalese, of Indo-Aryan origin, comprise 74 percent of the population; the Sri Lankan Tamils of Dravidian origin, who had migrated to the island, are 12.6 percent; the Indian Tamils, descendants of migrant workers from South India recruited in the last century by the British 5.5 percent; the Moors, descendants from Arab traders who arrived in the island from about the 12th century AD 7.1 percent; and others, who include Burghers, descendants of the Dutch and Portuguese 0.8 percent. Sinhalese and Tamil are official languages while English is the national language. Four major religions are freely practiced in Sri Lanka. Buddhists account for 69.3 percent of the population, Hindus 15.5 percent, Christians 7.6 percent and Muslims 7.5 percent.

At the time of independence, Sri Lanka adopted a Westminster system of Parliamentary government with a House of Representatives, a Senate and a Cabinet headed by a Prime Minister. The British monarch was retained as constitutional head of state, and was represented in the Island by a Governor-General. In 1972, a Republican Constitution was adopted with a single legislature (the National State Assembly) and a constitutional President thus formally severing links with the British Crown. Following the amendment of Constitution in 1978, an Executive Presidential system of government prevails.

The President of Sri Lanka is both the Head of State and Head of Government. The President is directly elected by the people for a term of six years. The supreme legislative body is a unicameral parliament consisting of 225 members elected by a system of proportional representation. A multi-party system prevails and many smaller parties are allied to either the government or the opposition group. The leader of the majority party in the parliament is elected as the Prime Minister.

Ninety percent of the economy of the country at independence depended on the export of the three plantation crops of tea, rubber and coconut. Since the late 1970s, the economy has been progressively liberalized. Industrial policy has shifted from import substitution to export-oriented production. The service center now accounts for 52% in the sectoral composition of the GDP; the manufacturing sector 16.5%; agriculture 21.1%; construction 7.6%; and mining 1.9%.

Colombo is the largest Tea Auction Centre in the world since London auctions ceased to function in June 1998. Other exports include textiles and garments, coconut products, spices, cocoa, coffee, essential oils, gems, fishery products, rubber, machinery, footware and leather products and petroleum by-products. Major imports include rice, wheat and sugar, fertilizer, crude oil and investment goods such as raw materials, building materials, transport equipment and machinery.

Source: SAARC Secretariat

Annexures

Annexure 1

Charter of SAARC

Do hereby agree to establish an organisation to be known as South Asian Association for Regional Cooperation hereinafter referred to as the association, with the charter of the South Asian Association for Regional Cooperation.

We, the Heads of State or Government of Bangladesh, Bhutan, India, Maldives, Nepal, Pakistan and Sri Lanka;

1. Desirous of promoting peace, stability, amity and progress in the region through strict adherence to the principles of the UNITED NATIONS CHARTER and NON-ALIGNMENT, particularly respect for the principles of sovereign equality, territorial integrity, national independence, non-use of force and non-interference in the internal affairs of other States and peaceful settlement of all disputes;
2. Conscious that in an increasingly interdependent world, the objectives of peace, freedom, social justice and economic prosperity are best achieved in the SOUTH ASIAN region by fostering mutual understanding, good neighbourly relations and meaningful cooperation among the Member States which are bound by ties of history and culture;
3. Aware of the common problems, interests and aspirations of the peoples of SOUTH ASIA and the need for joint action and enhanced cooperation within their respective political and economic systems and cultural traditions;
4. Convinced that regional cooperation among the countries of SOUTH ASIA is mutually beneficial, desirable and necessary for promoting the welfare and improving the quality of life of the peoples of the region;

5. Convinced further that economic, social and technical cooperation among the countries of SOUTH ASIA would contribute significantly to national and collective self-reliance;
6. Recognising that increased cooperation, contacts and exchanges among the countries of the region will contribute to the promotion of friendship and understanding among their peoples;
7. Recalling the DECLARATION signed by their Foreign Ministers in NEW DELHI on August 2, 1983, and noting the progress achieved in regional cooperation;
8. Reaffirming their determination to promote such cooperation within an institutional framework; following objectives, principles, institutional and financial arrangements:

Article 1: Objectives

The objectives of the ASSOCIATION shall be:

a) to promote the welfare of the peoples of SOUTH ASIA and to improve their quality of life;
b) to accelerate economic growth, social progress and cultural development in the region and to provide all individuals the opportunity to live in dignity and to realise their full potentials;
c) to promote and strengthen collective self-reliance among the countries of SOUTH ASIA;
d) to contribute to mutual trust, understanding and appreciation of one another's problems;
e) to promote active collaboration and mutual assistance in the economic, social, cultural, technical and scientific fields;
f) to strengthen cooperation with other developing countries;
g) to strengthen cooperation among themselves in international forums on matters of common interests; and
h) to cooperate with international and regional organisations with similar aims and purposes.

Article 2 : Principles

1. Cooperation within the framework of the ASSOCIATION shall be based on respect for the principles of sovereign

equality, territorial integrity, political independence, non-interference in the internal affairs of other States and mutual benefit.

2. Such cooperation shall not be a substitute for bilateral and multilateral cooperation but shall complement them.
3. Such cooperation shall not be inconsistent with bilateral and multilateral obligations.

Article 3 : Meetings of the heads of State or Government

The Heads of State or Government shall meet once a year or more often as and when considered necessary by the Member States.

Article 4 : Council of Ministers

1. A Council of Ministers consisting of the Foreign Ministers of the Member States shall be established with the following functions:
   a) formulation of the policies of the Association;
   b) review of the progress of cooperation under the Association;
   c) decision on new areas of cooperation;
   d) establishment of additional mechanism under the Association as deemed necessary;
   e) decision on other matters of general interest to the Association.
2. The Council of Ministers shall meet twice a year. Extraordinary session of the Council may be held by agreement among the Member States.

Article 5 : Standing Committee

1. The Standing Committee comprising the Foreign Secretaries shall have the following functions:
   a) overall monitoring and coordination of programme of cooperation;
   b) approval of projects and programmes, and the modalities of their financing;
   c) determination of inter-sectoral priorities;
   d) mobilisation of regional and external resources;
   e) identification of new areas of cooperation based on appropriate studies.

2. The Standing Committee shall meet as often as deemed necessary.
3. The Standing Committee shall submit periodic reports to the Council of Ministers and make reference to it as and when necessary for decisions on policy matters.

Article 6 : Technical Committees

1. Technical Committees comprising representatives of Member States shall be responsible for the implementation, coordination and monitoring of the programmes in their respective areas of cooperation.
2. They shall have the following terms of reference:
   a) determination of the potential and the scope of regional cooperation in agreed areas;
   b) formulation of programmes and preparation of projects;
   c) determination of financial implications of sectoral programmes;
   d) formulation of recommendations regarding apportionment of costs;
   e) implementation and coordination of sectoral programmes;
   f) monitoring of progress in implementation.
3. The Technical Committees shall submit periodic reports to the Standing Committee.
4. The Chairmanship of the Technical Committees shall normally rotate among Member States in alphabetical order every two years.
5. The Technical Committees may, inter-alia, use the following mechanisms and modalities, if and when considered necessary:
   a) meetings of heads of national technical agencies;
   b) meetings of experts in specific fields;
   c) contact amongst recognised centres of excellence in the region.

Article 7 : Action Committees

The Standing Committee may set up Action Committees comprising Member States concerned with implementation of projects involving more than two but not all Member States.

Article 8 : Secretariat

There shall be a Secretariat of the Association.

Article 9 : Financial Arrangements

1. The contribution of each Member State towards financing of the activities of the ASSOCIATION shall be voluntary.
2. Each Technical Committee shall make recommendations for the apportionment of costs of implementing the programmes proposed by it.
3. In case sufficient financial resources cannot be mobilised within the region for funding activities of the association, external financing from appropriate sources may be mobilised with the approval of or by the Standing Committee.

Article 10 : General Provisions

1. Decisions at all levels shall be taken on the basis of unanimity.
2. Bilateral and contentious issues shall be excluded from the deliberations.

In faith whereof we have set our hands and seals hereunto. Done in Dhaka, Bangladesh, on this the eighth day of December of the year one thousand nine hundred eighty five.

Hussain Muhammad Ershad President of the People's Republic of Bangladesh, Jigme Singye Wangchuk King of Bhutan, Rajiv Gandhi Prime Minister of the Republic of India, Maumoon Abdul Gayoom President of the Republic of Maldives, Birendra Bir Bikram Shah Dev King of Nepal, Muhammad Zia-ul-Haq President of the Islamic Republic of Pakistan, Junius Richard Jayewardene President of Democratic Socialist Republic of Sri Lanka.

Annexure 2

Dhaka Summit—1985

Declaration

Salient points of the Dhaka Declaration issued on 8th December, 1985.

Introduction

1. The Heads of State or Government underscored the historic significance of their first ever South Asian Summit meeting. They considered it to be a tangible manifestation of their determination to cooperate regionally, to work together towards finding solutions towards their common problems in a spirit of friendship, trust and mutual understanding and to the creation of an order based on mutual respect, equity and shared benefits.
2. The Heads of State or Government reaffirmed that their fundamental goal was to accelerate the process of economic and social development in their respective countries through the optimum utilization of their human and material resources, so as to promote the welfare and prosperity of their peoples and to improve their quality of life. They were conscious that peace and security was an essential prerequisite for the realization of this objective.
3. Acknowledged that the countries of South Asia, who constituted one-fifth of humanity, were faced with the formidable challenges posed by poverty, underdevelopment, low levels of production, unemployment and pressure of population compounded by exploitation of the past and

other adverse legacies. They felt that, bound as their countries were by many common values rooted in their social, ethnic, cultural and historical traditions, regional cooperation provided a logical response to these problems. They were conscious of their individual and regional strengths, their potential as a huge market, their substantial human and natural resources and the complementarities of their economies. They were confident that with effective regional cooperation, they could make optimum use of these capacities for the benefit of their peoples, accelerate the pace of their economic development and enhance their national and collective self-reliance. They were convinced that their countries, which had made important contributions to the enrichment of human civilization, could together play their due role in international relations and influence decisions which affected them.

4. Emphasised that strengthening of regional cooperation in South Asia required greater involvement of their peoples. They agreed to increase interaction and further promote people-to-people contacts at various levels among their countries. To this end, they decided to take steps to create awareness and public opinion in the region.

5. Welcomed the progress already made in the implementation of the Integrated Programme of Action in the nine mutually agreed areas. They expressed their desire to consolidate and further expand cooperative efforts within an appropriate institutional framework in a spirit of partnership and equality.

6. The leaders were convinced that they could effectively pursue their individual and collective objectives and improve the quality of life of their peoples only in an atmosphere of peace and security. In this context, they expressed concern at the deteriorating international political situation. They were alarmed at the unprecedented escalation of arms race particularly in its nuclear aspect. They recognized that mankind today was confronted with the threat of self extinction arising from a massive accumulation of the most destructive weapons ever produced. The arms race

intensified international tension and violated the principles of the UN Charter. The leaders called upon the nuclear weapons-states for urgent negotiations for a comprehensive Test Ban Treaty leading to the complete cessation of testing, production and deployment of nuclear weapons. In this connection, they welcomed the recent meeting between President Reagan and General Secretary Gorbachev in Geneva and expressed the hope that the meeting would have a positive effect on international peace and security.

7. The Heads of State or Government were conscious of the historic importance of the Dhaka Summit and reiterated their conviction that the launching of the South Asian Association for Regional Cooperation (SAARC), which they had established at this meeting, would place regional cooperation on a firm foundation, play an important role in accelerating the pace of economic and social development of their countries, promote the objectives of individual and collective self reliance and further the cause of peace, progress and stability in their region and the world.

Annexure 3

Bangalore Summit—1986

Salient points of the Bangalore Declaration issued on November 17, 1986.

1. The Heads of State or Government reiterated their desire of promoting peace, stability, amity and progress in the region through strict adherence to the principles of the United Nations Charter and Non-alignment, particularly respect for the principles of sovereign equality, territorial integrity, national independence, non-use of force and non-interference in the internal affairs of other States and peaceful settlement of disputes.
2. Reaffirmed the will of their peoples and Governments to work together in accordance with the SAARC Charter to devise common policies and approaches for finding common solutions to the shared problems that all of them face. They stressed that mutual trust, goodwill and understanding must animate their cooperative effort under SAARC. Progress and prosperity in each country would redound to the benefit of others. This was what constituted the SAARC spirit.
3. The leaders reaffirmed that the principal goal of SAARC was to promote the welfare of the peoples of South Asia, to improve their quality of life, to accelerate economic growth, social programmes and cultural development in the region and to provide all individuals the opportunity to live in dignity and to realize their full potential.
4. Recalled that the countries of South Asia had been linked by age-old cultural, social and historical traditions. These had led to enriching interaction of ideas, values, culture

and philosophies. These commonalities constituted solid foundations for regional cooperation for addressing more effectively the economic and social problems.

5. Noted with satisfaction that considerable progress had been achieved in the implementation of SAARC Integrated Programme of Action. They expressed their firm commitment to consolidate and streamline further the implementation of the IPA. They agreed that a progressive movement towards more concrete and action-oriented projects and programmes was essential to ensure more tangible benefits from SAARC to the peoples of the region. The Heads of State or Government emphasized the importance of expanding cooperative endeavours under SAARC. They welcomed the establishment of the Technical Committees on Women in Development, and on the Prevention of Drug Trafficking and Drug Abuse.
6. Welcomed the signing of the Memorandum of Understanding on the establishment of the SAARC Secretariat by the Council of Ministers and their decision to locate the Secretariat in Kathmandu and appoint Ambassador Abul Ahsan of Bangladesh as the first Secretary-General of SAARC. They were convinced that the establishment of the Secretariat would assist in the coordination of SAARC activities and more fruitful implementation of its programmes and projects.
7. Recognised that meeting the needs of all children was the principal means of human resources development. Children should, therefore, be given the highest priority in national development planning. The Heads of State or Government underlined the importance of enhancing public consciousness and building a national political consensus on the rights of the children. In this context they called for an early conclusion and adoption of the UN Convention on the Rights of the Child.
8. Agreed that co-operation among SAARC States was vital if terrorism was to be prevented and eliminated from the region. They unequivocally condemned all acts, methods and practices of terrorism as criminal and deplored their impact on life and

property, social economic development, political stability, regional and international peace and co-operation. They recognized the importance of the principles laid down in UN Resolution 2625 which among others required that each State should refrain from organizing, instigating, assisting or participating in acts of civil strife or terrorist acts in another State or acquiesing in organized activities within its territory directed towards the commission of such acts.

9. Expressed their concern at the crisis facing the United Nations system. They reiterated their deep commitment to the purposes and principles of the United Nations Charter and their support for and faith in the United Nations as the most important international forum for addressing issues of peace, disarmament and development and an essential instrument for bringing about justice and equity in international political and economic relations. They resolved to concert their efforts in all multilateral fora within the United Nations system to preserve and strengthen the Organisation and to prevent erosion of its role, functions and principles.

10. Reiterated their deep commitment to the principles and objectives of the Non-aligned Movement and underlined the historic role the Movement had been playing in strengthening international peace, promoting development, establishing equitable and just economic relations and strengthening international co-operation in all fields.

11. The leaders of the South Asian countries were convinced that an environment of peace, security and respect for international law was essential for their growth and stability. Unfortunately, this environment had become increasingly adverse for the pursuit of their cherished goals. The international political scene was marred by strife and tension due to Great Power policies and practices of domination and intervention as well as the increased resort to the threat or use of force, aggression, occupation, pressure, economic coercion and interference in flagrant violation of the principles and purposes of the Charter of the United Nations. The arms race, particularly the nuclear arms race,

had escalated to a point where it jeopardizes the most fundamental of all human rights - the right to live.

12. The Heads of State or Government were deeply concerned that the world economy continued to be in the throes of crisis, with particularly harsh and severe consequences for the economies and development prospects and aspirations of the developing countries. They endorsed the Declaration of the SAARC Ministerial Meeting on International Economic Issues held in Islamabad and its analysis of the exceptionally adverse external economic environment which retards the development of the South Asian and other developing countries. These negative factors include depressed commodity prices, rising protectionism, global recession, lower export earnings, net outflow of financial resources from developing countries and an aggravated debt crisis.

13. Noted with satisfaction that at the SAARC Ministerial Meeting on International Economic Issues a number of priority objectives of the SAARC countries have been identified. These include: enlarged concessional assistance, the doubling in three years of the financial flows for the development of developing countries, amelioration of official debts, trade liberalization, especially in textiles and agriculture, commodity price stabilization, transfer of technology and special treatment for least developed SAARC countries. The Heads of State or Government agreed that the SAARC members should closely and regularly consult and co-operate in relevant international economic conferences and institutions in order to promote the above mentioned objectives. They recognised that an important opportunity in this context would be provided by UNCTAD VII.

14. Reiterated their determination and will to expand and strengthen their co-operation under SAARC. They underlined their belief that SAARC reflected a resurgence of the South Asian consciousness which had inspired the peoples of this region over several millenia. The leaders expressed their deep conviction that South Asian regional co-operation would not only have a salutary effect on bilateral relations between the countries of the region, but also impart strength and stability to these relations.

Annexure 4

Kathmandu Summit—1987

Salient points of the Kathmandu Declaration issued on November 4, 1987.

1. The Heads of State or Government recalled with pleasure the launching of SAARC which marked the beginning of a new era of regional cooperation for the promotion of peace and progress, mutual trust and goodwill in South Asia and underlined the importance of annual meetings at their level, as a prime mover, in consolidating and accelerating the pace and process of overall social, economic and cultural development in the region. They renewed their commitment to the SAARC Charter. They reiterated their desire of promoting peace, stability, amity and progress in the region through strict adherence to the principles of the United Nations Charter and Nonalignment, particularly respect for the principles of sovereign equality, territorial integrity, national independence, non-use of force and non-interference in the internal affairs of other States and peaceful settlement of disputes.
2. Emphasized that a fundamental goal of SAARC was to promote the welfare of the peoples of South Asia and to provide them with the opportunity to live in dignity and realise their full potential. They were conscious of the formidable tasks ahead of eradicating poverty, hunger, disease, illiteracy and unemployment and alleviation of environmental degradation facing South Asia today. They

were convinced that the peoples and governments of South Asia could, acting in unison, surmount these challenges.

3. Expressed their faith in and commitment to the principles and purposes enshrined in the United Nation Charter. They further believed that the United Nations has an important role to play in promoting universal trust, understanding and concerted actions for the attainment of lasting peace, global development and general disarmament. They reiterated their concern at the crisis facing the United Nations. They expressed their commitment to the multilateral negotiating process and called upon all states to help strengthen the UN system. They reaffirmed their belief that SAARC will reinforce this process by promoting South Asian cooperation.
4. Also reaffirmed their deep commitment to the principles and objectives of the Non-Aligned Movement.
5. The Heads of State or Government believed that the escalation in military expenditure was a major constraint on world development. In this regard they noted that the UN Conference on Disarmament and Development had clearly established a link between disarmament and development and had provided a valuable framework for future action in this vital area.
6. They welcomed the understanding reached between the United States and the Soviet Union on Intermediate Nuclear Forces. This should be a precursor of further accords between them to reduce drastically their strategic nuclear missiles and to refrain from extending the arms race to Outer Space. They called for the early conclusion in the Geneva Conference on Disarmament of a Comprehensive Test Ban Treaty and a Convention to Ban Chemical Weapons. They declared their intention to continue their efforts to contribute to the realisation of the objective of halting the nuclear arms race and eliminating nuclear weapons. They declared their resolve to support every effort to conclude a treaty prohibiting vertical and horizontal proliferation of nuclear weapons.

7. The Heads of State or Government reviewed with satisfaction the progress made so far in the implementation of the SAARC Integrated Programme of Action and emphasised the need to further consolidate and streamline the process.
8. Expressed satisfaction at the launching of the SAARC Audio Visual Exchange programme coinciding with the opening of the Third SAARC Summit in Kathmandu. While taking note of the dates for the institution of the SAARC Chairs, Fellowships and Scholarships and the commencement of Organised Tourism among SAARC member countries, they directed that the schemes for the SAARC Documentation Centre and the SAARC Youth Volunteer Programme be implemented at the earliest.
9. Noted with satisfaction the signing of the Agreement establishing a South Asian Food Security Reserve and expressed confidence that this will provide a much-needed cushion against food shortages and scarcity situations in the region.
10. Expressed happiness at the signing of the SAARC Regional Convention on Suppression of Terrorism and considered it a historic step towards the prevention and elimination of terrorism from the region. In this regard, they also reiterated their unequivocal condemnation of all acts, methods and practice of terrorism as criminal and expressed their abhorrence of their impact on life and property, socio-economic development, political stability, regional peace and cooperation.
11. The Heads of State or Government were conscious of the aspirations of the peoples of South Asia to communicate and cooperate with each other at the people-to-people level. They recognised that academics, researchers, non-governmental organizations and others have an important role to play in promoting the SAARC spirit and giving impetus to regional programmes and projects. They further observed that the interest and enthusiasm so far demonstrated by the increased interactions and exchange of information at the inter-governmental level should be capitalised and translated into tangible programmes and

projects. They recognised the vast potential for the generation of friendship, goodwill and trust through interactions between the peoples which would foster harmonious relations in South Asia.

12. The Heads of State or Government were conscious that SAARC should be increasingly oriented to the people's needs and aspirations so that the masses of the region could be drawn to a greater extent into the mainstream of SAARC activities. This, they firmly held, would help bring about a qualitative improvement in the general atmosphere of the region contributing to peace, friendship and cooperation in the areas.

Annexure 5

Islamabad Summit—1988

Salient points of the Islamabad Declaration issued on 31st December, 1988.

1. The Heads of State of Government expressed their deep satisfaction at the progress achieved by the Association since the last Summit. They reiterated their commitment to the SAARC Charter and renewed their determination to cooperate in promoting the welfare of the peoples of South Asia and to improving their quality of life by eradicating poverty, hunger, disease, illiteracy, unemployment and environmental degradation.
2. They recalled that their countries were linked by cultural, social and historical ties and they had at their disposal substantial human and natural resources. They recognised that these provided a sound basis as well as immense opportunities for regional cooperation. They therefore expressed their determination to make optimal use of their resources for the benefit of their people by working jointly to pursue their shared objectives. They were aware that by acting in concert they could realise the full potential for regional progress, taking into account complementarities and growing inter-dependence.
3. The leaders endorsed the decision of the Council of Ministers that any country in the region subscribing to the objectives and principles of the SAARC Charter may be admitted as a member of the Association by a unanimous decision of the Heads of State of Government.

4. Expressed satisfaction at the progress so far made in the implementation of the SAARC Integrated Programme of Action. They underlined the need for closer cooperation in the activities undertaken under this programme. They took note of the measures to streamline and re-orient various SAARC activities to make them more action-oriented so as to improve the quality of life of their peoples. They directed that the Secretary General may submit recommendations to the Standing Committee which should in turn decide how to streamline SAARC activities and make them more effective. They welcomed the establishment of the SAARC Agricultural Information Centre (SAIC), as well as the steps being taken for the establishment of other regional institutions.
5. The Heads of State of Government expressed satisfaction that the South Asian Food Security Reserve had become operational on 12 August, 1988. The Reserve would serve as a cushion against food shortages and was a tangible manifestation of the spirit of cooperation in the region.
6. Noted with satisfaction that the SAARC Convention on Suppression of Terrorism had been ratified and had come into effect on 22 August, 1988, thus reflecting the sincere desire on the part of the Member States to enter into meaningful cooperation to eliminate the scourge of terrorism from the South Asian region. They called for the adoption of enabling measures by Member States to implement the Convention at the earliest.

Annexure 6

Male Summit—1990

Salient points of the Male Declaration issued on 23rd November, 1990.

1. The Heads of State or Government reiterated that cooperation among the countries of South Asia was necessary for improving the quality of life of the peoples of the region. They recalled their conviction that the objectives of peace and stability in South Asia could be best served by fostering mutual understanding, cooperation and good neighbourly relations. They reaffirmed their commitment to the purposes and principles of the South Asian Association for Regional Cooperation and renewed their resolve to intensify cooperation under its aegis in pursuit of their common objectives.
2. Expressed satisfaction that the launching of SAARC in 1985 and the initiatives under the Integrated Programme of Action for strengthening regional cooperation in South Asia had generated much enthusiasm and hope in their peoples, and that the South Asian consciousness necessary for the success of regional cooperation was gradually permeating the region. They reiterated their resolve to make optimal use of the positive forces of goodwill, trust and understanding existing among their peoples and to turn SAARC into a dynamic instrument for achieving its objectives and creating an order based on mutual respect, equity, cooperation and shared benefits.

3. Recognizing that environment had emerged as a major global concern, the Heads of State or Government noted with alarm the unprecedented climatic changes predicted by the Intergovernmental Panel on Climate Change (IPCC).
4. The Heads of State or Government approved the recommendations of the Council of Ministers regarding Special SAARC Travel Document and decided to launch the scheme.
5. The Heads of State or Government expressed concern that Member States were compelled to divert their scarce resources in combating terrorism. They called for expeditious enactment of enabling measures for the implementation of the SAARC Regional Convention on Suppression of Terrorism. They also urged Member States to continue to cooperate in accordance with the Convention.
6. The Heads of State or Government, noting the vital importance of biotechnology for the longterm food security of developing countries as well as for medicinal purposes, decided that cooperation should be extended to this field and, in particular, to the exchange of expertise in genetic conservation and maintenance of germplasm banks. In this connection, they welcomed India's offer of training facilities and agreed that cooperation in the cataloguing of genetic resources stored in different SAARC countries would be mutually beneficial. Taking note of the proposal made by the Group of Fifteen Developing Countries (G15) for the establishment of a gene bank for developing countries, they agreed to participate in this venture.
7. The Heads of State or Government welcomed the idea of setting up of a Fund for regional projects which could make available credit on easy terms for the identification and development of regional projects. They agreed that representatives of the national development banks of the Member Countries should get together to work out the precise modalities for the source of funds and the manner

in which these could be related to joint venture projects. They accepted India's offer to host this meeting.

8. Noted with satisfaction that the initiative of the Government of the Maldives for the Protection and Security of Small States at the UN in 1989, which they all supported, had also received overwhelming support of the international community. They agreed that, because of their particular problems, small states merited special measures of support in safeguarding their independence and territorial integrity.

Annexure 7

Colombo Summit—1991

Salient points of the Colombo Declaration issued on 21st December, 1991.

1. The Heads of State or Government reaffirmed their commitment to the principles and objectives enshrined in the Charter of SAARC. They resolved to promote regional cooperation for the benefit of their people, in a spirit of mutual accommodation, with full respect for the principles of sovereign equality, independence and territorial integrity of all States and in strict adherence to the principles of nonuse of force, the peaceful settlement of disputes and noninterference in each other's internal affairs. They also reiterated their commitment to the principles of the United Nations Charter and the Nonaligned Movement.
2. The Heads of State or Government also exchanged views on the priorities of their respective national economies. They identified, for the further development of their economies, the importance of securing less restrictive trading and marketing opportunities for their products, more extensive technology and resource transfers to South Asia, debt relief and access on favourable and on more concessional terms to resources from multilateral financial institutions. They agreed to keep an open dialogue on these aspects through mutual consultations.
3. In the context of the SAARC Charter objective to strengthen cooperation among Member States in international fora, the Heads of State or Government resolved to encourage

consultations among delegations of SAARC countries at all international fora and to promote articulation of joint positions where such action would be in the interests of all. They felt that the development of a collective position in international fora would accord them greater credibility and enhance the international profile of South Asia.

4. The Heads of State or Government welcomed the Report presented by the Chairman of the Fifth SAARC Summit, the President of Maldives, and the Head of Government of Bangladesh on the adoption of a more business like and functional approach in the conduct of SAARC meetings, as well as the Report submitted by the Chairman of the Ninth Session of the Council of Ministers, the Foreign Minister of Maldives, on rationalizing SAARC activities. The Heads of State or Government also considered other proposals submitted by Member States and by the Secretariat to make the Association a more effective instrument for the realisation of the aspirations of the people of South Asia.

5. The Heads of State or Government requested the Standing Committee at its Special Session to study the question of cooperation between SAARC and appropriate international and regional organizations taking into account the evolution of SAARC activities in the core economic areas and to report to the Eleventh Session of the Council of Ministers.

6. Noted the progress made by the Integrated Programme of Action (IPA) in expanding to cover a number of sectors crucial for the economic and social progress of the peoples of South Asia. They were of the view that the challenge facing the IPA was to achieve its identified targets within specific time periods. The Heads of State or Government welcomed the proposals made and the discussions proceeding in SAARC to heighten the effectiveness of the IPA.

7. Recognising that a great majority of these people remain below the poverty line, they evinced keen interest in a "Daal-

Bhaat", or assured nutritional standards approach towards the satisfaction of basic needs of the South Asian poor.

8. The Heads of State or Government decided to establish an independent South Asian Commission on Poverty Alleviation consisting of eminent persons from each SAARC Member State to conduct an indepth study of diverse experiences of the seven countries on poverty alleviation, and to report to the Seventh Summit, their recommendations on the alleviation of poverty in South Asia.

9. The Heads of State or Government approved that the Inter Governmental Group (IGG) set up on the recommendation of the Committee on Economic Cooperation should formulate and seek agreement on an institutional framework under which specific measures for trade liberalisation among SAARC Member States could be furthered. It should also examine the Sri Lankan proposal to establish a SAARC Preferential Trade Arrangement (SAPTA) by 1997. They directed that the IGG should meet as early as possible and report to the Committee on Economic Cooperation.

10. The Heads of State or Government welcomed the recommendation on the establishment of a shelter information network to be called "SHELTERNET".

11. The Heads of State or Government welcomed the adoption of the Plan of Action for 1991 2000 A.D. as the SAARC Decade of the Girl Child. They requested the Council of Ministers to ensure an annual review of the status of implementation of the Plan of Action during the decade.

12. The Heads of State or Government expressed serious concern on the spread of terrorism in the region affecting the security and stability of all Member States and unequivocally condemned all acts, methods and practices of terrorism as criminal. They deplored all such acts for their impact on life, property, socio-economic development and political stability as well as on regional and international peace and cooperation.

13. They recognised that cooperation among SAARC States was vital if terrorism was to be prevented and eliminated from the region. In this regard they urged Member States to take all necessary measures to give full effect to their obligations under the SAARC Regional Convention on Suppression of Terrorism. They stressed in particular, the urgent need for the expeditious enactment of enabling legislation by those Member States which had not yet done so, for the implementation of the Convention and the need for a constant dialogue and interaction among the concerned agencies of Member States, including submission of periodic recommendations to the Council of Ministers.
14. The Heads of State or Government welcomed the setting up of a SAARC Fund for Regional Projects (SFRP) for identification and development of regional projects. They noted that the Fund would be managed by a Regional Council of Development Financing Institutions of the SAARC Member States and that the First Meeting of the Council would take place in India.
15. The Heads of State or Government requested the Secretary-General of SAARC to set up a panel of experts to examine the proposal of His Majesty the King of Bhutan to undertake a prefeasibility study for the establishment of a South Asian Development Fund, taking into account the views of all Member States.
16. The Heads of State or Government noted with satisfaction that the Scheme in regard to the entitled categories of Members of Parliament, Judges of the Supreme Court, Heads of national academic institutions and the accompanying spouses and dependent children will become operational from 1st March, 1992. They called for expeditious action to implement the scheme as well as to consider other categories eligible for exemption.

Annexure 8

Dhaka Summit—1993

Salient points of the Dhaka Declaration issued on 11th April, 1993.

1. The Heads of State or Government reiterated their commitment to the principles and objectives of the South Asian Association for Regional Cooperation (SAARC), to the five principles of peaceful co-existence, the UN Charter and non-alignment. The Heads of State or Government noted the progress achieved in regional cooperation under the aegis of SAARC. They felt that time was now opportune for SAARC to provide a further dynamic impetus to activities in the core areas of economic, social and cultural cooperation in the SAARC region.
2. The Heads of State or Government welcomed the Report of the Independent South Asian Commission on Poverty Alleviation established at the Colombo Summit. The Report provided valuable insight and illustrative examples of successful poverty alleviation programmes in individual Member States.
3. The Heads of State or Government committed their Governments unequivocally to the eradication of poverty in South Asia, preferably by the year 2002 A.D. through an Agenda of Action.
4. The Heads of State or Government stressed that within the overall conceptual approach of 'Daal-Bhaat', the right to work and the right to primary education should receive priority.

Trade, Manufactures and Services

5. The Heads of State or Government reaffirmed the need to liberalize trade as early as possible through a step by step approach. They underscored that this should be done in such a manner that all countries in the region could share the benefits of trade expansion equitably.

6. In this context, the Heads of State or Government welcomed the finalization of the framework Agreement on SAARC Preferential Trading Arrangement (SAPTA). They expressed their deep satisfaction over the signing of the framework Agreement. The Leaders stressed that all necessary steps should be taken to begin the first round of trade negotiations to exchange trade preferences among Member States under the Arrangement.

7. The Heads of State or Government further underlined the critical importance of urgently promoting intra-regional cooperation, particularly in the area of manufactures in order to enhance the productive capacity of the Member Countries, and to promote sustained growth and development to prevent the marginalization of South Asia's trade interest in the larger global context.

8. Recognizing the sovereign right of all countries to promote, adopt and implement their population policies and mindful of their cultures, values and traditions, the Heads of State or Government stressed the need to integrate demographic objectives and population strategies in the formulation of the development strategies of Member Countries. In this context, they also noted the importance of adequate investment in the health and education sectors for the success of their population programmes. They agreed that cooperation among Member States should be strengthened, both through sharing experiences and in other practical ways, to enhance their capacity to deal with the population problem.

9. The Heads of State or Government emphasized that cooperation in the field of Science and Technology was of

utmost importance in order to accelerate the process of development in South Asia.

10. The Heads of State or Government reiterated their unequivocal condemnation of all acts, methods and practices of terrorism as criminal. They strongly deplored the adverse consequences of terrorism.

11. They noted with grave concern that the efforts to combat the growing threat of terrorism had resulted in the diversion of valuable scarce resources from urgent development programmes.

12. The leaders reiterated the need to give high priority to the enactment of enabling legislation at the national level to give effect to the SAARC Regional Convention on Suppression of Terrorism, while urging the Member States which had not yet done so, to make every effort to finalize this matter before the Eighth SAARC Summit.

Drug Trafficking and Drug Abuse

13. The Heads of State or Government reiterated their grave concern at the growing menace of drug trafficking in the region and the aggravation of the problem of drug abuse among the South Asian population, particularly the youth.

14. The Heads of State or Government stressed the need to further promote people-to-people contact in order to ensure increased involvement of peoples of South Asia in the process of regional cooperation. In this context, they noted that the formulation of guidelines and procedures for extending recognition to regional apex bodies would facilitate participation of these bodies in promoting regional cooperation at the people-to-people level.

15. The leaders expressed the hope that the recent recognition of the SAARC Chamber of Commerce and Industry would contribute positively to enhancing

cooperation in the crucial areas of trade and economic relations.

16. The Heads of State or Government expressed their appreciation to the Government and people of India for hosting the First South Asian Festival of SAARC Countries in 1992. The Festival provided the people of the region the opportunity to share in the rich cultural heritage of South Asia. The Heads of State or Government hoped that the South Asian Festival would become a regular feature.

17. The Heads of State or Government welcomed the initiative of the Speakers of Parliaments of SAARC Countries in forming an "Association of SAARC Speakers and Parliamentarians". They were of the view that the establishment of this Association would add another important dimension to the process of regional cooperation.

South Asian Development Fund

18. The Heads of State or Government endorsed the recommendation of the Council of Ministers for the establishment of an Inter-Governmental Group (IGG) on South Asian Development Fund (SADF) on an ad-hoc basis. They directed that the IGG define in clear terms the size, structure, resources and operational modalities of the proposed Fund. They also directed the IGG to examine the complementarities between the SAARC Fund for Regional Projects (SFRP) and SADF, and their relationship, including the possibility of their merger. They welcomed the offer of the Maldives to host the meeting of IGG.

19. The Heads of State or Government were of the view that greater consultations among the delegations of SAARC Countries in all international fora on the major issues of common concern to them would be in the interest of all their countries. They felt that the development of collective positions on such issues in the international fora would

enhance the international profile of South Asia and would enable the countries in the region to articulate their position on them more effectively. They reiterated their common resolve to concert their position in all international fora and negotiations with a view to deriving maximum benefits from them in accordance with their needs and common priorities.

Observer Status

20. The Heads of State or Government decided that an Expert Group of the Member States will examine the various requests for observer status at SAARC/SAARC meetings in all its aspects on the basis of a working paper to be prepared by the Secretariat and make appropriate recommendations to the Nineteenth Session of the Standing Committee. In this respect, they welcomed the offer of Sri Lanka to host the Expert Group Meeting.

Annexure 9

New Delhi Summit—1995

Salient points of the New Delhi Declaration issued on 4th May, 1995.

1. The Heads of State or Government expressed their satisfaction on the achievements of the First Decade of SAARC and resolved to celebrate its completion of the First Decade both in the individual Member States and collectively. They endorsed the proposal of the Council of Ministers to convene a Commemorative Session of the Council on the theme "SAARC- Vision for the Second Decade" to identify the areas on which SAARC should focus in its Second Decade.
2. The Heads of State or Government reaffirmed their commitment to the eradication of poverty in South Asia, preferably by the year 2002 A.D. through an Agenda of Action.
3. The leaders endorsed the recommendations of the Finance/ Planning Ministers' Meeting held in Dhaka in July 1994, which recommended that a mechanism should be set up which would act as a forum for exchange of information on poverty eradication programmes, in the context of the policies and strategies adopted, particularly exchange of information on technologies that are relevant to efforts at poverty eradication. They agreed that this process could be strengthened by sharing and exchanging relevant studies carried out by independent research institutions and experts. This mechanism would be in the form of a three-

tier institutional structure as recommended in the Report and would meet once a year. They noted that such a mechanism has been set up enabling the procedures of exchange of information to commence and welcomed the offer of India to host the first round of the three-tier mechanism.

4. In this context, they decided to declare 1995 as the "SAARC Year of Poverty Eradication".

SAARC Preferential Trading Arrangement (SAPTA)

5. The Heads of State or Government noted with satisfaction that subsequent to the signing of the Framework Agreement on SAARC Preferential Trading Arrangement (SAPTA) during their Seventh Summit in Dhaka in April 1993, the first round of trade negotiations to exchange trade concessions among Member States has been completed. They directed that all necessary steps should be taken to facilitate ratification by all Member States and operationalise SAPTA by the end of 1995 as mandated.

6. The leaders reiterated their firm belief that the operationalisation of SAPTA will herald the beginning of a new and significant process of regional cooperation and would lend strength to SAARC as an institution for promoting the welfare of the peoples of South Asia.

7. The Heads of State or Government noted that illiteracy is one of the major causes of poverty, backwardness and social injustices and called on the Member States to initiate more concrete programmes aimed at eradicating illiteracy in the region preferably by the year 2000 A.D. They decided to observe 1996 as the "SAARC Year of Literacy".

8. The Heads of State or Government noted that although some work has been carried out in the area of disseminating information on the problems of environmental degradation and their impact on the region, progress in the implementation of the recommendations of the SAARC Regional Study on the Causes and Consequences of Natural Disasters and the Protection

and Preservation of the Environment and the Regional Study on Greenhouse Effect and its Impact on the Region, which were completed in 1992, had been slow. They stressed the importance of effective and speedy implementation of the recommendations of the two studies and requested Member States to take all necessary steps without further delay in vital areas such as sharing and developing scientific capabilities to protect and manage the environment. They further directed the Technical Committee on Environment to monitor the progress made in the implementation of the recommendations of the two studies, and submit a report to the Ninth Summit through the Council of Ministers.

Terrorism

9. The Heads of State or Government expressed serious concern on the spread of terrorism in and outside the region and reiterated their unequivocal condemnation of all acts, methods and practices of terrorism as criminal. They deplored all such acts for their ruinous impact on life, property, socio-economic development and political stability as well as on regional and international peace and cooperation.

10. The Heads of State or Government once again emphasised that highest priority should be accorded to the enactment of enabling legislation at the national level to give effect to the SAARC Regional Convention on Suppression of Terrorism. They urged Member States, which had not yet done so, to enact expeditiously enabling legislation at the national level to implement the convention and reiterated the need for a constant dialogue and interaction among the concerned agencies of Member States, including submission of periodic recommendations to the Council of Ministers.

11. They underlined that cooperation among SAARC Member States was vital if the scourge of terrorism was to be eliminated from the region.

12. The Heads of State or Government recognised that drug abuse and drug trafficking with its linkages with organised crime, illicit arms trade and terrorism continues to pose a serious threat to the security and stability in the region.
13. The leaders welcomed the ratification of the SAARC Convention on Narcotic Drugs and Psychotropic Substances by all Member States and entry into force of the Convention in September 1993. They urged all Member States to take necessary follow-up action for effective implementation of the Convention.
14. The leaders noted that SAARCLAW (an association for persons of the legal communities of SAARC countries) had been accorded recognition by SAARC. The leaders hoped that SAARCLAW would play an effective role in fostering closer cooperation among the legal communities in the region.
15. The leaders noted with satisfaction that the SAARC Chamber of Commerce and Industry (SCCI) has been functioning satisfactorily. They expressed hope that the SAARC Chamber and its constituent units in the Member States will do their utmost to promote trade and economic cooperation in the SAARC region. The leaders commended the SAARC Chamber for disseminating information on the scope, content and potentials of SAARC Preferential Trading Arrangement (SAPTA) among the business community in the region.
16. The Heads of State or Government expressed satisfaction that the SAARC Visa Exemption Scheme is being implemented smoothly and has enhanced the scope of people-to-people contacts.
17. The Heads of State or Government endorsed the establishment of a three-window South Asian Development Fund with the merger of SAARC Fund for Regional Projects and the SAARC Regional Fund and a third window for social development and infrastructure development.

18. Appreciating the role of some SAARC Member States in the UN Peace Keeping Operations in various parts of the world, the Heads of State or Government felt that such participation had contributed towards maintenance of peace and security in the world.
19. The Heads of State or Government reiterated their firm commitment to the principles and objectives of the Non-aligned Movement and underlined the continued validity and relevance of these principles and objectives in the contemporary world.
20. The Heads of State or Government noted that while the international community had successfully created the norms against chemical and biological weapons, it had, unfortunately, been unable to do the same with regard to nuclear weapons. The leaders were convinced that more needs to be done and at a far greater pace. Reiterating that the utmost priority was to be given to nuclear disarmament, given the danger posed by nuclear weapons, they urged the Conference on Disarmament to negotiate an international convention prohibiting the use or threat of use of nuclear weapons under any circumstances and undertake negotiations for the complete elimination of all nuclear weapons within a time bound framework.

Annexure 10

Male Summit—1997

Salient points of the Male Declaration issued on 14th May, 1997.

1. The Heads of State or Government reiterated their commitment to SAARC and resolved to accelerate regional cooperation in order to realise the aims and objectives of the Association. They reaffirmed their commitment to the principles enshrined in the SAARC Charter, especially to the principles of sovereign equality, territorial integrity, national independence, non-use of force and non-interference in each others' internal affairs. They were convinced that regional cooperation was indispensable in an interdependent world for the realisation of the full potential of the South Asian region.
2. The Heads of State or Government welcomed the holding of the Commemorative Session of the Council of Ministers in New Delhi in December 1995, to mark the First Decade, on the theme "SAARC - Vision for the Second Decade". They observed that over the past decade SAARC has matured as an institution and the scope and volume of cooperative activities have expanded. They expressed satisfaction that in addition to continued cooperation in agreed areas, SAARC has now moved into the core areas of economic cooperation.
3. The Heads of State or Government noted that, in the twelve years of its existence, SAARC has seen progress in various fields of its endeavour. They directed that a Group

of Eminent Persons (GEP) be constituted, with distinguished backgrounds in activities pertaining to regional cooperation, comprising one representative from each Member State, with the discretion of each Member State to appoint an additional representative. This Group, to which the SAARC Secretary-General will be invited, will undertake a comprehensive appraisal of SAARC, and identify measures including mechanisms to further vitalise and enhance the effectiveness of the Association in achieving its objectives. They further decided that the Group may develop a long-range vision and formulate a perspective plan of action including a SAARC Agenda for 2000 and Beyond which will spell out the target that can and must be achieved by the year 2020. The Group may report to the Heads of State or Government at the Tenth SAARC Summit.

4. They agreed that a climate of mutual accommodation and purposeful cooperation was needed to impart further impetus to the SAARC process during the second decade of SAARC in order to address the developmental challenges facing the region.

5. The Heads of State or Government were unequivocal in their commitment to the eradication of poverty in South Asia at the earliest, preferably by the year 2002 A.D. through an Agenda of Action.

Acceleration of Economic Cooperation

6. The Heads of State or Government noted with satisfaction the entry into force of the Agreement on SAARC Preferential Trading Arrangement (SAPTA) on 7 December, 1995. They recognised the importance of achieving a free trade area by the year 2001 A.D. and reiterated that steps towards trade liberalisation must take into account the special needs of the smaller and the Least Developed Countries and that benefits must accrue equitably.

7. While expressing satisfaction at the conclusion of the two Rounds of Trade Negotiations under SAPTA, the Heads of State or Government welcomed the decision to launch the Third Round of Trade Negotiations shortly. They agreed

that preferential tariff concessions should cover products which are being actively traded amongst Member States. They further agreed that the Third Round should deepen tariff concessions along with the removal of non-tariff barriers and structural impediments in order to move speedily towards the goal of SAFTA.

8. The leaders welcomed the holding of the First Meeting of the Commerce Ministers and the First SAARC Trade Fair in New Delhi in 1996 and noted the decision of the Commerce Ministers to meet annually. They further welcomed the offer of Pakistan to host the second SAARC Trade Fair to coincide with the SAARC Commerce Ministers' Meeting.

9. The Heads of State or Government agreed that the efforts to enhance trade and economic co-operation in the region would be further strengthened by initiating specific steps to promote and protect investment, increase complementarities in economic activities of Member States and other measures supportive of promotion of SAARC joint ventures. They also welcomed the offer of India to host a meeting on promotion and protection of investment and the offer of Pakistan to host a meeting on avoidance of double taxation. They also welcomed measures of cooperation in the areas of customs standardisation, arbitration and enhancing industrial economy and management.

10. The Heads of State or Government reaffirmed their determination to encourage the private sector in the region to contribute increasingly to the strengthening of intra-SAARC links in key areas of trade, investment and finance. They welcomed the decision by the SCCI to convene annually an Economic Cooperation Conference in conjunction with the annual meeting of SAARC Commerce Ministers and SAARC Trade Fairs.

11. The Heads of State or Government emphasised the need to make the Integrated Programme of Action (IPA) more effective through the selection of target-oriented and time-bound activities within an overall framework of enhanced

co-operation among Member States. In this context, they noted that the Secretary-General had been authorised by the Council of Ministers to constitute a Group of Experts to review the IPA.

12. The Heads of State or Government noted that Regional Centres have an important role to play in harnessing the resources and capabilities within the SAARC region in addressing specific and shared concerns of Member States. They welcomed the decision of the Council of Ministers to establish a Human Resource Development Centre in Pakistan.

Terrorism and Drug Trafficking

13. Recognising that terrorism and drug trafficking pose a serious threat to security and stability of Member States, the Heads of State or Government reiterated their firm commitment to combat these activities in the region. They emphasised the urgent need to complete enabling legislation in order to implement the SAARC Regional Conventions on Suppression of Terrorism and on Narcotic Drugs and Psychotropic Substances.

14. The Heads of State or Government recalled the adoption of the 1996 UN Declaration on Measures to Eliminate International Terrorism and urged all Member States to work towards its implementation. They called for international action to prevent the abuse of Refugee Conventions and to halt activities which help terrorist groups to collect funds for their activities in South Asia.

15. The Heads of State or Government noted the establishment of the SAARC Terrorist Offences Monitoring Desk (STOMD) and the SAARC Drug Offences Monitoring Desk (SDOMD) in Colombo. They agreed on the need to maintain regular flow of relevant information to enable the Monitoring Desks to function effectively.

16. The Heads of State or Government noted with appreciation the convening of the First SAARC Conference on Cooperation in Police Matters in Colombo during July

1996. They endorsed the outcome of the Conference, particularly, the call for sharing of expertise with regard to the different areas of police investigation and investigation of organised crime and drug related crimes. They welcomed the offer of the Maldives to host the second Conference in 1997.

17. The Heads of State or Government reiterated their conviction that enhanced people-to-people contact would contribute to strengthening mutual understanding and goodwill among the people in the region. In this context, they noted the positive contribution made by SAARC Chamber of Commerce and Industry (SCCI) and SAARCLAW.

South Asian Development Fund (SADF)

18. While expressing satisfaction that the South Asian Development Fund (SADF) had been established in June 1996, initially with its headquarters in Dhaka, Bangladesh, the Heads of State or Government recognised the need to make the Fund operational at the earliest.

19. The Heads of State or Government reiterated their commitment to develop collective SAARC positions in international fora on issues of common concern, in order to enhance the international profile of South Asia as well as to enable Member States to articulate their position on such issues in a more effective manner. In this regard, they noted with satisfaction the collective SAARC positions finalised and presented prior to the Fourth World Conference on Women held in Beijing in September 1995, HABITAT II held in Istanbul in June 1996, and World Food Summit held in Rome in November 1996. They also expressed satisfaction with the formulation of a SAARC common position before the forthcoming Special Session of the United Nations General Assembly to Review and Appraise the Implementation of Agenda 21.

Annexure 11

Colombo Summit—1998

Salient points of the Colombo Declaration issued on 31 July, 1998, in Colombo.

1. The Heads of State or Government re-affirmed their firm commitment to the objectives, principles and provisions of the Charter of the South Asian Association for Regional Cooperation (SAARC) and to the pursuit of regional cooperation on the basis of their acceptance of the principles of sovereign equality, territorial integrity of States, political independence, non-interference in each other's internal affairs, non-use of force, the peaceful settlement of all disputes and mutuality of benefit.
2. The Heads of State or Government recognized that South Asia, while reflecting a rich, complex and varied plurality of cultural and religious traditions, was heir to a profound common civilizational continuum of great antiquity which constitutes a historical basis for sustaining harmonious relations among the people of the region. They acknowledged that the SAARC process could draw more deeply from the vitality and strength of South Asia's shared cultural heritage as a source influencing and enhancing creative energies in all fields.
3. The Heads of State or Government welcomed the offer of Sri Lanka to host a meeting of the Ministers of Cultural Affairs of SAARC to prepare a practical Action Plan to network the national institutes of cultural relations and to establish a South Asian Cultural Center to promote the

distinctive arts of South Asia. They requested the Government of Sri Lanka to circulate a concept paper on the issues to be addressed by the meeting including financing arrangements for the proposed institute.

4. The Heads of State or Government reiterated their commitment to the promotion of mutual trust and understanding and, recognising that the aims of promoting peace, stability and amity and accelerated socio-economic cooperation may best be achieved by fostering good neighbourly relations, relieving tensions and building confidence, agreed that a process of informal political consultations would prove useful in this regard. The Heads of State or Government further recognized that this process would contribute to the appreciation of each other's problems and perceptions as well as for decisive action in agreed areas of regional cooperation.

5. The Heads of State or Government continued their review of the nature, extent, and effectiveness of the cooperative activities of SAARC. They considered the Report and Recommendations of the Group of Eminent Persons mandated by the Ninth Summit in Male to undertake a comprehensive appraisal of SAARC and to develop an Agenda for 2000 and beyond. They expressed appreciation for the Chairman of the Ninth Summit, His Excellency Mr. Maumoon Abdul Gayoom, the President of the Maldives, for convening the Group of Eminent Persons (GEP) and encouraging them to complete their work within the time-frame given to them by the Ninth SAARC Summit.

6. The Heads of State or Government noted the initiation of links between SAARC and economic unions and trading groups that were emerging in the wake of globalization and liberalization and considered how best relationships of mutual benefit could be established.

7. Against this background of the need to address systemic issues, they agreed on the vital imperative for strengthened cooperation among SAARC Members to identify, analyze and effectively contend with the complex multi-faceted challenges inherent in the global economic environment

that is changing so radically, particularly in this last decade preceding the new millennium. They acknowledged the need to enhance the collective capacity of SAARC in respect of policy analysis, with a specific emphasis on international financial, monetary, trade and investment issues and their domestic ramifications.

8. They stressed the need for more efficient capacity building to enable informed decision-making in these areas to enable innovative collective intervention to safeguard South Asian interests in international negotiations, as well as to develop some edge for effective leverage in such negotiations. The Heads of State or Government agreed on the urgent need for harnessing the rich intellectual and resource capacity of South Asia for this purpose.

Acceleration of Economic Cooperation

9. The Heads of State or Government assessed progress made in the two rounds of negotiations already undertaken under SAPTA. They decided that the third round should be concluded well before the Twenty-first Session of the Council of Ministers. The Heads of State or Government decided that to accelerate progress in the next round of SAPTA negotiations, deeper preferential tariff concessions should be extended to products which are being actively traded, or are likely to be traded, among Members; that discriminatory practices and non-tariff barriers should be simultaneously removed on items in respect of which tariff concessions are granted or have been granted earlier. Measures to remove structural impediments should also be taken in order to move speedily towards the goal of SAFTA. They also directed that domestic content requirements under SAPTA Rules of Origin should be reduced and that the SAPTA Committee of Participants should meet by mid-October '98 in Colombo to finalise the extent of reduction in keeping with the decision of the Second SAARC Commerce Ministers' Meeting. The Heads of State or Government reaffirmed that measures to enable smaller and Least Developed Countries to benefit equitably from economic liberalization were specially important.

10. The Heads of State or Government reiterated the importance of achieving SAFTA as mandated by the Ninth SAARC Summit. To this end they decided that a Committee of Experts, in consultation with Member States, be constituted with specific Terms of Reference (TOR) to work on drafting a comprehensive treaty regime for creating a free trade area. The Heads of State or Government expressed the view that such a treaty must incorporate, among other things, binding time-frames for freeing trade, measures to facilitate trade, and provisions to ensure an equitable distribution of benefits of trade to all states, especially for smaller and least developed countries, including mechanisms for compensation of revenue loss. They emphasised the importance of finalising the text of the regulatory framework by the year 2001.

11. Agreed that the benefits of economic liberalization would be more extensive and better balanced through the promotion of trade- creating joint ventures, investment and trade in services such as tourism.

12. Noted with satisfaction the outcome of the Second Meeting of the SAARC Commerce Ministers in Islamabad and welcomed their decision to coordinate SAARC's position on issues of common concern at the WTO. They welcomed in this connection the Declaration issued by the SAARC Commerce Ministers on the eve of the Second WTO Ministerial Meeting in Geneva, setting out a SAARC approach on these issues. Recognizing that critical issues would be decided at the Third WTO Ministerial Conference in the USA in 1999, the Heads of State or Government urged SAARC Commerce Ministers to work closely with a view to evolving better co-ordinated positions on all issues. They directed the Consultative Group of SAARC Permanent Representatives to the WTO at Geneva to consult closely with like-minded countries to advance the interests of developing countries at all WTO Conferences.

13. They welcomed the contribution made by the SAARC Chamber of Commerce and Industry in facilitating the

engagement of the private sector in regional economic interaction as well as initiating linkages with other regions for the purpose of promoting SAARC exports. The Heads of State or Government noted that a document entitled "Road Map to SAFTA" was presented by the President of the SAARC Chamber of Commerce and Industry (SCCI) to the Chairperson of the Twentieth Session of the Council of Ministers.

Links with International and Regional Organizations

14. The Heads of State or Government noted links initiated between SAARC and other international and regional organizations. They considered the prospects for the development of SAARC projects and programmes in association with such organizations with which SAARC has cooperative arrangements as well as through other forms of cooperation. The Heads of State or Government were of the view that priority needs to be given in establishing contact with those regional groupings which have experience in economic cooperation and functional regional cooperation.

15. The Heads of State or Government also noted proposals for developing cooperation between SAARC and individual States outside the region. They requested the Council of Ministers to consider such proposals with a view to developing such contacts on the basis of mutual benefit and for the advancement of SAARC objectives.

16. The Heads of State or Government were in agreement that illiteracy was a major impediment to economic development and social emancipation and that the eradication of illiteracy in the Region including through co-operative endeavours within SAARC must continue to be pursued resolutely.

17. The Heads of State or Government reiterated the commitment of SAARC to the eradication of poverty in the Region at the earliest possible, preferably by the year 2002. They emphasised the need to encourage maximum participation by target groups in the formulation and

implementation of poverty eradication programmes. The Heads of State or Government were of the view that such participation is essential for success of efforts in this field. They stressed the need for effective utilisation of the SAARC Three-Tier Mechanism on Poverty Eradication and in that context welcomed the offer of the Government of Pakistan to host the next meeting of the SAARC Finance/Planning Ministers under the Mechanism in October 1998.

18. The Heads of State or Government reviewed the progress made in the social sector by SAARC and determined that, in order to increase effectiveness, it would be necessary to develop, beyond national plans of action, a regional dimension of action including a specific role for SAARC. In this context, they agreed that it would be necessary for SAARC to develop a Social Charter, which would focus on drawing up targets with a broad range to be achieved across the region in the areas of poverty eradication, population stabilisation, the empowerment of women, youth mobilisation, human resource development, the promotion of health and nutrition and the protection of children. The Heads of State or Government further directed the Council of Ministers to initiate work on drawing up a Social Charter.

Tourism

19. The Heads of State or Government recognized that further efforts were required for South Asia to effectively tap the economic potential afforded by the global tourist industry as well as to encourage intra-SAARC tourism. They welcomed the convening of the First SAARC Tourism Ministers' Meeting in Colombo as a step towards this end and called for the effective implementation of its decisions, including the encouragement of active private sector participation in the promotion of tourism, both intra-regionally and internationally, simplification of visa-procedures for tourists and pilgrims, more convenient air and other travel links among SAARC countries including special regional fares and the co-ordination of activities of tour operators.

20. The Heads of State or Government identified the need to strengthen the existing air services between their respective capitals, with a view to both facilitating tourism as well as people to people contacts. They called in this regard, for an early meeting of the Chairpersons/Chief Executive Officers of the national airlines.

21. The Heads of State or Government noted that the development of a regional self-reliance capability for South Asia in scientific research and development was essential, given a global context in which barriers to the free flow of technology still remained in place. The Heads of State or Government appreciated the efforts to foster under the SAARC umbrella, collective co-operation in this field.

22. The Heads of State or Government reiterated their earlier call for the effective and rapid institutionalization of SAARC co-operation in the field of bio-technology. They pointed out that South Asia with its vast reservoir of bio-diversity and tropical climate, has substantial potential for bio-industry development on a sustainable basis. Many of the food and nutritional needs of the SAARC region could be met by the application of bio-technology. Contemporary developments in intellectual property and patent law, moreover, heightened the need for vigilance against encroachment on the regional bio-diversity heritage by external entities.

23. The Heads of State or Government condemned the exploitation of children by terrorist groups in hostilities and called for special measures for the psychological, physical and social rehabilitation of child victims. In this respect, the Heads of State or Government noted the initiative taken by Maldives in pursuance of their directive at the Ninth SAARC Summit in drafting the Convention on Regional Arrangements for the Promotion of Child Welfare in South Asia. They welcomed the offer of Maldives to hold an Expert Group Meeting to finalise the draft Convention for its adoption at the Eleventh SAARC Summit.

24. The Heads of State or Government recalled that the Ninth SAARC Summit expressed concern at the trafficking of women and children within and between countries and pledged to coordinate efforts of Member States to take effective measures to address this problem. In this context, they welcomed the finalisation of the draft text on the Regional Convention on Combating the Crime of Trafficking in Women and Children for Prostitution and noted that this would be a vital instrument in dealing with this problem. They approved that the Convention be signed at the Eleventh SAARC Summit.

25. The Heads of State or Government called for concerted endeavours for the promotion of practical programmes among South Asian countries, including through professional organizations, in the field of information and media exchanges benefitting from technological advances. Such action would help promote deeper understanding of issues common to the region, as well as to project a more balanced view of developments in the region. They welcomed the offer of India to host the First Meeting of SAARC Editors and Journalists.

Terrorism and Drug Trafficking

26. The Heads of State or Government recognized that the Member States and peoples of South Asia continue to face the serious threat of terrorism in all its forms and manifestations and drug trafficking. They reiterated their firm commitment to combat these activities in the region. They emphasized the urgent need to complete enabling legislation in order to implement the SAARC Regional Conventions on Suppression of Terrorism and on Narcotic Drugs and Psychotropic Substances.

27. The Heads of State or Government urged all Member States to enhance cooperation against terrorism, wherever, by whomever, against whoever it occurs and to fully observe and implement the SAARC Regional Convention on Terrorism.

28. The Heads of State or Government affirmed that criminal acts intended to provoke a state of terror in the general public, a group of persons or particular persons, for whatever purposes, are unjustifiable in any circumstances.

29. The Heads of State or Government recalled the adoption of the 1996 UN Declaration on Measures to Eliminate International Terrorism and urged all Member States to work towards its implementation. They called for international action to prevent the abuse of Refugee Conventions and to halt activities which help terrorist groups to collect funds for their activities in South Asia.

30. The Heads of State or Government noted the outcome of the recent UN Diplomatic Conference on the establishment of an International Criminal Court and the fact that the Conference had not addressed such issues as the crime of drug trafficking and the crime of terrorism with its use of indiscriminate violence aimed at innocent civilians and use of weapons of mass destruction. They emphasised the need to ensure that the proposed Court should respect the sovereignty of States consistent with the principle of complementarity with national jurisdiction on which the Statute of the Court is based.

Annexure 12

Kathmandu Summit—2002

Salient points of the Kathmandu declaration issued on 6th January, 2002.

1. The Heads of State or Government reaffirmed their commitment to regional cooperation through SAARC and underscored the importance of annual Summit meetings in charting common strategies for the realization of the objectives and principles set out in the Charter of the Association. Meeting for the first time at the dawn of the new millennium, they solemnly renewed their pledge to strengthen the Association and make it more cohesive, result oriented, and forward looking, by adopting clearly defined programs and effective implementation strategies in line with popular expectations. To give effect to the shared aspirations for a more prosperous South Asia, the leaders agreed to the vision of a phased and planned process eventually leading to a South Asian Economic Union.
2. Reiterating their resolve to promote South Asian regional identity and to strengthen cooperation at the international level, the Heads of State or Government also reemphasized the need to evolve common positions on issues of shared interest at the international fora.

Cooperation in the Economic Sector

3. The Heads of State or Government agreed to accelerate cooperation in the core areas of trade, finance and investment to realize the goal of an integrated South Asian

economy in a step-by-step manner. They expressed their determination to make full use of regional synergy to maximize the benefits of globalisation and liberalization and to minimize their negative impacts on the region. While recognizing that trade and economic expansion is closely inter-linked, the leaders made a commitment to widen and deepen the scope of regional networks of activities in trade and financial matters.

4. The Heads of State or Government noted with satisfaction the outcomes of the successive meetings of the SAARC Commerce Ministers aimed at enlarging the scope of cooperation in the core areas. They recognised the importance of achieving a free trade area and reaffirmed that the treaty regime for creating a free trade area must incorporate, inter alia, binding timeframes for freeing trade, measures to facilitate trade and provisions to ensure an equitable distribution of benefits of trade to all states, especially for small and least developed countries, including mechanisms for compensation of revenue loss.

5. Recognising the need to move quickly towards a South Asian Free Trade Area, the Heads of State or Government directed the Council of Ministers to finalize the text of the Draft Treaty Framework by the end of 2002. They also directed that in moving towards the goal of SAFTA, the Member States expedite action to remove tariff and non-tariff barriers and structural impediments to free trade. They also instructed to conclude the meeting of the Inter Governmental Group on Trade Liberalization for the Fourth Round of Trade Negotiations under SAPTA as early as possible as per the decision of the Tenth SAARC Summit in Colombo.

6. The Heads of State or Government renewed their commitment to encourage the participation of the private sector and assured their full support for their socially responsible economic initiatives. While welcoming the practice of holding trade fairs in cooperation with the private sector at the regional level, they appreciated the efforts of the SAARC Chamber of Commerce and Industry

to promote regional economic cooperation in the spirit of public and private sector partnership.

7. The Heads of State or Government also decided to instruct the Secretary-General to facilitate the early finalization of a regionally agreed investment framework to meet investment needs of the SAARC Member States.
8. The Heads of State or Government recognized the immense tourism potential of South Asia and underlined the need to take measures to promote South Asia as a common tourist destination through joint efforts in areas such as upgrading of infrastructure, air linkages, simplification and harmonization of administrative procedures and training and joint marketing.
9. The Heads of State or Government reiterated the need for an early finalisation of the SAARC Social Charter and instructed the Inter Governmental Expert Group to expedite their work on the basis of the draft to be submitted by the Secretary-General, as a working paper for its consideration and to complete the draft framework of the Charter as early as possible for consideration at the next meeting of the Council of Ministers. In drawing up the Charter, they also directed the Council of Ministers to include the important areas of poverty eradication, population stabilization, the empowerment of women, youth mobilization, human resources development, the promotion of health and nutrition and the protection of children as decided at the Tenth Summit.
10. The Heads of State or Government agreed to establish, on the basis of recommendations of the Regional Task Force responsible for the implementation of the provisions of the SAARC Convention on Preventing and Combating Trafficking in Women and Children for Prostitution, a voluntary fund with contributions from Member States, individuals, and donor countries and agencies for the rehabilitation and reintegration of the victims of trafficking.
11. The Heads of State or Government were of the view that stability, peace and security in South Asia should be

promoted together with efforts to improve the global security environment. They underscored their commitment to general and complete disarmament including nuclear disarmament on a universal basis, under effective international control. They agreed that global non-proliferation goals could not be achieved in the absence of progress towards nuclear disarmament and in this context called upon all nuclear weapon states, whether party or non-party to the NPT, to engage constructively through a transparent and credible process of negotiations at the Conference on Disarmament. The leaders also recognized the linkage between disarmament and development.

12. The Heads of State or Government recognized that due to their particular vulnerability, small states require special measures for support from the international community for the safeguarding of their sovereign independence and territorial integrity.

13. The Heads of State or Government were convinced that terrorism, in all its forms and manifestations, is a challenge to all states and to all of humanity, and cannot be justified on ideological, political, religious or on any other ground. The leaders agreed that terrorism violates the fundamental values of the United Nations and the SAARC Charter and constitutes one of the most serious threats to international peace and security in the Twenty-first century.

14. The Heads of State or Government emphasized the need for the urgent conclusion of a Comprehensive Convention on Combating International Terrorism. They also emphasized that international co-operation to combat terrorism should be conducted in conformity with the UN Charter, international law and relevant international conventions.

15. The Heads of State or Government reiterated their support to the United Nations Security Council Resolution 1373 of September 28, 2001, and affirmed their determination to redouble efforts, collectively as well as individually, to prevent and suppress terrorism in all its forms and

manifestations, including by increased cooperation and full implementation of the relevant international Conventions relating to terrorism to which they are parties. In this context, they called on all states to prevent and suppress the financing of terrorist acts by criminalizing the collection of funds for such acts and refraining from organizing, instigating, assisting or participating in terrorist acts in states or acquiescing in organized activities within its territory directed towards the commission of such acts. The leaders reaffirmed that the fight against terrorism in all its forms and manifestations has to be comprehensive and sustained.

16. The Heads of State or Government were unanimous in recognizing the distinct ominous link between terrorism, drug-trafficking, money laundering and other trans-national crimes and emphasized the need to coordinate efforts at the national and regional levels to strengthen the global response to this serious challenge and threat to international security. They called upon the international community to assist Member States of SAARC to deal effectively with the adverse economic effects of terrorism in general and to meet the rising insurance and security related costs in particular.

17. The Heads of State or Government reaffirmed their commitment to SAARC Regional Convention on Suppression of Terrorism, which, among others, recognizes the seriousness of the problem of terrorism as it affects the security, stability, and development of the region. They also reiterated their firm resolve to accelerate the enactment of enabling legislation within a definite time-frame for the full implementation of the Convention, together with strengthening of SAARC Terrorist Offences Monitoring Desk and the SAARC Drug Offences Monitoring Desk in an effective manner.

Report of the Group of Eminent Persons

18. The leaders noted with appreciation that the Report of the Group of Eminent Persons (GEP) was an important

contribution in the on-going process of introspection into the functioning of the Association as well as in setting out a perspective plan of action for that purpose. They endorsed the report of the Council of Ministers on the implementation of the recommendations of the GEP Report, and directed the Council of Ministers to undertake a review of progress in this regard.

Enhancing Political Cooperation

19. The Heads of State or Government reaffirmed their commitment to the promotion of mutual trust and understanding and, recognizing that the aims of promoting peace, stability and amity and accelerated socio-economic cooperation may best be achieved by fostering good neighbourly relations, relieving tensions and building confidence, agreed that a process of informal consultations would prove useful in this regard. The leaders further recognized that this process would contribute to the appreciation of each other's problems and perceptions as well as for decisive action in agreed areas of regional cooperation. They underlined the importance of informal political consultations in promoting mutual understanding and reinforcing the confidence building process among the Member States.

Sub-regional Cooperation

20. The Heads of State or Government reaffirmed the validity of the idea of encouraging the development of specific projects relevant to the individual needs of three or more Member States under the provisions of Articles VII and X of the SAARC Charter.

South Asian Development Fund (SADF)

21. The Heads of State or Government underlined the urgent need to make the South Asian Development Fund operational by making utilization of the existing funds. They also instructed the Secretary-General to submit a proposal for seeking possible assistance from regional and international sources for the implementation of specific regional poverty alleviation priority projects.

People-to-People Contact

22. The Heads of State or Government were unanimous in recognizing the need for further promoting a sense of regional identity amongst the peoples of the region. The leaders lauded the roles played by intellectuals, professionals and eminent persons in promoting people-to-people contacts within the region and agreed to encourage such endeavours as a healthy sign of regional cohesion and fraternity. In this context, they took note of the activities of the SAARCLAW including other recognized bodies. They also took note of the First Meeting of the Chief Election Commissioners of SAARC Countries held in Kathmandu in February 1999, and appreciated the initiative on free and fair election. The leaders instructed the Secretary-General to collect on a regular basis study reports and other relevant documents and information from the civil society on matters relating to regional cooperation for dissemination to Member States.

SAARC Award

23. The Heads of State or Government noted with appreciation the proposal made by Nepal to institute a SAARC Award to honour the outstanding work of individuals and organizations within the region in the fields of peace, development, poverty alleviation and regional cooperation, and requested His Majesty's Government of Nepal to submit a concept paper for consideration by the next session of the Council of Ministers.

Annexure 13

Islamabad Summit—2004

Salient points of the Islamabad Declaration issued on 6th January, 2004.

1. We renew our commitment to the objectives and principles of SAARC and pledge to reinvigorate cooperation to realize peace, amity, progress and prosperity of all peoples of South Asia.
2. We affirm our determination to create an inclusive, just and equitable partnership for peace, development and prosperity. Satisfactory progress has been made in the SAARC Preferential Trading Arrangement (SAPTA). The signing of the Framework Agreement on the South Asian Free Trade Area (SAFTA) is a major milestone. It is important to maintain this momentum and move towards further broadening of economic cooperation and to ensure equitable distribution of benefits of trade and cater to the special needs of the small and LDC Member States by providing them special and deferential treatment.
3. We reiterate our commitment made at the 11th SAARC Summit at Kathmandu in January 2002, for the creation of a South Asian Economic Union. In this context, we underline that creation of a suitable political and economic environment would be conducive to the realization of this objective.
4. A study on creating a South Asian Energy Cooperation including the concept of an Energy Ring should be undertaken by the Working Group on Energy.

5. For accelerated and balanced economic growth it is essential to strengthen transportation, transit and communication links across the region.
6. Public and private sector cooperation, particularly joint ventures, holds great promise. It is important to move towards project ccoperation under SAARC. Prospects for setting up of a South Asian Development Bank should be examined by the SAARC FINANCE and report through the Council of Ministers.
7. Priority attention should also be given to the need for harmonization of standards, simplification of custom procedures, as well as cooperation among the central banks.
8. Development of tourism within South Asia could bring economic, social and cultural dividends. There is a need for increasing cooperation to jointly promote tourism within South Asia as well as to promote South Asia as a tourism destination, inter alia, by improved air links. To achieve this and to commemorate the twentieth year of the establishment of SAARC, the year 2005 is designated as "South Asia Tourism Year", for the success of which, each member would individually and jointly organize special events.
9. SAARC members should continue to safeguard their collective interests in multilateral forums by discussing, coordinating and exchanging information with a view to adopting common positions, where appropriate, on various issues.

Poverty Alleviation

10. We recognise poverty alleviation as the greatest challenge facing the peoples of South Asia and declare poverty alleviation as the overarching goal of all SAARC activities. It is imperative to relate regional cooperation to the actual needs of the people.
11. The reconstituted Independent South Asian Commission for Poverty Alleviation (ISACPA) has done commendable work. An effective strategy should be devised to implement suggestions made in its Report "Our Future Our

Responsibility". In this context, ISACPA should continue in an advocacy role. It should prepare and submit to the next SAARC summit a comprehensive and realistic blueprint setting out SAARC Development Goals for the next five years in the areas of poverty alleviation, education, health and environment giving due regard, among others, to the suggestions made in the ISACPA report.

12. Investment in human resources is critical for future development of South Asia. It is, therefore, essential to establish a network of centres of higher learning and training, and Skill Development Institutes (SDIs) across South Asia. In this context, the role of the SAARC Human Resource Development Centre (SHRDC) is important.
13. Strengthening of scientific and technological co-operation across the region is fundamental to accelerating the pace of economic and social development.
14. We hail the signing of the SAARC Social Charter as a historic development, which would have a far-reaching impact on the lives of millions of South Asians. Issues covered under the Charter, such as poverty alleviation, population stabilization, empowerment of women, youth mobilization, human resource development, promotion of health and nutrition, and protection of children are keys to the welfare and well being of all South Asians.
15. Progress has been made in the constitution of SAARC Autonomous Advocacy Group of Prominent Women Personalities (SAWAG). To enable women to contribute to the socio-economic development, there is a need for SAARC to encourage women entrepreneurs in the region.
16. We take pride in the rich cultural mosaic of the peoples of South Asia and underline the need for preservation of traditional skills and crafts, and promotion of cultural exchanges between nations.
17. We welcome the establishment of a SAARC Cultural Centre in Kandy, which will serve as a symbol of South Asian shared cultural heritage.

Combating Terrorism

18. We condemn terrorist violence in all its forms and manifestations and note that people of South Asia continue to face a serious threat from terrorism.

19. We are convinced that terrorism, in all its forms and manifestations, is a challenge to all states and to all of humanity, and cannot be justified on any ground, whatsoever. Terrorism violates the fundamental values of the United Nations and the SAARC Charter and constitutes one of the most serious threats to international peace and security. We agree to fully implement the relevant international conventions to which we are parties.

20. We reaffirm our commitment to the SAARC Regional Convention on Suppression of Terrorism, which, among others, recognizes the seriousness of the problem of terrorism as it affects the security, stability, and development of the region.

21. The signing of the Additional Protocol to the SAARC Regional Convention on Suppression of Terrorism to deal effectively with financing of terrorism is a further manifestation of our determination to eliminate all forms and manifestations of terrorism from South Asia.

22. We recognize the vital role that information and media can play in the promotion of peace, progress and harmony in South Asia. In this context, the initiatives for introducing regular 'SAARC Roundup' and 'SAARC News' programmes for telecast and broadcast on National TV and Radio Channels respectively in Member Countries is a welcome development. We agree to the establishment of a SAARC Information Centre in Kathmandu.

23. We note with satisfaction the progress achieved in regional cooperation through SIPA. The commitment to SIPA must be matched by a corresponding allocation of resources for it.

24. We express our determination to develop mutually beneficial links between SAARC and other regional and

international organizations, bodies and entities and agree to establish dialogue partnership with other regional bodies and with states outside the region, interested in SAARC activities.

25. We envision South Asia to be a peaceful and stable region where each nation is at peace with itself and its neighbours and where conflicts, differences and disputes are addressed through peaceful means and dialogue.

26. We reaffirm our pledge to promote good neighbourly relations on the basis of the principles of sovereign equality, territorial integrity and national independence, non-use of force, non-intervention and non-interference and peaceful settlement of disputes and recognize the importance of informal political consultations in promoting mutual understanding and reinforcing confidence building process among Member States.

27. We are particularly mindful of the security concerns of small states that arise, inter alia, from their particular vulnerabilities, which should be firmly addressed by scrupulous adherence to the UN Charter, rules of international law and strict adherence to the universally accepted principles and norms related to sovereign rights and territorial integrity of all states. This should be ensured by all, both severally and collectively, through appropriate actions.

Selected Readings and References

1. *Policy making in European Union*, 4th edition, edited by Helen Wallace, Oxford University Press, April, 2000
2. *Theories of European Integration*, Ben Rosament, Palgrave, London
3. Europa: Gateway to the European Union; An European Union portal site.
4. The EU foreign policy: Making a difference in the world; Christopher Patten: External Relations Commissioner, European Commission
5. European Policy Centre: Website of Independent think tank
6. European Union in the US: EU news web. Delegation of the EC to the USA
7. Neill Nugent, 199. *The government and politics of the European Union*, Durha, N.C.; Duke University Press
8. *The European Union*: *Politics and Policies* by John Mc Cormick. West View Press, 1996
9. *The Expanding European Union: Past, present and future.* Edited by John Redmond, Glenda G. Rosenthal, Lynne Reinner, 1998
10. *The European Union in the 1990's* by Paul Taylor, Oxford University Press
11. *The Rebirth of Europe*; by Elizabeth Pond; The Brookings Institution, 2000

12. *The European Parliament, the National Parliament and European Integration*; edited by Richard S. Katz and Bernhard Wessels, Oxford University Press

13. *A concise history of Euroepan monetary integration: From EPU to EMU*; by Hornst Unger; Quorum books, 1997

14. *The road to Maastricht: Negotiating Economic and Monetary Union* by Kenneth Dyson, Kevin Featherstone. Oxford University Press, 1999

15. *The political economy of Euroepan monetary unification*; by Barry Eichengreen , Jeffery A. Frieden, Westview Press, 2001.

16. Economic policy in the EMU, A study by the European Commission services. By Barco Buti Andre Sapir, Oxford, 1998

17. Observing European elections by Demetrius Andreas Floudas, *Contemporary Review*, Vol, 268. May, 1996

18. *Policing the European Union* by Malcolm Anderson and others Clarendon Press, Oxford 1995

19. Securing South Asia by Lakshman Kadirgamar, *The Hindu* 29th Dec, 2003, Chennai

20. Council of European Union: The EU an exporter of peace and security

21. European Security Strategy: A secure Europe in a better world, Dec, 2003 EU Institute of Security Studies, Paris

22. How the EU works: A citizen's guide to the EU institutions; European documentation, 2003

23. SAFTA an analysis : A study report by Federation of Indian Chambers of Commerce and Industry, March 2004

24. The impact of SAARC on regional integration in South Asia By Calistus A. Christian, 1995

25. More Unity and more diversity: The EU's biggest enlargement, European Communities, 2003

26. A Constitution for Europe: European Communities, 2004

27. South Asia can go the EU way: By K. Subrahmaniam, *The Times of India* 23rd Dec, 2003
28. The Single South Asian currency; *Hindustan Times* Tarun Das and S. Akbar Zaidi 21st Dec, 2003
29. EU - India trade relations; EU-India update, Jan, 2004
30. South Asia: Regional economic and trade cooperation: A Study report by Confederation of Indian Industries, December 2003
31. Status Paper: India-Pakistan economic relations, 2003 A report by FICCI
32. Churchill and the Unification of Europe; Inside the journals (Edited by John G. Plumpton. 1998)
33. SAFTA: A perspective; Muchkund Dubey. *The Hindu*, 10th Jan, 2004
34. Nuclear neighbours: By V.R.Raghvan 23rd Dec, 2003 *The Hindu*, Chennai
35. India Pakistan economic relations : A FICCI report, March, 2004
36. Thessaloniki European Council 19&20th June, 2003 Presidency conclusions: European documentation

Index